WORDS THAT SHOOK THE WORLD

100 Years of
Unforgettable Speeches and Events

Richard Greene

with Florie Brizel

To the magical, creative force that, every once in a while, shines through the thoughts, passions, and words of mere mortals, lifting them—and all of us—to experience the divine.

And to my beautiful, wise and precious daughter Chiara and our next generations—may the legacy of these great words inspire you to even greater heights.

—Richard Greene

Prentice Hall Press

A member of Penguin Putnam Inc.

Prentice Hall® is a registered trademark of Pearson Education, Inc.

375 Hudson Street

New York, New York 10014

www.penguinputnam.com

Library of Congress Cataloging-in-Publication Data

Greene, Richard 1954–

Words that shook the world : 100 years of unforgettable speeches and events /
Richard Greene with Florie Brizel.

p. cm.

Includes bibliographical references and index.

ISBN 0-7352-0296-6

1. Speeches, addresses, etc. 2. Speeches, addresses, etc.—History and criticism.
I. Brizel, Florie. II. Title.

PN6122 .G75 2002   808.85—dc21

Printed in the United States of America

10 9 8 7 6 5 4 3 2 1

CONTENTS

PREFACE

In January of 1984, a young attorney walked up to me at the end of one of my seminars and complimented me on my speaking ability. He shared that he was moved by the power of my words and how I was able to touch so many with the force of my communication. At the time I was twenty-three years old and my career was only five years old. I had hoped at that point to make a measurable difference in the world by communicating the message of what power our creator has given us human beings to change the quality of our lives, our families, our organizations, and communities if we chose to speak from our true passion and our hearts.

The attorney offered me legal support for my business at that early stage and we soon became friends and colleagues. That young attorney was the author of *Words That Shook the World*, Richard Greene. I must say I never saw him as an attorney because he didn't use language as most attorneys do—to confuse. Instead, Richard always focused on how to communicate better, to be more open and more passionate. He was on a mission and still is. The mission was to share with the world the power of how words can change lives in a positive way. In *Words That Shook the World*, Richard has selected speeches that do just that.

Richard and I both believe that what is said in public can define a human being, a moment or an era, and that, at its best, a speech can define who we are, shape a society, a community, and the world.

We believe that language makes human beings special and that a speech offers amazing insight into the personality and soul of the person giving it; that a speech distills the essence of a person down into a few hundred or a few thousand words, each one capable of revealing that individual's thoughts, feelings, pains, and joys.

There is much to learn from these speeches—lessons that can help all of us become even better communicators in our personal and professional lives.

You will be inspired by the amazing lives of those who wrote and spoke these words, and you will discover the secrets that allowed each of the speakers to be so effective in touching others then, and why they touch us still today.

You will be inspired by the artistry of the language, the alchemy that occurs when simple words are turned into thoughts and emotions that transform and change our lives. You will savor the experience of stepping into some of the most powerful moments in human history—living and reliving them as if you were there.

You will be transported to Yankee Stadium to soak in the simple, but sweet words of baseball hero Lou Gehrig, as he faces a devastating illness that forced him to leave the game he loved and say goodbye to his fans. You'll be swept inside historic Westminster Abbey for a eulogy that touched the billions who heard it—the words of a brother mourning the death of a sister and mother while celebrating the life of an exceptional woman, Diana, Princess of Wales.

In London you will also hear the new Prime Minister Winston Churchill lift the spirits of Parliament and all of Britain with his personal dedication to give the full measure of his own "blood, sweat, toil, and tears" to defeat the German onslaught threatening Britain and the world; and in postwar Berlin twenty-three years later, an emotional forty-four-year-old John F. Kennedy, angered by the sight of the Berlin Wall, declares his oneness with Berliners and rallies the world to his cause. You will tingle to the poetic speech-making of Martin Luther King, Jr., as he shares his dream of freedom and brings 250,000 to the "snowcapped peaks of Colorado" and the "curvaceous peaks of California"—oratory unmatched in our lifetime.

The speeches in *Words That Shook the World*, and the pictures and audios that capture them, encapsulate pivotal moments and events in the history of the past century. They can be studied, read and re-read, listened to, discussed, and appreciated. Richard has provided fascinating background material that will make you feel you were there and his analysis will provide insights into what made each speech so powerful. This book and its companion CDs can and should be a wonderful tool and a reminder of the heights we can reach when we communicate with heart, with intellect, and especially, with passion.

Anthony Robbins
La Jolla, California

FOREWORD

We know that memorable words can move a mountain and motivate us toward great goals. They are most often spoken by political leaders who are trying to rally the people to their cause. And their eloquent, sometimes electrifying, addresses are long remembered only by one line. But they are lines that give hope and inspiration in times of great need. They touch a personal chord that also imbues us with a new strength and a sense of belonging.

I remember when I came to Washington in search of a newspaper job in the summer of 1942. The old-timers were still talking about the greatest of the politician-orators of the times—Franklin D. Roosevelt. A teletype operator told me that when he was out of work like millions of others during the Great Depression, he was ready to become a Socialist. He said he stood in a crowd to hear the uplifting words of Franklin D. Roosevelt in his inaugural address, broadcast on radio, March 4, 1933, and took great heart when he heard: ". . . let me assert my firm belief that the only thing we have to fear is fear itself—nameless, unreasoning, unjustified terror which paralyzes needed efforts to convert retreat into advance."

I often think how reassuring those words are today in the new atmosphere of fear and terrorism. I was sitting at a press table on January 20, 1961, in front of the Capitol. It was a bitterly cold day in the aftermath of a blizzard that paralyzed Washington and I listened to John F. Kennedy's inaugural address: "Ask not what your country can do for you; ask what you can do for your country." Those lines have been repeated through the years, and gave young people the impetus and inspiration to go into public service.

I was covering the White House on the day that civil rights leader Martin Luther King, Jr. marched on Washington in 1963 and delivered his immortal "I have a dream" speech. Later, he came to the White House and as he went through the receiving line, I remember a smiling President Kennedy shook his hand and said: "I have a dream." And a year later in 1964, I shall never forget that chilling moment while covering the Republican National Party convention in the Cow Palace in San Francisco when the GOP presidential nominee said: "I would remind you that extremism in defense of liberty is no vice. And let me remind you also that moderation in the pursuit of justice is no virtue."

When Robert F. Kennedy was assassinated in 1968, his brother Senator Edward Kennedy recalled the George Bernard Shaw lines that "Bobby" recited during his presidential campaign: "Some men see things as they are and say (ask) why. I dream of things as they never were and say why not." That quote was our signal that he was winding up his speech and it was time to run for the press bus.

And who has not read the immortal speech that British Prime Minister Winston Churchill delivered to the House of Commons? Along with FDR's "Day of Infamy" address to Congress the day after the Japanese bombing of Pearl Harbor on December 7, 1941, the Churchill oration is one of the best known from World War II and rallied Britain in its hour of peril. He said, "I have nothing to offer but blood, toil, tears, and sweat."

President Ronald Reagan was renowned as a "great communicator" with his timing and phrasing. It was a natural for his speechwriters and researchers to go to the best-loved poem "High Flight" of the Air Force, posted at all the bases when the space shuttle *Challenger* blew up. He said that the crew prepared for the journey and waved goodbye and "slipped the surly bonds of earth" to "touch the face of God." There was not a dry eye at the White House as we listened to that speech, or I dare say, in the country, for that matter.

I think that Richard Greene has made a tremendous contribution by compiling *Words That Shook The World,* representing 100 years of unforgettable speeches and events. It is my fondest wish that every schoolchild will read these superb enduring addresses and remember some of the great moments in history.

Helen Thomas

FOREWORD

On a warm August afternoon in 1963, I stood in back of some 200,000 people as a young black minister began to speak. As Martin Luther King, Jr. talked, I found myself pulled forward, along the length of the reflecting pool, up toward the Lincoln Memorial. Long before King reached his rhetorical climax—the "I have a dream" refrain that has long since become so familiar—the hair on the back of my neck had (literally, I now think) stood up. Along with everyone else in that crowd, I knew this was a Big Moment. And it was a moment etched into history by the power of the spoken word.

I could not have imagined then that less than four years later, I would be sitting in a cramped cubby in a Senate office building, helping to craft speeches for Senator Robert Kennedy. I could not have imagined that I would be spending a good chunk of the next decade of my life as a political speechwriter. I could not have imagined that I would spend the quarter century after that as a political journalist, tending to some of the most memorable speeches of our time. Indeed, as I look back, it seems as if my entire adult life has been bound up with the spoken word. Those that I helped craft took shape in plush New York offices—and on a tiny airplane flying to an Indian reservation in Arizona, its landing strip illuminated by lines of parked cars, as my colleague and I pounded out text on two bulky manual typewriters, finishing seconds before the plane landed.

They included phrases shaped for a moment, quickly forgotten—and words that have endured. In the mid-1980s, in South Africa, I interviewed a young dissident who was a fugitive from the white minority government, with a price on his head. He was a young man committed to non-violence—a belief, he said, shaped by the days he had spent driving through the black township of Soweto with a loudspeaker mounted on his car, playing speeches by King and Robert Kennedy.

We are told now that, with the conquest of television, we live in a "post-rhetorical" age, a time when we lack the patience to sit through a lengthy oration without reaching for the remote. I do not believe this. Yes, we are a few millennia removed from Pericles's Funeral Oration, or Cicero's phillippics but again and again in my lifetime, I have witnessed what the power of the spoken word can do.

I watched a young, new president suddenly grow in stature with an inaugural address that, literally, changed the way we expected our leaders to speak to us. And in the fall of 1963, I heard that same president tell the nation that a limited nuclear-test ban treaty had been reached with the Soviet Union, proclaiming "a shaft of light has cut into the darkness." In the summer of 1964, I heard the newly crowned Republican Presidential nominee, Barry Goldwater, declare that "extremism in the defense of liberty is no vice," and learned that memorable rhetoric also has the power to shock, as well as to appeal. Twenty-four years after that, I stood on a Convention floor and saw a charismatically challenged Vice President Bush redefine himself with a single acceptance speech—temporarily and not entirely accurately—as a bold, decisive leader. And thirteen years after that, we all saw his son help rally a shaken nation with words of steel.

Why does the spoken word still have the power to move us. In part, I think, it is because so much of our public dialogue has been compressed into ten- and five- and three-second slogans. Hearing a well-crafted, sustained piece of oratory is like tasting a five-course meal for the first time after a lifetime of potato chips and Ring Dings.

The speeches I've mentioned, and those you're about to encounter, are sustained *arguments*. They state premises, marshal evidence, and then reach conclusions. "I have a dream" as a slogan is empty; as the conclusion to a speech about race in America that contains both an indictment and the hope of redemption, it is the perfect summation. Similarly, when President Johnson proclaimed "we *shall* overcome" during his speech to Congress in 1965 on civil rights, he did more than the adopt a movement's slogan as the nation's own; he acknowledged that all of us—white and black—had to overcome the crippling legacy of racism.

The appeal, however, is more than the gift of sustenance. Speech is the way we touch each other's deepest emotions and beliefs. A picture may be worth a thousand words, but a few hundred words, properly crafted, can move us far beyond the image. For all of the technological wizardry of computer graphics to dazzle the eye, I still believe nothing can match the power of the spoken word to move us to the core.

For those of you who doubt this, here is a simple invitation: Turn the page.

Jeff Greenfield

INTRODUCTION

What is contained in these pages is the same thing that Michael Jordan, Pablo Piccaso, Steven Spielberg, Katharine Hepburn, Luciano Pavarotti, and Tiger Woods bring to their audiences. Perfection. Grace. Indescribable emotion. Power. Exhilaration. In other words, a peak experience.

We throng to stadiums and performance halls, squeeze ourselves in with hundreds or thousands of our fellow humans and wait for the peak experiences—the climax of a slam dunk, the emotional catharsis of a perfectly acted scene, the tenor's-soul-lifting crescendo. And here, too, in written and spoken forms, are those experiences. That is what this book is all about. Twenty brief moments in the past 100 years when time stood still. Twenty brief moments in our history when geniuses put together mere words that have been taken for granted for thousands of years and turned them into goose bumps. Twenty bona fide peak experiences waiting for you to enjoy and savor them.

As much as a stirring athletic or artistic performance, the words in this book and CDs represent a sort of perfection that should make every human being proud. So, drink in what lies before you. Feel the words stimulate your mind and tug at your heart as these remarkable individuals use words for what they truly are—experiences waiting to happen.

For eighteen years I have gently prodded—and even pushed—my clients to move beyond words as we understand them and go to a place where words are magic. Words in a speech are not there simply to convey information. They are there to generate a feeling. The biggest challenge I have with my clients—be they prime ministers or presidents, CEOs or celebrities, royalty or regional managers—is this distinction between information and emotion. The natural tendency in public speaking, unfortunately, is to try to tell everything one knows about a subject in a speech.

But, in my opinion, a technically perfect talk—one that conveys all the essential data but one in which nobody is moved to do anything with the information—is a useless speech. It's better to fax or e-mail the information and stay home.

The secret in writing or giving a speech is to generate emotion. It is through emotion that human beings are moved in their gut and in their heart. And only when human beings are moved in this way do they change how they think and change what they do. That is the true purpose of public speaking. That, too, is the secret of all communication. The brilliant communicator uses words not as markers for denotative meaning but rather as vehicles to carry the emotional content that will, in fact, generate changes in thought, feeling, or action. The word *emotion* says it all, but "e-motion" is how it should be spelled. "E," the first letter in "energy," in "motion."

So, read these speeches, and listen to them, with this core secret in mind. Read and listen to these speeches as tools to stimulate your energy, to generate Energy in Motion. Try the following:

- Look and listen for the rhythm. Does it carry you? Does it evoke "e-motion"? Great speakers know that rhythm is one of the most important ways to carry and generate emotion.

- As you read and listen to these speeches, look for the secrets these great speakers employ to create that rhythm—the repetition of words, the repetition of phrases, the parallel structure of words and phrases, the arrangement of phrases into groups of three ("triplets"). For great examples, see the speeches of Churchill, MacArthur, JFK, King, and Jordan.

- Look and listen for the structure of the speech. If you really think about it, Beethoven, Mozart, and Tchaikovsky actually wrote "speeches" with their orchestras while King, John Kennedy, and Churchill wrote symphonies with their words. The symphonies of master composers and the speeches of master orators establish a theme, in precisely the same way, and then build on it. There is direction and movement that turns sounds and words into emotion, grabbing us by the heart, and taking us with them.

- Look and listen for the perfect balance between detail and emotion—just enough detail to support the theme. Nothing kills the rhythm or emotional potential of a speech as quickly as too much detail. Yet, if you speak only with emotion and no detail, no one will take you or your message seriously. Great speakers set a theme and a few sub-themes and support each with at least one fact, but not too many. All of the speeches included here succeed at doing this, but look especially at Theodore Roosevelt, FDR, JFK, King, Jordan, Reagan, and Bush.

- Finally, look and listen for perhaps the most important secret of powerful communication: authenticity. The importance of this cannot be overstated. When giving a speech, you are either 100% honest, genuine, real, speaking from your heart or you are not. There is no 99 percent. See Gehrig, Edward Kennedy, and Earl Spencer.

As you read and listen to these great speeches, ask yourself if these great speakers are "spinning"—that is, strategically forming their words and arguments from their heads—or are they marching forth with authentic emotion, carried on the winds of their own genuine passion? The former may be clever, but the latter is a peak experience, for both speaker and listener. I never want my clients to simply be clever, because "clever" fades. I want them to share 100 percent of who they are in every speech they give; if they can't, I ask them to sit down and not give it. It's that simple.

When a speaker taps into his or her emotional depths and gives 100 percent of him- or herself authentically from that place, everyone feels it, everyone is touched, and a peak experience is created that will never be forgotten. And, perhaps more importantly, when a speaker taps into his or her emotional depths, a tremendous gift is given. Whether that speaker is a Winston Churchill, John Kennedy, your English teacher, or the next guy to speak at the annual sales meeting, he shares something that is unique and irreplaceable when he fully shares himself. There will never be another Winston Churchill or John Kennedy. The combination of DNA, life experiences, time, and place in history and soul that created Churchill or Kennedy—or you—is a singular event. That makes reading and listening to these speeches such fun—each speaker brings something historically significant and irreplaceable.

These twenty speeches are, of course, a mere fraction of the truly great and inspirational speeches that have touched people during the last century. Many others were given in the classrooms or meeting rooms or even restaurants and bars with no cameras or tape recorders to record them. Even if it were possible to list all of the great speeches—large and small—that is not our goal. Rather, our goal is to offer the top twenty guaranteed, life-affirming peak experiences from twenty of the greatest speakers in the past 100 years.

To that end, we have decided to omit from our list some speakers whose messages were not, in our view, inspirational and life affirming. Adolph Hitler, one of the most gifted speakers of all time, is not here for this reason, regardless of his prowess. The same is true for others, such as Mao, Lenin, and Stalin, whose life works have, in many cases, been the antithesis of that of lifting the human spirit.

Read and listen to Martin Luther King, Jr.'s "I have a dream" speech and watch as your emotions soar with rhetoric and passion unmatched in its brilliance and power.

Read and listen to Lou Gehrig's "luckiest man" speech and you will be humbled by a chilling demonstration of graciousness and gratitude that will send chills down your spine.

Read and listen to John F. Kennedy's passionate "Ich bin ein Berliner" speech and you will feel the exhilaration that sent over one million Germans into an ecstatic celebration of their freedom.

Read and listen to the remaining speeches and you will feel different but equally powerful emotional responses to each one.

And then, I hope, you will enjoy these speeches in the same way you would a Michael Jordan slam dunk, a Picasso painting, a Katharine Hepburn performance, or a Pavarotti aria, as life-affirming peak experiences that touch the soul.

When you have experienced even a few of these, you will become, as we are, fans of this truly remarkable art form and the "word artists" who have the awesome talent to turn words into goose bumps and create words that shake the world.

Richard Greene

HOW WE CHOSE THE 20 SPEECHES THAT SHOOK THE WORLD

Part of the fun of culling through thousands of great speeches was anticipating the questions that were sure to come. "How come you didn't include . . . ?" or "Why in the world would you include . . . ?"

Well, you, the reader, are certainly invited to weigh in on our choices and, in fact, we would love to hear from you. But before you criticize or compliment, you might want to know what the criteria for inclusion were. For a speech to end up in this collection it had to:

1. Be a positive, uplifting, inspiring speech that helped make the world a better place—a speech that we, ourselves, would want on our coffee table.

2. Similarly, we wanted speeches from positive, uplifting, inspiring individuals—people we looked up to as exhilarating examples of human achievement. Again, we only included people we would want to invite into our living room to take residence on our coffee table.

3. The event or issues that surrounded the speech had to, in some way, shake the world or, at the very least, move it.

4. The speech or the speaker, or preferably both, had to truly move us. We wanted only speeches that gave us "goose bumps" and speakers who make us feel proud to share this planet with them.

5. We had a strong preference for speeches that were given in English because excerpts of the speeches would be included on the companion CDs.

6. We wanted this book to be a historic collector's item, and, therefore, we were committed to including the entire text of these wonderful speeches, rather than excerpts. As a result, the primary speech had to be of reasonable length. Unfortunately there were some wonderful speeches that had to be eliminated because the speaker, on an emotional roll as it were, went on for hours.

7. So that there was a wide range of speakers and topics, we decided to only feature one speech from any one speaker. Especially when it came to very prolific and extraordinary orators like Churchill or Martin Luther King, Jr., or JFK or Reagan, this made for some very difficult choices. Where a speaker has given many wonderful speeches, we decided to include excerpts of other speeches to give you a taste of the extraordinary talent of these orators.

Now that you know our thoughts, please feel free to comment, in any way, on our selections. E-mail them to *rhgreene@aol.com*. In fact, we'd love to know about other speeches that really moved you. We might just end up including them in our next book!

THEODORE ROOSEVELT

"Leave it as it is.
You can not improve on it."

AMERICA'S FIRST CONSERVATIONIST

Few would disagree that Theodore "Teddy" Roosevelt is one of America's most colorful presidents and one of the century's great personalities. Not only was the 26th president the man for whom the teddy bear was named, he was the force behind the Panama Canal (begun in 1904), the first real consumer legislation ("Pure Food and Drug Act," 1906), the break-up of corporate monopolies ("trust busting"), the United States' expanded role in international affairs ("Speak softly but carry a big stick"), and the creation of five National Parks and eighteen National Monuments (including the Grand Canyon, the Petrified Forest, and Muir Woods).

Teddy himself was a force of nature. Born into a wealthy New York family, young Roosevelt's life was marred by asthma, which often left him bedridden and occasionally near death. He also suffered from extremely poor eyesight. Unwilling to give in to illness, he learned to ride, shoot, and box, and went on to build a career that might have sapped the strength of healthier men: Harvard, Phi Beta Kappa, father of six, naval historian, biographer, essayist, paleontologist, taxidermist, conservationist, ornithologist, big-game hunter, editor, critic, rancher, orator, civil service reformer, socialite, patron of the arts, Colonel of the Rough Riders in Cuba, a leading expert on big-game mammals in North America, New York State Assemblyman at age 23, candidate for Mayor of New York City, member of the U.S. Civil Service Commission, President of New York City Board of Police Commissioners, Assistant Secretary of the Navy, Governor of New York, winner of the 1906 Nobel Peace Prize, vice president and youngest president of the United States.

President; September 6, McKinley shot and dies September 14; Roosevelt sworn in as the 26th President of the United States

1902 Orders antitrust suit under Sherman Act to dissolve Northern Securities Company (first of 45 antitrust suits); designates Crater Lake as a National Park, first of many he establishes; signs Newlands Reclamation Act, leading to first 21 federal irrigation projects

1903 Pelican Island, Florida, first of 51 federal bird reservations established; settles Alaskan Boundary dispute; recognizes the Republic of Panama after Panama's secession from Colombia; signs treaty with Panama for building of canal (completed in 1914)

1904 Reelected President over Democrat Alton B. Parker; pledges not to run again

1905 Wichita Forest, Oklahoma, made first federal game preserve; media-tion by TR leads to signing of Portsmouth Treaty ending Russo-Japanese War

1906 Signs National Monument Act, establishing first of 18 "National Monuments"; signs Pure Food and Drug Act and federal meat inspection law; awarded Nobel Peace Prize for role in ending Russo-Japanese War in 1905—first American to win Nobel Prize

1909 Second term ends on March 4 with inauguration of William Howard Taft

1912 Announces candidacy for Republican nomination; Republican National Convention renominates Taft; National Progressive party ("Bull Moose" party) nominates TR for president; shot while campaigning; Democrat Woodrow Wilson elected president; TR came in second, receiving the largest percentage of votes of any third-party candidate

1919 Dies in his sleep on January 6 at Sagamore Hill

Not listed in that bio are his amazing personal habits. Teddy was a gargantuan eater, often polishing off a dozen or more eggs at a sitting; a voracious reader, reading between one and three books every day; a prodigious writer, writing over 150,000 personal letters and publishing hundreds of works including 36 books as well as over 1,000 articles on everything from history to travel; and a fervent exercise enthusiast, known for his "White House walks" and nude swims across the Potomac.

Drawn into politics because of his San Juan Hill heroics during the Spanish-American War, Roosevelt's ascent from New York Governor in 1898 to Vice President in 1901 and then President later that same year after the assassination of William McKinley was as dizzying as the pace of his life.

Nothing was impossible for TR. In his view the President as "steward of the people" should take whatever action necessary for the public good unless expressly forbidden by law or the Constitution. In his seven years as president, Roosevelt championed the worker against the growing economic power of industry, emerged as a "trust buster," forcing the dissolution of the great railroad trust in the Northwest, and pushed the United States into world politics in a bold new way: "Speak softly and carry a big stick."

He arranged for the construction of the Panama Canal, reached a "gentleman's agreement" on immigration with Japan, and won the Nobel Peace Prize for mediating the Russo-Japanese War.

First President to Win Medal of Honor

On January 16, 2001, by unanimous vote by the United States House and Senate, Roosevelt was posthumously awarded the Medal of Honor for bravery in battle at San Juan Heights, Cuba, during the Spanish-American War.

Theodore Roosevelt wanted, but was denied, the medal in 1898, perhaps because he offended the Secretary of War, perhaps because of the envy of regular army officers who received less press than the flamboyant volunteer, perhaps because of bad politics. In his lifetime, it was not to be.

An application was made to the Department of the Army in 1998 to award him the medal on the 100th anniversary of the Spanish-American War and the Rough Riders. The Army again refused to give TR the award. Finally, both houses of Congress in 1998 voted to give the Medal to TR. Yet, even after the bill was passed and signed by President Clinton, the Army still hesitated, taking two more years to approve the medal.

The Medal of Honor was presented in the Roosevelt Room of the West Wing of the White House. In giving the award, President Clinton stated, "TR was a larger-than-life figure, who gave our nation a larger-than-life vision of our place in the world."

A portrait of Theodore Roosevelt in his Rough Rider uniform, a unit he helped form to fight in the Spanish-American War in 1898. His charge up San Juan Hill made him a hero, but it was only in 2001 that he was posthumously awarded the Medal of Honor.

Theodore Roosevelt / "Leave it as it is. You can not improve on it."

2

(above) Lieutenant Colonel Theodore Roosevelt with his First Volunteer cavalry stand on San Juan Hill (1898).

(left) TR's decision not to shoot a bear while on a hunting trip became the inspiration for the original "Teddy Bear."

With all these accomplishments, many believe that his most lasting was his work on behalf of conservation (now called preservation). In his seven and one half years as president, TR, almost single-handedly, created 150 national forests, 51 federal bird reservations, 4 national game preserves, 5 national parks, and 18 national monuments.

When TR entered the White House, only 43 million acres of national forest had been set aside as public land in the preceding 125 years. In less than eight years as president, he increased that figure by more than 450 percent to about 194 million acres or a combined land mass greater in area than the countries of France, Belgium, and The Netherlands! To protect it forever, he created the United States Forest Service.

To do this in the face of strong special interests, who had become accustomed to a "do as you please" attitude on the part of the federal government, he used every means in his power. In 1907, for example, a strongly worded amendment to an agricultural appropriations bill stated that the President could not set aside any more national forests in six Western states. Roosevelt knew the bill would pass; he also knew he had to sign it. Still, there were 16 million acres of forest in those states that he wanted to protect. Just days before the bill passed the Senate, TR cleverly proclaimed the new national forests. In his 1913 autobiography, Roosevelt proudly writes:

> And when the friends of the special interests in the Senate got their amendment through and woke up, they discovered that sixteen million acres of timberland had been saved for the people by putting them in the National Forests before the land grabbers could get at them.

President Theodore Roosevelt speaks to a crowd in Willimantic, Connecticut, 1902.

Continuing, he rather gleefully tells us that the opponents of the National Forests "turned handsprings in their wrath."

Roosevelt was also a pragmatist and believed that when natural resources could be safely and predictably restored, farmers or ranchers or lumber companies could use those resources if they had a policy and practice that did, indeed, replenish them. This philosophy became known as "use conservation."

Visiting the Grand Canyon for the first time, part of a nine-state tour of the West, Roosevelt used the picturesque backdrop and an enthusiastic crowd of 800 to promote his environmental cause. Back home in Washington, he was having a hard time getting Congress to make the Grand Canyon a national park. Three years later, however, in 1906, Teddy got the power to turn certain sites on federal land into "national monuments" with the passage of The National Monuments Act. On January 11, 1908, TR declared the Grand Canyon a National Monument, saving the area until it was later designated a national park.

Theodore Roosevelt / "Leave it as it is. You can not improve on it."

4

Theodore Roosevelt and naturalist John Muir in front of Yosemite National Monument. Roosevelt was one of America's greatest environmentalists creating five national parks and eighteen national monuments including Yosemite.

"He was so alive at all points, and so gifted with the rare faculty of living intensely … in every moment."

Edith Wharton, at Roosevelt's burial, January 1919

After leaving the presidency in March 1909, Roosevelt served as Special Ambassador to England, traveled around the world, including a long safari in Africa, edited *Outlook* magazine, and, then—disenchanted with his own Republican Party—returned to politics, founding the Progressive Party, nicknamed the "Bull Moose" party after TR described himself "fit as a bull moose." He ran for a third term in 1912, but although he received the most votes of any third-party candidate in U.S. history (27.4 percent), he finished second to Democrat Woodrow Wilson.

Today that race may be most remembered for the attempt on his life, his "miraculous" escape, and TR's characteristic response to it. The former Colonel, who led the Rough Riders up San Juan Hill during the Spanish-American War, was unfazed by the experience. Despite a bullet lodged in his chest, he pushed his aides away, refused to go to the hospital, and declared that he was going to "give this speech even if I die!"

Turning down the nomination of his party in 1916, at the age of 58, he petitioned President Wilson in 1917 to allow him to raise, equip, and lead a volunteer division in France in World War I. Ignoring him for three months, Wilson finally refused, angering and embarrassing TR greatly. TR's youngest son, a fighter pilot, was killed in France the next year.

Poised to garner the Republican nomination in 1920, his 1912 run was to be his last campaign. This man of action died in his sleep on January 6, 1919 at the age of 60.

The portraits of American presidents at the Mount Rushmore memorial. Theodore Roosevelt is third from the left.

"...it takes more than that to kill a Bull Moose."

Excerpts from the Campaign Speech that Saved TR'S Life, October 14, 1912

Roosevelt was on the last leg of his uphill campaign as he approached the meeting hall in Milwaukee where an enthusiastic crowd of 5,000 was waiting. Out of the shadows, a crazed anti-third-term fanatic neared the former President and, point-blank, fired a .45 directly into his chest. Astonishingly, the bullet passed through Roosevelt's leather-covered metal eyeglass case, through the thick folded manuscript of the speech he was going to give, and only then into his chest, lodging itself less than an inch from his right lung. Medical experts agreed that had it gone that extra inch and perforated the lung, Roosevelt most likely would have bled to death.

Although urged to go to the hospital, he instead borrowed a clean handkerchief, pushed it into the hole in his chest, held up the manuscript demonstrating the bullet hole, told everyone that the bullet was inside of him (it was never removed), and then delivered a different, completely ad-libbed speech for an hour and a half. Undoubtedly, one of the most heroic and extraordinary moments in speech making.

Friends, I shall ask you to be as quiet as possible. I don't know whether you fully understand that I have just been shot; but it takes more than that to kill a Bull Moose. But fortunately I had my manuscript. …

The bullet is in me now, so that I cannot make a very long speech, but I will try my best. …

I have altogether too important things to think of to feel any concern over my own death; and now I cannot speak to you insincerely within five minutes of being shot. I am telling you the literal truth when I say that my concern is for many other things. …

It was just as when I was colonel of my regiment. … I cannot understand a man fit to be a colonel who can pay any heed to his personal safety when he is occupied as he ought to be with the absorbing desire to do his duty. …

Now, friends, I am not speaking for myself at all, I give you my word, I do not care a rap about being shot; not a rap. …

I have had a good many experiences in my time and this is one of them. What I care for is my country. …

Don't you waste any sympathy on me. I have had an A-1 time in life and I am having it now. …

I am all right—I am a little sore. Anybody has a right to be sore with a bullet in him. You would find that if I was in battle now I would be leading my men just the same. Just the same way I am going to make this speech. …

I ask you to look at our declaration and hear and read our platform about social and industrial justice and then, friends, vote for the Progressive ticket without regard to me, without regard to my personality, for only by voting for that platform can you be true to the cause of progress throughout this Union.

"MANIAC IN MILWAUKEE SHOOTS COL. ROOSEVELT; HE IGNORES WOUND, SPEAKS AN HOUR, GOES TO HOSPITAL."

The New York Times, Tuesday, October 15, 1912

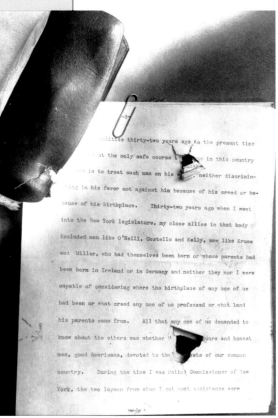

"The Speech That Saved Teddy Roosevelt's Life." Folded in half in his coat pocket, this thick manuscript and an eyeglass case slowed the assassin's bullet just enough to keep it from piercing his lungs. Despite bleeding from the bullet in his chest, TR pushed away his aides and declared, "I'm going to give this speech even if I die!" And a magnificent, totally ad-libbed speech it was!

"Leave it as it is. You can not improve on it."

Speech at the Grand Canyon, Grand Canyon, Arizona, May 6, 1903

On his first visit to the Grand Canyon and Arizona, President Roosevelt's train stopped near the edge of the massive canyon carved out by the rushing Colorado River. Eight hundred people were waiting for him at a hotel overlooking the canyon.

The very short speech he delivered that day breaks ground in two important ways. It establishes the theme of conservation (recognizing both the need to "preserve" and at the same time to "use" the land and its resources), and marks the first time that Roosevelt used the phrase "square deal," which became a cornerstone of his administration's philosophy. To Roosevelt those words embodied the philosophy that government had to be fair and honest in its dealings with individuals and not simply the protector of business and special interests.

An undisciplined speaker, TR frequently, as here, ad-libbed his remarks and, unable to curtail his bubbling enthusiasm, often rambled, sometimes talking for well over an hour. In this short but significant speech, Roosevelt seems uncharacteristically precise and to the point. Unpretentious and straightforward, it succeeds because TR is unafraid to bring his own unabashed personality into every word.

ANALYSIS

Roosevelt begins with short, focused sentences that are nevertheless made poetic by his obvious affection for the men who have served in the military and particularly Arizona's governor, Bucky O'Neill.

Starting with the most immediate concern for Arizona, TR mentions irrigation. Within the past year, TR had signed an act that would eventually create 21 federal irrigation projects across the country.

Notice the personal passion contained in these few sentences. Rarely do we find a leader as personal in an entire speech as TR is in this one paragraph. Each sentence begins with or contains the word *I*. Part of TR's effectiveness as a speaker derives from the way he brings the full force of his beliefs and his enormous energy into everything he says. A personal, from-the-heart statement, which this is, carries significantly more weight than any theoretical or academic argument ever could.

These two short sentences say it all: that the Grand Canyon is God's work, that it is divine, that it is irreplaceable, that human beings can never reproduce or improve on nature. All in 11 words!

SPEECH

Mr. Governor, and you, My Fellow Citizens:

I am glad to be in Arizona today. From Arizona many gallant men came into the regiment which I had the honor to command. Arizona sent men who won glory on hard-fought fields, and men to whom came a glorious and honorable death fighting for the flag of their country. As long as I live it will be to me an inspiration to have served with Bucky O'Neill. I have met so many comrades whom I prize, for whom I feel respect and admiration and affection, that I shall not particularize among them except to say that there is none for whom I feel all of respect and admiration and affection more than for your Governor.

I have never been in Arizona before. It is one of the regions from which I expect most development through the wise action of the National Congress in passing the irrigation act. The first and biggest experiment now in view under that act is the one that we are trying in Arizona. I look forward to the effects of irrigation partly as applied by and through the government, still more as applied by individuals … profiting by the example of the government, and possibly by help from it—I look forward to the effects of irrigation as being of greater consequence to all this region of country in the next fifty years than any other material movement whatsoever.

In the Grand Canyon, Arizona has a natural wonder which, so far as I know, is in kind absolutely unparalleled throughout the rest of the world. I want to ask you to do one thing in connection with it in your own interest and in the interest of the country—to keep this great wonder of nature as it now is. I was delighted to learn of the wisdom of the Santa Fe railroad people in deciding not to build their hotel on the brink of the canyon. I hope that you will not have a building of any kind, not a summer cottage, a hotel, or anything else, to mar the wonderful grandeur, the sublimity, the great loneliness and beauty of the canyon.

Leave it as it is. You can not improve on it.

The ages have been at work on it, and man can only mar it. What you can do is to keep it for your children, your children's children, and for all who come after you, as one of the great sights which every American if he can travel at all should see.

Continuing, he now tells us what he wants his audience to do and why.

We have gotten past the stage, my fellow-citizens, when we are to be pardoned if we treat any part of our country as something to be skinned for two or three years for the use of the present generation, whether it is the forest, the water, the scenery. Whatever it is handle it so that your children's children will get the benefit of it.

With non-diplomatic directness the President expresses his anger at those who destroy the country's natural resources. What a great visual image and what a wonderful analogy: to equate the country with a trophy animal—how especially apt it is coming from someone who is not only an expert hunter, but an expert taxidermist.

If you deal with irrigation, apply it under circumstances that will make it of benefit, not to the speculator who hopes to get profit out of it for two or three years, but handle it so that it will be of use to the home-maker, to the man who comes to live here, and to have his children stay after him. Keep the forests in the same way. Preserve the forests by use; preserve them for the ranchman and the stockman, for the people of the Territory, for the people of the region round about. Preserve them for that use, but use them so that they will not be squandered, that they will not be wasted, so that they will be of benefit to the Arizona of 1953 as well as the Arizona of 1903.

He now moves from admonition to prescription—from a warning against mistreating the environment to prescribing, rather precisely, how to use it. This is, again, very unusual for a world leader to be so personal and so specific, further evidence of the extraordinary heartfelt connection that TR has with this subject.

To the Indians here I want to say a word of welcome. In my regiment I had a good many Indians. They were good enough to fight and to die, and they are good enough to have me treat them exactly as squarely as any white man. There are many problems in connection with them. We must save them from corruption and from brutality; and I regret to say that at times we must save them from unregulated Eastern philanthropy. All I ask is a square deal for every man. Give him a fair chance. Do not let him wrong any one, and do not let him be wronged.

TR's personal passions and human compassion made him a great leader as well as a compelling speaker. Here, off the top of his head, he digresses from irrigation policy to conservation and now to his personal perspective on the Indians who had come to greet him. In acknowledging them for their heroic efforts, he may seem to contemporary ears paternalistic, but in 1903 his advocacy of giving "Indians" a "square deal" was considered quite progressive.

I believe in you. I am glad to see you. I wish you well with all my heart, and I know that your future will justify all the hopes we have.

He began this speech with very personal remarks, and now ends it on a warm, very personal note—again, notice the four uses of the word *I*.

Theodore Roosevelt

THE SPEECH—WHAT TO LOOK FOR: The speech shows his personal passion and his own revolutionary beliefs. Because he had the courage to say what he really felt and speak from the heart, we get to know the real TR in just a few words.

THE DELIVERY—WHAT TO LISTEN FOR: Although this 1903 speech was never recorded, we know from later recordings that TR's voice was high pitched and his delivery impassioned.

THE PERSON—QUALITIES OF GREATNESS: He promoted causes and ideals many decades ahead of his time with gargantuan energy, passion, and style.

FRANKLIN DELANO ROOSEVELT

"... the only thing we have to fear ... is fear itself."

HIGHLIGHTS

1882 Born on January 30 at Hyde Park, New York

1905 Marries Eleanor Roosevelt

1910 Elected to New York State Senate; reelected in 1912

1913 Appointed Assistant Secretary of the Navy by President Woodrow Wilson

1914 Defeated in run for U.S. Senate

1919 Attends Versailles Peace Conference with President Wilson

1920 Runs for Vice President on Democratic Ticket with James N. Cox; resigns as Assistant Secretary of Navy; Harding–Coolidge defeat Cox–FDR

NEW PRESIDENT RALLIES NATION WITH "NEW DEAL"

Franklin Delano Roosevelt—fifth cousin to Theodore Roosevelt, the 26th president—is regarded as one of the greatest leaders the United States ever had. He played center stage for the 12 difficult years—from the Depression to almost the end of World War II—he was President. He charmed the entire world with his jaunty style, positive attitude, dashing demeanor, and great sense of humor. His keen intelligence, pragmatic approach to problems, and stubborn determination to succeed against real odds made him practically unbeatable.

FDR's political career started in 1910 when he was asked to run as a Democrat for the New York State Senate. When he determined that cousin Teddy, a Republican, would not campaign against him, he agreed to run and won. He next served as Assistant Secretary of the Navy (coincidentally a position previously occupied by Teddy) and was tapped as the party's 1920 candidate for Vice President running alongside presidential candidate James Cox. They lost, handily, to Warren Harding.

FDR was stricken with polio in 1921 and, for a time, was almost completely paralyzed. Instead of retreating into retirement, he sent his wife, Eleanor, to speak on his behalf, a job she did so effectively that in 1928 FDR again followed cousin Teddy's path and was elected Governor of New York. Four years later, carrying the hopes of Depression-ridden America, Franklin Roosevelt defeated Herbert Hoover in one of the nation's biggest landslides (472 to 59 electoral votes) and then went on to win three more terms, becoming the first, and only, U.S. President to win more than two terms.

1921	Stricken with polio while vacationing at Campobello Island
1928	Elected Governor of New York; reelected in 1930
1932	November 8, elected President, defeating incumbent Herbert Hoover
1933	March 4, inaugurated as the 32nd U.S. President; March 9, Emergency Banking Relief Act passes; first legislation under the New Deal; March 12, delivers first "fireside chat"
1935	Creates the Works Progress Administration (WPA); the Social Security Act, the most significant New Deal legislation, is passed
1940	Engineers the Lend-Lease Act, giving military aid to Britain
1941	Secretly meets with Winston Churchill, resulting in the Atlantic Charter; on December 7 Japan attacks Pearl Harbor; U.S. enters WWII
1942	Signs Executive Order #9066 interning 120,000 Japanese
1943	At the Casablanca Conference, FDR and Churchill announce they will accept nothing less than an unconditional surrender from the Axis powers; meets with Churchill and Stalin in Teheran—first "Big Three" conference—to discuss the Allied invasion of western Europe
1944	Reelected to a fourth term as President
1945	Meets with Churchill and Stalin at the Yalta Conference to discuss the future of Europe, Asia, and the United Nations; dies on April 12 of a stroke in Warm Springs, Georgia; buried April 15 at Hyde Park

The thirty-second President's tenure began during the depths of the Depression. Thirteen million or more were unemployed, hundreds of thousands were homeless, and banks were failing. Many feared that the country would never recover. Roosevelt's first task was to restore national optimism. At his nomination in 1932, he promised "a New Deal for the American people." He immediately proposed and got Congress to enact legislation to create jobs in construction and industry (Civilian Conservation Corps), improve the country's infrastructure by building highway and power systems (Tennessee Valley Authority), and, in 1935, inaugurated perhaps the best-known program, the Works Progress Administration, which employed more than 8.5 million people on 1.4 million public projects, from building bridges to recording music, creating theater, art, photography, and other cultural activities. Although these and the other programs he implemented, while helpful, did not end the Depression, they helped restore confidence and morale to a deeply frightened nation.

In the end, the quality that perhaps most helped Franklin Roosevelt reassure and inspire America was his understanding and use of the media to get his message out. The first "media president," he wisely controlled how he was portrayed to

Breadlines: Long lines of people waiting to be fed, New York City.

"I pledge you, I pledge myself, to a new deal for the American people. Let us all here assembled constitute ourselves prophets of a new order of competence and of courage. This is more than a political campaign; it is a call to arms. Give me your help, not to win votes alone, but to win in this crusade to restore America to its own people."

FDR accepting nomination, July 2, 1932

(above) Dust Storm in Rolla, Kansas; "5/6/35: Dear Mr. Roosevelt, Darkness came when it hit us. Picture taken from water tower one hundred feet high. Yours Truly, Chas. P. Williams."

(left) Homeless family, tenant farmers in 1936.

(far left) Farm foreclosure sale.

"... one-third of a nation ill-housed, ill-clad, ill-nourished."

Excerpts from Second Inaugural Address, January 17, 1937

Let us ask again: Have we reached the goal of our vision of that fourth day of March 1933? Have we found our happy valley? …

But here is the challenge to our democracy: In this nation I see tens of millions of its citizens—a substantial part of its whole population—who at this very moment are denied the greater part of what the very lowest standards of today call the necessities of life.

I see millions of families trying to live on incomes so meager that the pall of family disaster hangs over them day by day.

I see millions whose daily lives in city and on farm continue under conditions labeled indecent by a so-called polite society half a century ago.

I see millions denied education, recreation, and the opportunity to better their lot and the lot of their children.

I see millions lacking the means to buy the products of farm and factory and by their poverty denying work and productiveness to many other millions.

I see one-third of a nation ill-housed, ill-clad, ill-nourished.

It is not in despair that I paint you that picture. I paint it for you in hope—because the Nation, seeing and understanding the injustice in it, proposes to paint it out. … The test of our progress is not whether we add more to the abundance of those who have much; it is whether we provide enough for those who have too little.

---

the public. Never allowing the press to take pictures of him in his wheelchair and only permitting photos from the waist up if he was standing, FDR's public image was one of great strength wrapped in natural ebullience. He brilliantly used the relatively new medium of radio, inaugurating weekly "Fireside Chats" to communicate with and comfort a nation whose spirit was unraveling. He allowed himself to be seen frequently on local movie screens in the famous MovieTone™ newsreels, and on April 30, 1939, he opened the World's Fair in New York with a televised broadcast—the first televised presidential address, and the first of many regular broadcasts by NBC.

FDR's 12-year "reign," as those who disliked him called it, began on a dismal, gray Inaugural Day, March 4, 1933. With his flair for image-making, FDR reintroduced a long-discarded tradition of a grand inaugural parade, despite the fact someone had tried to assassinate him just three weeks before. Although sharpshooters lined the rooftops of the buildings along the route, people from all over the country crowded into Washington, filled with hope and wild enthusiasm. Many who came had no money; many did not know how they would pay to get home. Nevertheless, street vendors reported record sales of buttons, pins, and banners. Excitement filled the air, and everyone wanted an FDR souvenir.

Despite his legendary reputation and the fact that—in the end—he won four successive elections, opinions about FDR varied widely then and now. Some thought him a saint; others, the devil incarnate. Some thought him too far to the left; others, too far to the right, but as he delivered his first inaugural address he was an inspiration to a nation in crisis. After his decisive victory over Hoover in 1932, Roosevelt defeated Alfred M. Landon by a landslide in 1936, and won an unprecedented third term when he defeated Wendell L. Willkie in 1940. Although quite ill, he won his last election by beating Thomas E. Dewey in 1944. FDR died on April 12, 1945.

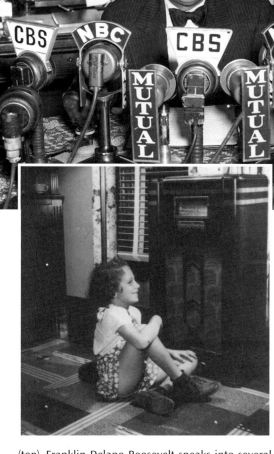

The "Four Freedoms"

Excerpts from State of the Union Address, January 6, 1941

When Roosevelt ran for reelection in 1940, he had promised the parents of America that he would not send their boys into foreign wars. Nevertheless, he had become convinced that to preserve itself, the United States had to assist Britain and the other nations fighting Germany. Knowing the people, just recovering from the Depression, were loathe to enter another European war, Roosevelt devised a plan to lend equipment to the allies, who would repay the loans in goods and services after the war. FDR's aim in this first State of the Union of his unprecedented third term is to sell what might have been an unpopular idea to Congress and the country.

… [A]t no previous time has American security been as seriously threatened from without as it is today. …

In times like these it is immature—and incidentally untrue—for anybody to brag that an unprepared America, single-handed, and with one hand tied behind its back, can hold off the whole world. …

As a nation we may take pride in the fact that we are soft-hearted; but we cannot afford to be soft-headed. We must always be wary of those who with sounding brass and the tinkling cymbal preach the "ism" of appeasement. We must especially beware of that small group of selfish men who would clip the wings of the American eagle in order to feather their own nests.

… [T]he tempo of modern warfare could bring into our very midst the physical attack which we must expect if the dictator nations win this war. …

Our most useful and immediate role is to act as an arsenal for them as well as for ourselves. They do not need manpower. They do need billions of dollars worth of the weapons of defense. …

Let us say to the democracies: "We Americans are vitally concerned in your defense of freedom. We are putting forth our energies, our resources and our organizing powers to give you the strength to regain and maintain a free world. We shall send you, in ever increasing numbers, ships, planes, tanks, guns. That is our purpose and our pledge."…

As men do not live by bread alone, they do not fight by armaments alone. Those who man our defenses and those behind them who build our defenses, must have the stamina and courage which come from an unshakable belief in the manner of life which they are defending. …

[W]e look forward to a world founded upon four essential human freedoms.

The first is freedom of speech and expression everywhere in the world.

The second is freedom of every person to worship God in his own way everywhere in the world.

The third is freedom from want, which, translated into world terms, means economic understandings which will secure to every nation a healthy peacetime life for its inhabitants everywhere in the world.

The fourth is freedom from fear, which, translated into world terms, means a world-wide reduction of armaments to such a point and in such a thorough fashion that no nation will be in a position to commit an act of physical aggression against any neighbor anywhere in the world.

That is no vision of a distant millennium. It is a definite basis for a kind of world attainable in our own time and generation. …

Freedom means the supremacy of human rights everywhere. Our support goes to those who struggle to gain those rights or keep them. Our strength is in our unity of purpose.

To that high concept there can be no end save victory.

(top) Franklin Delano Roosevelt speaks into several network microphones.

(above) Little girl by radio.

"He lifted the U.S. out of economic despair and revolutionized the American way of life. Then he helped make the world safe for democracy."

Arthur Schlesinger, Jr., *Time 100*, "Leaders & Revolutionaries: Twenty people who helped define the political and social fabric of our times," June 14, 1999

First Inaugural Address, March 4, 1933

Roosevelt's inaugural address was the shortest inaugural on the record books, offering only broad themes and few specifics. But because it filled a beaten-down America with confidence at a moment when it was most needed, many then and since have compared FDR's first inaugural address favorably with some of the world's greatest political orations.

ANALYSIS	SPEECH
	President Hoover, Mr. Chief Justice, my friends:
FDR wastes no time and begins by talking right to the American people in plain, clear language that gives the speech a sense of urgency and provided stark contrast to the sense of inaction they had about former President Hoover.	This is a day of national consecration, and I am certain that my fellow Americans expect that on my induction into the Presidency I will address them with a candor and a decision which the present situation of our Nation impels.
Especially when times are bad, truth and honesty are what people crave, and Roosevelt takes pains to assure them that that is what they are going to get. As if to prove that these were not empty words, and at the same time to reassure them, he goes directly to the problem that is on everyone's minds. Note the word *shrink*. FDR is saying, "yes, some of this may be frightening," but with the truth we can face it.	This is pre-eminently the time to speak the truth, the whole truth, frankly and boldly. Nor need we shrink from honestly facing conditions in our country today.
A sentence later, he reassures them directly—the country will *endure, survive,* and *prosper.*	This great nation will endure as it has endured, will revive and will prosper.
After winning their trust, he assumes the tone a father might calming a child who is afraid of the dark. In this, only his fifth sentence as president, in what has become one of his most famous sentences, he names the only thing that can defeat them: their own *fear.* There is a pause before he repeats the word and continues the phrase; note the cadence of the triplet—*nameless, unreasoning, unjustified*; note how he then upgrades the word *fear* to *terror* for increased emphasis.	So, first of all, let me assert my firm belief that the only thing we have to fear is fear itself, nameless, unreasoning, unjustified terror which paralyzes needed efforts to convert retreat into advance.
In the same vein, he demonstrates that he (a frank and vigorous leader) is taking over and is in control, but, interestingly, he also tells them that they have a role to play (so that the burden is now on the people to fully support him) if he is to succeed.	In every dark hour of our national life a leadership of frankness and vigor has met with that understanding and support of the people themselves which is essential to victory.

I am convinced that you will again give that support to leadership in these critical days.	Notice that in this paragraph and the paragraph above, he didn't say *me*, instead he uses the more impersonal, stronger word *leadership*—a word that commands respect. Having made it clear who the leader is, he tells them "we're a team now."
In such a spirit on my part and on yours we face our common difficulties. They concern, thank God, only material things. Values have shrunken to fantastic levels; taxes have risen; our ability to pay has fallen; government of all kinds is faced by serious curtailment of income; the means of exchange are frozen in the currents of trade; the withered leaves of industrial enterprise lie on every side; farmers find no markets for their produce; the savings of many years in thousands of families are gone.	Together they must fight a host of ills. Here, he uses short phrases and poetic imagery, which makes hard-to-understand financial concepts accessible and the battle more lofty and noble, even if it is about money!
More important, a host of unemployed citizens face the grim problem of existence, and an equally great number toil with little return.	Last, and definitely not least for his audience, he addresses the financial issue they all understand and all dread—unemployment.
Only a foolish optimist can deny the dark realities of the moment.	Without specifically mentioning Herbert Hoover's failed pie-in-the-sky optimism, he pointedly criticizes it. He is not a *foolish optimist* because he is not, by implication, *denying the dark realities*. Yet despite this swipe at Hoover, the overall tone of this entire inaugural is one of great optimism.
Yet our distress comes from no failure of substance. We are stricken by no plague of locusts. Compared with the perils which our forefathers conquered because they believed and were not afraid, we have still much to be thankful for.	First, a biblical reference, *plague of locusts*, and then a historical reference—both intended to compare what others suffered and survived and to assure the people that they, too, will prevail.
Nature still offers her bounty and human efforts have multiplied it. Plenty is at our doorstep, but a generous use of it languishes in the very sight of the supply. Primarily this is because the rulers of the exchange of mankind's goods have failed, through their own stubbornness and their own incompetence, have admitted their failure, and abdicated.	Still further reassurance—at a time that the country was suffering severe agricultural problems (the Dust Bowl) and farmers were losing their farms—Roosevelt tells the nation that, in essence, God has not forsaken them; corporate greed and mismanagement has, and those are solvable problems. Nor have they themselves failed; it is the *rulers of the exchange of mankind's goods*—a wonderful use of language that lets everyone know who is to blame without naming the culprits.
Practices of the unscrupulous money changers stand indicted in the court of public opinion, rejected by the hearts and minds of men.	And using another vivid religious analogy, he also places the blame on the banks (the *money changers*) who have thrown farmers off their land for failure to pay mortgages.

He convicts them with powerful, rythmic prose. They are "old school" that won't try new things; they are greedy, and worst of all they are blind.	True they have tried, but their efforts have been cast in the pattern of an outworn tradition. Faced by failure of credit they have proposed only the lending of more money. Stripped of the lure of profit by which to induce our people to follow their false leadership, they have resorted to exhortations, pleading tearfully for restored confidence. They know only the rules of a generation of self-seekers. They have no vision, and when there is no vision the people perish.
Here, Roosevelt returns to the Biblical *money changers*, and wisely does not compare himself to Jesus. Rather *we* (all of us) will drive them out of the temple.	The money changers have fled their high seats in the temple of our civilization. We may now restore that temple to the ancient truths.
Having planted spiritual references, he harvests them, like a preacher addressing his congregation. At the same time, having identified the devil, he changes his theme and knowing that the Depression will not go away overnight, focuses the country on the things that are more important than money.	The measure of the restoration lies in the extent to which we apply social values more noble than mere monetary profit.
And here he tells them what those things are—his definition of happiness.	Happiness lies not in the mere possession of money; it lies in the joy of achievement, in the thrill of creative effort. The joy and moral stimulation of work no longer must be forgotten in the mad chase of evanescent profits.
As you read the following sentence, do you hear another first inaugural address? Can you hear JFK's "Ask not what your country can do for you—ask what you can do for your country"?	These dark days will be worth all they cost us if they teach us that our true destiny is not to be ministered unto but to minister to ourselves and to our fellow men.
FDR goes on to propose a new standard of value—represented not by wealth or high position—and condemns those who, out of greed, abandon their *sacred trust*. President Theodore Roosevelt (the "trust buster") would have been very proud of his cousin as FDR takes on the banks and big business.	Recognition of the falsity of material wealth as the standard of success goes hand in hand with the abandonment of the false belief that public office and high political position are to be valued only by the standards of pride of place and personal profit; and there must be an end to a conduct in banking and in business which too often has given to a sacred trust the likeness of callous and selfish wrongdoing.
Blaming the old guard of businessmen, bankers, and politicians, FDR trumpets a return to old-fashioned values.	Small wonder that confidence languishes, for it thrives only on honesty, on honor, on the sacredness of obligations, on faithful protection, on unselfish performance; without them it cannot live.
Again, having told the audience the problem, he begins to outline his plan for massive action.	Restoration calls, however, not for changes in ethics alone. This Nation asks for action, and action now.

Our greatest primary task is to put people to work. This is no unsolvable problem if we face it wisely and courageously. It can be accomplished in part by direct recruiting by the government itself, treating the task as we would treat the emergency of a war, but at the same time, through this employment, accomplishing greatly needed projects to stimulate and reorganize the use of our natural resources.

Hand in hand with this we must frankly recognize the overbalance of population in our industrial centers and, by engaging on a national scale in a redistribution, endeavor to provide a better use of the land for those best fitted for the land.

An activist government will come to the rescue not with make-work, but real, *greatly needed* work. He begins by outlining the broad large-scale plans for industry and then agriculture.

The task can be helped by definite efforts to raise the values of agricultural products and, with this, the power to purchase the output of our cities. It can be helped by preventing, realistically, the tragedy of the growing loss through foreclosure of our small homes and our farms. It can be helped by insistence that the Federal, State, and local governments act forthwith on the demand that their cost be drastically reduced. It can be helped by the unifying of relief activities which today are often scattered, uneconomical, and unequal. It can be helped by national planning for and supervision of all forms of transportation and of communications and other utilities which have a definitely public character. There are many ways in which it can be helped, but it can never be helped merely by talking about it. We must act and act quickly.

Next, he offers some specific actions and, by repeating the phrase *can be helped by* six times in quick succession, he builds a powerful feeling of optimism, movement, and urgency which is reinforced in his last sentence.

Finally, in our progress toward a resumption of work we require two safeguards against a return of the evils of the old order; there must be a strict supervision of all banking and credits and investments; there must be an end to speculation with other people's money; and there must be provision for an adequate but sound currency.

The needy country must have loved hearing that FDR was going to do something and do it quickly. Now FDR needed something from them. He needed their support to get the Congress to enact sweeping legislation to control banking and business.

These are the lines of attack. I shall presently urge upon a new Congress in special session detailed measures for their fulfillment, and I shall seek the immediate assistance of the several States.

Rather than provide the details, which would have distracted from the momentum of his message, FDR wisely chose to stay away from them.

Through this program of action we address ourselves to putting our own national house in order and making income balance outgo. Our international trade relations, though vastly important, are in point of time and necessity secondary to the establishment of a sound national economy. I favor as a practical policy the putting of first things first. I shall spare no effort to restore world trade by international economic readjustment, but the emergency at home cannot wait on that accomplishment.

Instead, he is once again the protective father, assuring his "children" that he will take care of things at home.

The basic thought that guides these specific means of national recovery is not narrowly nationalistic. It is the insistence, as a first consideration, upon the interdependence of the various elements in all parts of the United States; a recognition of the old and permanently important manifestation of the American spirit of the pioneer.

Here it wasn't only Americans he was addressing. For the benefit of the country's allies, he does a little fancy footwork to justify his focus on domestic matters and at the same time reassure them.

Notice the emphatic effect produced by these three really short sentences. Grouped together they create a feeling of unshakable solidity.

It is the way to recovery. It is the immediate way. It is the strongest assurance that the recovery will endure.

Nothing inspires higher approval ratings than when a president assumes the mantle of "commander in chief," and speaks in war terms, even if the enemy is the country's domestic problems.

In the field of world policy I would dedicate this Nation to the policy of the good neighbor; the neighbor who resolutely respects himself and, because he does so, respects the rights of others; the neighbor who respects his obligations and respects the sanctity of his agreements in and with a world of neighbors.

If I read the temper of our people correctly, we now realize as we have never realized before our interdependence on each other; that we cannot merely take but we must give as well; that if we are to go forward, we must move as a trained and loyal army willing to sacrifice for the good of a common discipline, because without such discipline, no progress is made, no leadership becomes effective. We are, I know, ready and willing to submit our lives and property to such discipline because it makes possible a leadership which aims at a larger good. This I propose to offer, pledging that the larger purposes will bind upon us all as a sacred obligation with a unity of duty hitherto evoked only in time of armed strife.

With this pledge taken, I assume unhesitatingly the leadership of this great army of our people dedicated to a disciplined attack upon our common problems.

Here FDR appears to be preparing Americans for sweeping changes and sweeping criticism of some of the programs he has in mind. Indeed, he was criticized roundly and some felt that to achieve his aims he overstepped his Constitutional authority; some programs were ultimately declared to be unconsitutional by the Supreme Court.

Action in this image and to this end is feasible under the form of government which we have inherited from our ancestors. Our Constitution is so simple and practical that it is possible always to meet extraordinary needs by changes in emphasis and arrangement without loss of essential form. That is why our constitutional system has proved itself the most superbly enduring political mechanism the modern world has produced. It has met every stress of vast expansion of territory, of foreign wars, of bitter internal strife, of world relations.

Here he directly challenges the legislature to be flexible. His agenda here is subtle. Notice how he implies that a stronger role for the president might be necessary to meet the extraordinary circumstances—without saying it outright, he is saying, "you might not like it under other circumstances, but…"

It is to be hoped that the normal balance of executive and legislative authority may be wholly adequate to meet the unprecedented task before us. But it may be that an unprecedented demand and need for undelayed action may call for temporary departure from that normal balance of public procedure.

He proceeds to justify these potential actions very legally and poetically …

I am prepared under my constitutional duty to recommend the measures that a stricken nation in the midst of a stricken world may require.

These measures, or such other measures as the Congress may build out of its experience and wisdom, I shall seek, within my constitutional authority, to bring to speedy adoption. But in the event that the Congress shall fail to take one of these two courses, and in the event that the national emergency is still critical, I shall not evade the clear course of duty that will then confront me. I shall ask the Congress for the one remaining instrument to meet the crisis, broad Executive power to wage a war against the emergency, as great as the power that would be given to me if we were in fact invaded by a foreign foe.

For the trust reposed in me I will return the courage and the devotion that befit the time. I can do no less.

… And then gives strong and unmistakable warning to Congress about what his next step will be if they do not give him what he wants. Notice also that, at the same time, he is telling the people that he is prepared to wage war on their behalf. Had FDR not laid the groundwork with all that went before, these words would have been alarming; instead, they are reassuring.

We face the arduous days that lie before us in the warm courage of the national unity; with the clear consciousness of seeking old and precious moral values; with the clean satisfaction that comes from the stern performance of duty by old and young alike. We aim at the assurance of a rounded and permanent national life. We do not distrust the future of essential democracy.

Aware of the impact of what he has just said, he returns to wholesome imagery. Look at the adjectives he has chosen in this one sentence: arduous, warm, clear, old and precious, clean, stern. Notice, too, the very purposeful team-building use of the word we to start each of the following three sentences.

The people of the United States have not failed.

Again he reassures them. It is not their fault.

In their need they have registered a mandate that they want direct, vigorous action. They have asked for discipline and direction under leadership. They have made me the present instrument of their wishes. In the spirit of the gift I take it.

In this dedication of a Nation we humbly ask the blessing of God. May He protect each and every one of us. May He guide me in the days to come.

Now he does something astonishing. He shifts radically from first-person we to third-person they. He is not taking power; they—the people—have asked; more than asked, they have made him take it. Playing off of the indirect references to Jesus earlier in the speech, Roosevelt ends in an overtly spiritual way, fashioning himself as "the chosen one," the "present instrument of their wishes." He thus moves, in these last few seconds, from "reluctant dictator" to humble chosen servant and, because of his communication mastery, is able, remarkably, to sell both ideas at the same time as he sets the stage for an unprecedented twelve years of historic leadership.

Franklin Delano Roosevelt

THE SPEECH—WHAT TO LOOK FOR: Action-oriented, enormously confident words without a hint of doubt or vacillation caused this speech to lift and reassure a nation.

THE DELIVERY—WHAT TO LISTEN FOR: The strong, bold, confident tone of voice amplified the words, but it was, as always, FDR's rich, textured voice and brilliantly strategized pauses that gave people comfort and reassured them that the country was in good hands.

THE PERSON—QUALITIES OF GREATNESS: The speed of his wit, the power of his mind, the warmth and understanding he exuded, and the supreme self-confidence and conviction with which he spoke made him the perfect leader to buoy Americans during two of the country's greatest crises.

LOU GEHRIG

"... the luckiest man on the face of the earth."

HIGHLIGHTS

1903   Born on June 19 in New York City

1921   Football scholarship to Columbia

1925–May 2, 1939   NY Yankees, first baseman

1941   Died on June 2 in Riverdale, New York

CAREER STATISTICS

Jersey number   4 (first player ever to have his number retired)

Batting average   .340

Home runs   493

RBIs   1,995

"IRON HORSE" WOWS CROWD WITH HIS HEART — NOT HIS BAT

When legendary first baseman Lou Gehrig died on June 2, 1941, over 5,000 people filed past his casket at New York's Riverside Church in silent tribute to one of the greatest and most beloved athletes ever. In his fifteen years as a Yankee the team won nine American League pennants and eight World Series.

In 1939, when he retired, *New York Herald-Tribune* columnist Richards Vidmer said,

> ...only those who have been fortunate enough to have known him during his most glorious years will realize that he has stood for something finer than merely a great baseball player—that he has stood for everything that makes sports important in the American scene.

Even today, over sixty years after his death, Lou Gehrig remains one of the most impressive athletes of all time.

Known as the "Iron Horse," he earned a place in history not only for his extraordinary physical prowess, but also for downright common decency—strength of character and the positive attitude he displayed in the face of adversity.

Gehrig, by nature, was modest, and, because he played in the shadows of both Babe Ruth and Joe DiMaggio, he received less money than they did and, often, less attention than his talent deserved. Even on the day that he hit four consecutive home runs—the first time this had ever been accomplished in baseball—his place in the spotlight was eclipsed by the announcement of legendary Giants manager

Won Triple Crown 1934 (49 home runs, 165 RBIs and a .363 batting average—one of greatest seasons in the history of baseball)

Consecutive games played 2,130 (unbroken for 56 years until 1995 by Cal Ripkin, Jr.)

Home runs hit in a single game 4 (first player ever to achieve)

Grand slams 23 (all-time leader)

All-time Yankee leader in hits, doubles, triples, RBIs

American League MVP 1927, 1936

Salary $6,000 in 1927* (compared to Babe Ruth's $80,000)

Inducted into Baseball Hall of Fame by BBWAA (Special Election)—1939

While other members of the Yankees raise their arms and cheer, manager Joe McCarthy, right, shakes hands with Lou Gehrig and congratulates the veteran first baseman after he had played in his 2,000th consecutive game.

John McGraw's retirement. Even that didn't seem to bother Lou. A man of few words, he said his actions could speak louder than anything he might say. A filler of grandstands, he never grandstanded.

Indisputably, his incredible career statistics all prove that the "Iron Horse's" extraordinary ability at bat and on the field did speak far louder than any of his words. Until the day he said "goodbye"' to baseball.

Henry Louis Gehrig didn't leave baseball because he wanted to. Stricken with a degenerative neurological disease, amyotrophic lateral sclerosis (ALS), today often called "Lou Gehrig's disease," he was forced to retire.

Nevertheless, "Shy Lou" lived a wonderful life. He was born on June 19, 1903, to German immigrant parents in New York City and was accepted to Columbia University on a football scholarship. At Columbia, John McGraw (the Giants manager) scouted the strapping youth, who had played baseball in high school, recognized the southpaw's potential, and persuaded him to take an assumed last name (Lewis) and to start playing professional minor league baseball.

This may have been the only bad thing Gehrig ever did. And it landed him in lots of trouble. By going "pro," completely illegal under college rules, Gehrig inadvertently disqualified himself from playing college ball. As a result, he lost his scholarship. Fortunately, his coach valued Gehrig so much that he went to bat for him and convinced the Columbia faculty to reinstate him once he dissolved his pro contract.

In 1925, when Gehrig made the Yankee starting lineup, teams had long, 12- to 15-game road trips and, instead of lush private planes, traveled overnight by rail to reach their out-of-town destinations. Players were expected to sleep on the train, and be rested and ready for practice and play shortly after arrival.

"I did not go there to look at Gehrig. I did not even know what position he played. But he played in the outfield against Rutgers and socked a couple of balls a mile. I sat up and took notice. I saw a tremendous youth, with powerful arms and terrific legs. I said, … here is a kid who can't miss."
Yankee scout Paul Krichell

Babe Ruth hugs his former teammate Lou Gehrig, on the occasion of "Lou Gehrig Day" at Yankee Stadium.

"Let's face it. I'm not a headline guy. I always knew that as long as I was following Babe to the plate I could have gone up there and stood on my head. No one would have noticed the difference. When the Babe was through swinging, whether he hit one or fanned, nobody paid any attention to the next hitter. They all were talking about what the Babe had done."

Lou Gehrig

Without helmets, cushy gloves, or high-tech physical conditioning regimens, their injuries were more frequent and, without full-time medical staffs, they didn't receive the immediate treatment that athletes today take for granted. Under these conditions, it's amazing that Gehrig never had an injury, never had a cold or an infection, never had a family crisis, and never seemed to let anything interfere with his determination to show up and play in 2,130 consecutive games.

Suddenly, however, in the spring of 1939, Gehrig couldn't play as he did before. He couldn't connect at bat; his fielding wasn't as sharp; his throwing wasn't as reliable. Once, he even fell down at home plate. Finally, on May 2, 1939, knowing something was wrong and not wanting to hurt his team's chances, he took himself out of the lineup.

Some of the world's finest doctors examined young Gehrig, who was just shy of 36. Eventually, physicians at the Mayo Clinic made the frightening and tragic diagnosis: Lou Gehrig—the Iron Horse—had an incurable disease that would strip him of all physical control, although it would have no effect on his mind, and he would thus be fully aware of the continuous process of deterioration.

Gehrig officially retired from baseball on his 36th birthday, June 19, 1939. His teammates were devastated. The Yankees quickly organized a "Lou Gehrig Appreciation Day" for that July 4th.

Media coverage of the tribute was enormous. The ceremony took place between games of that day's double-header. Mayor Fiorello LaGuardia made a presentation, as did Gehrig's coaches, teammates, and other notables. By the time the ceremonies neared their conclusion, Gehrig stood physically exhausted and emotionally drained. He actually leaned on his friends for support. Although the crowd started chanting for him to speak, Master of Ceremonies Sid Mercer could see that Gehrig did not have the energy, and he graciously covered for him by announcing, "I shall not ask Lou Gehrig to make a speech. I do not believe that I should." Ed Barrow, president of the Yankees, took Gehrig aside and whispered something in his ear.

Shirley Povich, one of the greatest sportswriters of the day, and almost as beloved as Lou Gehrig himself, described best what followed:

They started to haul away the microphones. Gehrig half turned toward the dugout, with the ceremonies apparently at an end. And then he wheeled suddenly, strode back to the loud-speaking apparatus, held up his hand for attention, gulped, managed a smile, and then spoke.

"For weeks," [said Gehrig] "I have been reading in the newspapers that I am a fellow who got a tough break. I don't believe it. I have been a lucky guy. For sixteen years, into every ballpark in which I have ever walked, I received nothing but kindness and

(above) Lou Gehrig collapses at home plate at the beginning of his illness in 1939. Amyotropic Lateral Sclerosis (ALS), or Lou Gehrig's Disease.

(right) Mayor LaGuardia at microphone speaking as Lou Gehrig listens with bowed head at Yankee Stadium, July 4th—"Lou Gehrig Day."

(below) New York Yankees' manager Joe McCarthy (right) at Yankee Stadium on "Lou Gehrig Day," between games of the Yankee-Senator double-header, presenting Lou (left) with a trophy on behalf of the rest of the team.

encouragement. . . ."

Povich's overall impression of the day's events was quoted by Leonard Shapiro of the *Washington Post*, in a 1998 memorial tribute:

I saw strong men weep this afternoon, expressionless umpires swallow hard and emotion pump the hearts and glaze the eyes of 60,000 baseball fans in Yankee Stadium. ... Yes, and hard-boiled news photographers clicked their shutters with fingers that trembled a bit. All given spontaneously, it was without a doubt one of the most touching scenes ever witnessed on a ball field. ...

Another sportswriter of that era, John Drebinger of the *New York Times*, described Gehrig leaving Yankee Stadium following this day:

Long after the tumult and shouting had died and the last of the crowd had filed out, Lou trudged across the field for his familiar hike to his favorite exit gate. With him walked his bosom pal and teammate, Bill Dickey, with whom he always rooms when the Yanks are on the road. Lou walks with a slight hitch in his gait now, but there was supreme confidence in his voice as he said to his friend, "Bill, I'm going to remember this day for a long time."

Tragically, Gehrig did not have much time left. He died 23 months later with his devoted wife, Eleanor, his family, and his physician at his bedside.

"The Babe is one fellow, and I'm another and I could never be exactly like him. I don't try, I just go on as I am in my own right."
Lou Gehrig

Lou Gehrig / "... the luckiest man on the face of the earth."

22

". . . the luckiest man on the face of the earth"

Farewell Speech at Yankee Stadium, July 4, 1939

Reluctant and trembling, baseball icon Lou Gehrig summons the energy for perhaps his finest performance on a baseball field. After a career setting historic records of athletic achievement, Lou Gehrig's last appearance at Yankee Stadium, this time behind a microphone, set a standard of grace and humility that may exceed anything he ever did with a bat and a glove.

ANALYSIS	SPEECH
The words echoed off the walls of Yankee Stadium as Gehrig does what only the best speakers do—he speaks with his audience, addressing them in a warm, personal way and setting the stage for one of the most gracious and understated speeches in history.	Fans,
This line reverberates louder and longer in people's minds than even his remarkable 2,130 consecutive games. Its straightforward simplicity never fails to touch us. He and everyone else knew how ill he was, yet from the sincerity in his voice, the world knew this was how he truly felt.	For the past two weeks you have been reading about the bad break I got. Yet today I consider myself the luckiest man on the face of the earth.
His genuine humility comes through as he once again talks directly to his fans amd teammates.	I have been in ballparks for seventeen years and have never received anything but kindness and encouragement from you fans. Look at these grand men.
And here he establishes yet another powerful connection with the fans. Asking questions, even rhetorical ones, totally involves the audience and gives the whole speech an easy-to-listen-to conversational tone. Although Gehrig was hardly a seasoned orator, after this and each succeeding question, Gehrig returns to his main theme, "I'm lucky"—much like a brilliantly composed piece of classical music.	Which of you wouldn't consider it the highlight of his career just to associate with them for even one day? Sure I'm lucky.
Here, instead of simply stating what an honor it was to know the three men who hired and led him, he takes us through his life with them by asking us, again rhetorically, to put ourselves in his shoes. Notice, too, how he's not afraid to be informal and personal here.	Who wouldn't consider it an honor to have known Jacob Ruppert? Also, the builder of baseball's greatest empire, Ed Barrow? To have spent six years with that wonderful little fellow, Miller Huggins?
Watch how the triplet here starts to build momentum.	Then to have spent the next nine years with that outstanding leader, that smart student of psychology, the best manager in baseball today, Joe McCarthy?
The theme again.	Sure I'm lucky.

When the New York Giants, a team you would give your right arm to beat, and vice versa, sends you a gift—that's something!	Even the opposing team, the crosstown rivals, gets a compliment.
When everybody down to the groundskeepers and those boys in white coats remember you with trophies—that's something.	No one—not even the "little guys"—is left out. All are complimented with equal sincerity.
When you have a wonderful mother-in-law who takes sides with you in squabbles with her own daughter—that's something.	To compliment a mother-in-law is a warm and endearing thing, but look how much he tells us about their relationship by sharing a little example with his audience.
When you have a father and a mother who work all their lives so you can have an education and build your body—it's a blessing!	This acknowledgment of his parents is particularly poignant, particularly when you remember that the country had not yet fully emerged from the Great Depression and so many of his listeners had lived through hard times as struggling parents or the children of struggling parents.
When you have a wife who has been a tower of strength and shown more courage than you dreamed existed—that's the finest I know.	And he saves his last words of glowing tribute for his wife.
So I close in saying that I may have been given a bad break, but I have an awful lot to live for.	The last paragraph is the speech-making equivalent of a three-pitch strikeout to end the game. Notice how flawlessly he ties it up by echoing his very first sentence, hits a variation of his central theme and looks optimistically, like a kid who can't wait to get out there on the baseball diamond, to the future.

Lou Gehrig

THE SPEECH—WHAT TO LOOK FOR: So many beautiful human values in one short speech: humility, simplicity, unspoiled youthful enthusiasm and the pure, innocent love and gratitude he bestows upon his colleagues.

THE DELIVERY—WHAT TO LISTEN FOR: The emotion in his voice—so much emotion that he almost didn't give the speech. But beyond the emotional discomfort, even in so few words, you can hear the lack of pretense, the lack of ego, and the genuine humility of a simple man.

THE PERSON—QUALITIES OF GREATNESS: Strength, perseverance, courage, innocence, humility, and grace, even under spectacularly tragic personal circumstances

WINSTON CHURCHILL

". . .blood, toil, tears, and sweat"

PRIME MINISTER PREPARES NATION FOR WAR

Many believe Winston Churchill was the orator of the twentieth century. And he may have been, but even with so many memorable speeches filled with poetic phrases, fantastic cadence, great delivery, amazing voice, and powerful body language—conveying certitude and conviction—in the end it is Churchill's overwhelming personality that transcends even his most magical oratory.

Time magazine probably best described Churchill's impact on the world when they named him "The Man of the Half Century": "That a free world survived in 1950, with a hope of more progress and less calamity, was due in large measure to his exertions." Reading that, it's hard to believe that this was a boy who, according to his father, Lord Randolph, lacked "cleverness, knowledge and any capacity for settled work." Yet he also described him as boy who had "a great talent for show-off, exaggeration and make-believe," which may account, at least in part, for his great oratorical skill.

Born of an English father, whose ancestors were military heroes, and an American socialite mother, Winston was, indeed, a terrible student, almost failing out of the prestigious Harrow preparatory school. So unfocused was he in his youth, that the man who became one of the world's great wartime leaders failed the entrance exam to the Sandhurst Royal Military Academy twice before finally passing.

Like other leaders, it was in the heat of conflict that Winston Churchill showed almost unsurpassed daring and brilliance. At one point in his storied military career, Churchill risked his life to rescue an armored train during the Boer War in South Africa and was caught and imprisoned. After only 27 days in military prison he masterminded his escape, returning to England, for the first of many times, as a war hero.

In 1900, after a career as a soldier and journalist, Churchill's public life began when he was elected as a Conservative Member of Parliament. In 1904, he switched to the Liberal Party, only to return in 1924 to the Conservatives. Over the next eighteen years, he served in many capacities, ranging from Undersecretary of State for the Colonies to Chancellor of the Exchequer. By the 1930s, the years in which Adolf Hitler and the Nazi party achieved power in Germany, he was out of office.

From 1937, when Chamberlain became Prime Minister, until Germany invaded Poland in September 1939, Chamberlain had followed a policy of appeasement, agreeing to many of Hitler's demands for territory, in the belief that Hitler could be sated and an all-out war in Europe could be averted. After signing the Munich Agreement in September 1938, Chamberlain and many others believed he had achieved "peace in our time." Churchill, believing war was inevitable, strenuously disagreed, leaving him very unpopular and increasingly isolated during this period.

Covering the Boer War in South Africa as a war correspondent, Winston Churchill stands in the doorway of a tent.

The German army invaded Czechoslovakia in March 1939, significantly changing the mood in Britain and setting the stage for Churchill's return to the Government. On September 1, 1939, Hitler invaded Poland. Britain, France, Australia, and New Zealand declared war against Germany two days later, and

Franklin D. Roosevelt and Winston Churchill seated out-of-doors at news conference in Casablanca, Morocco.

Winston Churchill watches a flying German V-1 Buzz Bomb attack in Southern England with his daughter Mary during World War II.

Churchill was asked to join Chamberlain's wartime government in September 1939 as First Lord of the Admiralty. By April 1940, the Germans had invaded Denmark and Norway, and, on May 10, the Nazis invaded Belgium, The Netherlands, and France. Chamberlain resigned.

At 6:00 A.M. on May 10, 1940, Churchwill was summoned to Buckingham Palace where King George asked him at the age of sixty-five to head a Coalition Government. Three days later, in his first address as Prime Minister to the House of Commons, he offered the country everything he had—"I have nothing to offer but blood, toil, tears, and sweat"—and assured them of their ultimate victory.

Time magazine, in selecting Winston Churchill as its "Man of The Year" in 1940 (Hitler was the "runner-up"), said:

> Those eleven burning words summed up the nature of Britain's war, turned Britain's back on the weaknesses of the past, set her face toward the unknown future. Because of them the rest of that speech has been forgotten. It should not be forgotten, for it is not only a great example of Winston Churchill's eloquence, but the epitome of the movement which he leads.

Holland fell to the Nazis on May 15 and the situation in France was ominous. On May 26, the Allies began evacuating troops stranded in Europe from Dunkirk. Belgium fell on May 27. The evacuation ended on June 3 and was an astonishing

---

"… we shall fight on the beaches"

Excerpt from Speech to House of Commons, June 4, 1940

…Even though large tracts of Europe and many old and famous States have fallen or may fall into the grip of the Gestapo and all the odious apparatus of the Nazi rule, we shall not flag or fail. We shall go on to the end, we shall fight in France, we shall fight on the seas and oceans, we shall fight with growing confidence and growing strength in the air, we shall defend our Island, whatever the cost may be, we shall fight on the beaches, we shall fight on the landing grounds, we shall fight in the fields and in the streets, we shall fight in the hills; we shall never surrender…

Words That Shook the World

Winston Churchill visiting Coventry Cathedral after the German bombing of Coventry (November 14–15, 1940).

success—338,000 men were saved—made all the more remarkable because the 220 naval vessels crossing the English Channel were augmented by civilian fishing boats, barges, and paddle steamers.

Norway surrendered on June 10 and the Germans entered Paris on June 14. There were some in Churchill's own cabinet who thought the time had come to talk peace. Instead, Churchill braced the public for the likely invasion and the long war to come. The Battle of Britain actually began on July 10 and ended on October 30 after a 57-day blitz. Although outnumbered, but greatly aided by radar, and despite near constant bombardment of major cities, including London, the people of Britain did not give in, and while they did not win a decisive battle, they prevailed against overwhelming odds.

Although the Germans postponed their invasion plans, the war in Europe expanded. A pact among Germany, Japan, and Italy was signed in late September and Italy invaded Greece in late October. While the blitz had ended, intermittent heavy bombing of Britain continued with the bombing of Coventry on November 14–15 and massive bombings of London to end the year on December 29 and 30. In early 1941, there were some victories in Northern Africa and, although the United States was still not at war, Roosevelt signed the Lend-Lease Act, which provided much-needed aid to Britain. In May more bombings of London; this time the British retaliate by bombing Hamburg. Hitler invades the Soviet Union in June and the German Army sweeps through the country. The United States moves

"That a free world survived in 1950, with a hope of more progress and less calamity, was due in large measure to his exertions."

Time magazine, naming Churchill "Man of the Half Century," January 2, 1950 ("Winston Churchill: Through War & Peace")

"The master statesman stood alone against fascism and renewed the world's faith in the superiority of democracy."

John Keegan, *Time 100:* "Leaders & Revolutionaries: Twenty people who helped define the political and social fabric of our times," June 14, 1999

"We shall not fail or falter; we shall not weaken or tire. . . Give us the tools and we will finish the job."

Sir Winston Churchill, BBC radio broadcast, February 9, 1941

"Sinews of peace" (aka "The Iron Curtain Speech")

Excerpt froms Speech at Westminster College, Fulton, Missouri, March 5, 1946

… A shadow has fallen upon the scenes so lately lighted by the Allied victory. …

We understand the Russian need to be secure on her western frontiers by the removal of all possibility of German aggression. We welcome Russia to her rightful place among the leading nations of the world. We welcome her flag upon the seas…. It is my duty however, for I am sure you would wish me to state the facts as I see them to you, to place before you certain facts about the present position in Europe.

From Stettin in the Baltic to Trieste in the Adriatic, an iron curtain has descended across the Continent. Behind that line lie all the capitals of the ancient states of Central and Eastern Europe….

There is the solution which I respectfully offer to you in this Address to which I have given the title "The Sinews of Peace. …

Let no man underrate the abiding power of the British Empire and Commonwealth. … do not suppose that we shall not come through these dark years of privation as we have come through the glorious years of agony, or that half a century from now, you will not see 70 or 80 millions of Britons spread about the world and united in defense of our traditions, our way of life, and of the world causes which you and we espouse. … If we adhere faithfully to the Charter of the United Nations and walk forward in sedate and sober strength seeking no one's land or treasure, seeking to lay no arbitrary control upon the thoughts of men; if all British moral and material forces and convictions are joined with your own in fraternal association, the high-roads of the future will be clear, not only for us but for all, not only for our time, but for a century to come.

"… never, never, never give in"

Excerpt from speech to schoolchildren at The Harrow School, October 29, 1941

… [N]ever give in, never give in, never, never, never, never—in nothing, great or small, large or petty—never give in except to convictions of honour and good sense. Never yield to force; never yield to the apparently overwhelming might of the enemy. We stood all alone a year ago, and to many countries it seemed that our account was closed, we were finished….

Do not let us speak of darker days: let us speak rather of sterner days. These are not dark days; these are great days—the greatest days our country has ever lived; and we must all thank God that we have been allowed, each of us according to our stations, to play a part….

against the Axis and embargoes oil. Roosevelt and Churchill sign the Atlantic Charter in August, declaring that they were fighting the Axis powers to "ensure life, liberty, independence and religious freedom and to preserve the rights of man and justice." But still, the United States is not officially at war, and Britain is bearing the brunt of the fight.

On December 6, the tide in Russia begins to turn as the Soviet Army launches a massive counteroffensive. On December 7, Pearl Harbor is attacked and both the U.S. and Britain declare war on Japan. The war in Europe would continue for another three and a half years, but Britain was no longer in it alone. On May 7, 1945, Germany surrenders.

Even with general euphoria after the surrender, Churchill soon lost his governing coalition when the Labour party withdrew from his government. In the General Election that July, the Labour party won a decisive victory and Churchill was out of office. Although this was a devastating personal setback, he did not retire from public life, but remained on as Leader of the Opposition from 1945 to 1951.

(top) British Prime Minister Winston Churchill visits the U.S. 9th Army as they cross the concrete barrier of the Siegfried Line or West Wall into Germany, during World War II. With him are (left to right) General Simpson, Commander-in-Chief of the 9th Army, Field-Marshal Montgomery, and Field-Marshal Sir Alan Brooke.

(right) Winston Churchill, Harry S. Truman, and Joseph Stalin shake hands during the meeting of 'The Big Three' in Potsdam.

In 1945, Churchill was invited to speak at Westminster College in Fulton, Missouri. President Harry Truman, a Missourian, accompanied. There, in a gymnasium of the small-town college on March 5, 1946, Churchill ominously warned of the dangers inherent in the totalitarian regimes under Communism, suggesting that there be a western alliance that would achieve peace only through strength. The speech stimulated enormous controversy and criticism in the United States and abroad. Churchill was charged with being an alarmist, and worse.

To most people who remembered the wartime alliance, the Russians were perceived as an ally of the West, but Churchill had always been wary of them, and saw the alliance as a necessity. In fact, in a radio address seven years earlier, in October 1939, Churchill prophetically said of the Soviet Union, "I cannot forecast to you the action of Russia. It is a riddle wrapped in a mystery inside an enigma."

Interestingly, Churchill's speech not only immortalized the image of an "iron curtain" but it turned Fulton, Missouri, into a symbol as well. In 1992, the former president of the Soviet Union, Mikhail Gorbachev, went to Fulton to speak about the end of the Cold War and the collapse of the Soviet Union.

When all is said and done, Churchill was, indeed, a complex and fascinating figure: soldier, journalist, author, historian, lecturer, member of Parliament, Undersecretary of State, Home Secretary, Secretary of the Navy, Secretary of War, Chancellor of the Exchequer, Prime Minister (twice), Nobel Prize Laureate for Literature, and consummate statesman.

ANALYSIS

SPEECH

While Churchill's opening paragraphs may not be eloquent, they are extremely important because they achieve some very specific goals. Churchill must reassure a nation newly at war. He does so by first telling them that theirs is a government of unity. In record time he has created a War Cabinet to address the crisis, key government positions have been filled and the rest will be in a matter of days. Second, he assures them by providing great detail that there is no power vacuum, and that he, Churchill, is very much in charge.

On Friday evening last I received His Majesty's commission to form a new Administration. It was the evident wish and will of Parliament and the nation that this should be conceived on the broadest possible basis and that it should include all parties, both those who supported the late Government and also the parties of the Opposition. I have completed the most important part of this task. A War Cabinet has been formed of five Members, representing, with the Opposition Liberals, the unity of the nation. The three party Leaders have agreed to serve, either in the War Cabinet or in high executive office. The three Fighting Services have been filled. It was necessary that this should be done in one single day, on account of the extreme urgency and rigour of events. A number of other positions, key positions, were filled yesterday, and I am submitting a further list to His Majesty to-night. I hope to complete the appointment of the principal ministers during to-morrow. The appointment of the other ministers usually takes a little longer, but I trust that, when Parliament meets again, this part of my task will be completed, and that the administration will be complete in all respects.

I considered it in the public interest to suggest that the House should be summoned to meet today. Mr. Speaker agreed, and took the necessary steps, in accordance with the powers conferred upon him by the Resolution of the House. At the end of the proceedings today, the Adjournment of the House will be proposed until Tuesday, 21st May, with, of course, provision for earlier meeting, if need be. The business to be considered during that week will be notified to Members at the earliest opportunity. I now invite the House, by the Motion which stands in my name, to record its approval of the steps taken and to declare its confidence in the new Government.

He proceeds to tell them what the current situation is. In retrospect, it is interesting to note how right Churchill was: This was no short war they were facing and he pulls no punches as he tells the House of Commons and the nation that this is just the beginning. From the start, he sets the tone as he elevates the action to *one of the greatest battles in history*.

The closing line of this paragraph is not gratuitous. Typically Churchill's speeches were three to four times the length of this one, and his audience knew that. The shortness of the speech conveys a sense of urgency, which is a key aim of this address.

To form an Administration of this scale and complexity is a serious undertaking in itself, but it must be remembered that we are in the preliminary stage of one of the greatest battles in history, that we are in action at many other points in Norway and in Holland, that we have to be prepared in the Mediterranean, that the air battle is continuous and that many preparations, such as have been indicated by my Hon. Friend below the Gangway, have to be made here at home. In this crisis I hope I may be pardoned if I do not address the House at any length today.

Sir Winston Churchill—three portraits of the master orator in action.

I hope that any of my friends and colleagues, or former colleagues, who are affected by the political reconstruction, will make allowance, all allowance, for any lack of ceremony with which it has been necessary to act.

The phrase *lack of ceremony* reinforces that point, and takes it a step further when combined with *my friends and colleagues, or former colleagues*. Having changed parties, he is staving off criticism for having acted without consulting either group. Again he cites *necessity* for his unilateral actions.

I would say to the House, as I said to those who have joined this government: "I have nothing to offer but blood, toil, tears, and sweat."

With these "eleven burning words" as *Time* magazine called them, Churchill steps up as a true leader and sets an example for all of Britain to follow. With this one sentence, one of the most famous of the twentieth century, Churchill changed not only the tone of discourse in the House of Commons, but its purpose—it was to become a place of very real action and sacrifice.

Churchill loved bodily metaphors—remember his famous "Iron Curtain" speech? ("The Sinews of Peace")—and their use contributes to his earthy appeal and his oratorical power.

We have before us an ordeal of the most grievous kind. We have before us many, many long months of struggle and of suffering.

He wastes no time giving the bad news. Again, he reinforces the idea that this war will not end quickly and that it will not be easy. Having predicted the current crisis with Germany years before, Churchill speaks with tremendous credibility here and, as we know, his dire prediction would be proven accurate.

British Prime Minister Winston Churchill and other people survey bomb damage in London during the Battle of Britain. The blitzkrieg began July 10, 1939, and lasted until September.

Engaging the audience with this brilliant rhetorical question-and-answer technique, he is able to be conversational and to condense his entire strategy and philosophy into a tight few sentences.

> You ask, what is our policy?

Instead of straightforward answer, Churchill now becomes poetic and inspirational. The words are vigorous; the description, precise. Britain will wage war not only on all fronts—*land, sea and air*, but with *all their might*. And it's no ordinary enemy they're fighting but a *monstrous tyranny, never surpassed*; one, whose crimes include a *dark, lamentable catalogue*—clearly too many to mention in speech. The word artistry in that one sentence! And the concluding statement—no equivocation here.

> I can say: It is to wage war, by sea, land and air, with all our might and with all the strength that God can give us; to wage war against a monstrous tyranny, never surpassed in the dark, lamentable catalogue of human crime. That is our policy.

And he does it again.

> You ask, what is our aim?

I can answer in one word: It is victory, victory at all costs, victory in spite of all terror, victory, however long and hard the road may be; for without victory, there is no survival. Let that be realised; no survival for the British Empire, no survival for all that the British Empire has stood for, no survival for the urge and impulse of the ages, that mankind will move forward towards its goal.

Notice the use of repetition here and how indelibly he links *victory* (five uses) with *survival* (four uses). And it's not just victory; it is *victory at all costs*. Is there any doubt that he considers victory and survival inextricably intertwined? Again and again, Churchill hammers home the difficulty of achieving that victory. He clearly understands the power of repetition to cement the word or theme in the audience's mind, and the opportunity it gives him to build drama and momentum. In the end, he gives the audience what it needs: a reason to face the terror, a reason to fight and an extraordinary description of what is at stake. Notice how he leads into it with a short phrase followed by three, increasingly horrible consequences of the unthinkable failure—the loss of the empire, the loss of the values of the empire, and, rather dramatically and beautifully put, the loss of the future of mankind itself.

But I take up my task with buoyancy and hope. I feel sure that our cause will not be suffered to fail among men. At this time I feel entitled to claim the aid of all, and I say, "Come then, let us go forward together with our united strength."

He has certainly set the stage for what is to come and what is required. In summarizing, he condenses his message into two separate but important points: (1) his personal optimism (very important for a leader to communicate in a time of crisis); and (2) his presumption of unanimous support. He concludes with a rallying cry that reinforces the need for unity and not surprisingly, ends with the word so important to him—*strength*. A stirring, brilliantly crafted and important oration at a crucial moment in history.

Winston Churchill

THE SPEECH—WHAT TO LOOK FOR: The precision and poetry of the words lead the listener to an inescapable and rousing conclusion. His total commitment of his "blood, toil, tears, and sweat" is evident in every sentence and the question–answer technique rivets the audience to his ideas.

THE DELIVERY—WHAT TO LISTEN FOR: Long, purposeful pauses, great vocal variation, and deep resonant tones communicate gravitas and certitude and force us to listen and give weight to every word.

THE PERSON—QUALITIES OF GREATNESS: Passion, intelligence, conviction, and certainty of purpose demonstrated consistently over a lifetime of accomplishment.

Douglas MacArthur

"The entire world is quietly at peace."

HIGHLIGHTS

1880 Born January 26 on an army post in Little Rock, Arkansas

1903 Graduates from the United States Military Academy at West Point

1906 Appointed aide to President Theodore Roosevelt

1914 Takes part in the Vera Cruz raid; recommended for Congressional Medal of Honor

1918 Fighting in France; decorated nine times for heroism; appointed general; commands Rainbow Division

1919 Appointed superintendent of West Point

1922 Posted to the Philippines

1925 Promoted to major general

"OLD SOLDIER" SIGNALS END OF WWII WITH PRAYER FOR PEACE

It is no surprise that, in 1915, Douglas MacArthur became the first Public Relations officer of the United States Army. Few military men seemed to relish the institution of the army or the army life as much, and even fewer have had the gift for language and the flair for the dramatic that Douglas MacArthur brought to the military. Indeed, as the need for men to fight in World War I became clear, MacArthur is credited with "selling" the American public on what was a then-new concept of a military draft brought on by the Selective Service Act of 1917.

And it was true: The army had been MacArthur's life. Born in 1880, in Little Rock, Arkansas, to a distinguished Civil War hero, who was the son of the Governor of Wisconsin, he died at Walter Reed Army Hospital eighty-four event-filled years later in 1964.

In the years between, MacArthur was first in his class at West Point Academy (some say because his mother would rent rooms across the street to make sure he was studying), a White House aide to Theodore Roosevelt, WWI's most decorated soldier, Superintendent of West Point, Field Marshal and Chief of Staff in the Commonwealth of the Philippines Army, Army Chief of Staff under Herbert Hoover, the youngest full general in United States history, Supreme Military Commander of the Southwest Pacific during World War II, Supreme Commander of the Allied Powers in Japan (responsible for the highly successful occupation and rebuilding of that defeated country), and, finally, Supreme Commander of UN

1930	Becomes army Chief of Staff
1936	Becomes Philippine Field Marshal
1937	Marries Jean Marie Faircloth (second marriage); in December retires from active service, but continues as adviser to the Philippine government
1941	FDR recalls MacArthur to active duty as U.S. Far East commander; December 7, Japanese attack Pearl Harbor; MacArthur's air force destroyed on the ground
1941–1945	Leads American forces in Pacific campaigns
1942	Awarded Congressional Medal of Honor
1944	Becomes a five-star general
1945	Defies the Joint Chiefs, retakes central and southern Philippines;

	accepts Japan's unconditional surrender aboard battleship *Missouri*; appointed Supreme Commander of the Allied Powers in Japan
1948	Unsuccessful bid for the U.S. presidency
1950	Designated commander, United Nations Command in the Far East, upon North Korean invasion of South Korea; White House rejects his four-point plan to widen the war
1951	Stripped of all commands by President Truman
1952	Delivers keynote address at GOP national convention
1964	Dies on April 5 at Walter Reed Army Hospital in Washington, D.C.; body lies in state at Manhattan's Seventh Regiment Armory, the Capitol Rotunda, and the Naval Air station in Norfolk, Virginia; buried in Norfolk

Lt. Douglas MacArthur, Corps of Engineers, 1903.

forces in the Korean conflict (where his public disagreements with President Truman resulted in his dismissal and signaled the end of his 48-year military career).

Of all these accomplishments, it was an order from Franklin Roosevelt in 1942 that made Douglas MacArthur a household name.

With his air force and army in tatters shortly after the attack that rocked Hawaii on December 7, 1941, and completely surrounded by the Japanese on Corregidor Island in the Philippines, Roosevelt ordered MacArthur to leave the Philippines and head to Australia to command the forces there. Reluctant to leave his men, MacArthur ignored the request (foreshadowing his later conflict with Truman). Two weeks later at Roosevelt's insistence, he obeyed orders but vowed (famously) to return.

MacArthur's forces hung on for two and a half years.

And return he did. Marching through knee-deep water at Leyte in October 1944, MacArthur, true to his word, liberated his men ("I have returned. By the grace of Almighty God, our forces stand again on Philippine soil."), becoming a symbol of hope as well as heroism.

On August 6, 1945, the United States dropped the world's first atomic bomb on Hiroshima. Three days later, a second atomic bomb was dropped on Nagasaki. The Japanese at last acknowledged defeat. And, on Sunday, September 2, 1945, at 9:00 A.M., Japanese time—surrounded by hundreds of ships, 238 journalists, and representatives from the United States, Britain, France, The Netherlands, China, Australia,

> **"I shall return ..."**
> *Statement to Press*, **March 21, 1942**
>
> The President of the United States ordered me to break through the Japanese lines and proceed from Corregidor to Australia for the purpose, as I understand it, of organizing the American offensive against Japan, a primary objective of which is the relief of the Philippines. I came through and I shall return.

(above) Supreme commander of United Nations forces in Korea General Douglas MacArthur (center) accompanied by Vice Admiral Arthur Struble (left) and Marine Major General Oliver P. Smith (right) and other members of his staff go ashore in the Inchon area for an inspection of the front line.

(top left) Receiving DSC (Distinguished Service Cross) from General Pershing, September 7, 1918.

(left) St. Jovin, France. Beau Brummell of the AEF (American Expeditionary Force).

New Zealand, Canada, and the Japanese Empire—Douglas MacArthur, Commander in the Southwest Pacific and Supreme Commander for the Allied Powers, accepts the formal surrender of the Empire of Japan. The war in the Pacific is over.

After WWII MacArthur again figured prominently, this time as the United Nations Commander in Korea. His military successes, including the landing of 70,000 allied forces 100 miles behind North Korean enemy lines at Inchon Harbor, were overshadowed by his dramatic and very public disagreement with President Harry Truman over extending the conflict into China—something the Administration did not want to do. Truman, with the support of the Joint Chiefs, relieved him of his command. In a televised address on April 11, 1951, President Truman told the American people, "General MacArthur is one of our greatest military commanders. But the cause of world peace is more important than any individual."

Eight days after this "humiliation," Douglas MacArthur stood before a Joint Session of Congress to defend his actions. The next day, the day Truman was booed as he threw out the ceremonial first pitch of the 1951 baseball season in Washington, MacArthur and his family arrived in New York to the largest official welcoming ticker-tape parade (estimated at 7.5 million) in the city's history.

Truman may have lost the battle, but he won the war. MacArthur did fade from the minds of most Americans.

"Throughout his career he used words as weapons, often soaring to heights of grandiloquence in search of a phrase, inspirational in content, sonorous in tone, and evocative of his call to 'destiny.'"

The New York Times obituary, April 6, 1964

Words That Shook the World

"Old Soldiers Never Die," MacArthur addressing Congress.

". . . old soldiers never die"

Excerpts from Farewell Address to a Joint Session of Congress, April 20, 1951

I stand on this rostrum with a sense of deep humility and pride—humility in the weight of those great architects of our history who have stood here before me, pride in the reflection that this home of legislative debate represents human liberty in the purest form yet devised.

Here are centered the hopes and aspirations and faith of the entire human race.

I do not stand here as advocate for any partisan cause, for the issues are fundamental and reach quite beyond the realm of partisan considerations. They must be resolved on the highest plane of national interest if our course is to prove sound and our future protected. . . .

I address you with neither rancor nor bitterness in the fading twilight of life, with but one purpose in mind: to serve my country. . . .

I have constantly called for the new political decisions essential to a solution.

Efforts have been made to distort my position. It has been said in effect that I was a warmonger. Nothing could be further from the truth.

I know war as few other men now living know it, and nothing to me is more revolting. I have long advocated its complete abolition, as its very destructiveness on both friend and foe has rendered it useless as a means of settling international disputes. . . .

But once war is forced upon us, there is no other alternative than to apply every available means to bring it to a swift end. War's very object is victory, not prolonged indecision. In war, there is no substitute for victory.

There are some who, for varying reasons, would appease Red China. They are blind to history's clear lesson, for history teaches with unmistakable emphasis that appeasement but begets new and bloodier war. . . .

Why, my soldiers asked of me, surrender military advantages to an enemy in the field? I could not answer. . . .

I have just left your fighting sons in Korea. They have met all tests there, and I can report to you without reservation that they are splendid in every way.

It was my constant effort to preserve them and end this savage conflict honorably and with the least loss of time and a minimum sacrifice of life. Its growing bloodshed has caused me the deepest anguish and anxiety. Those gallant men will remain often in my thoughts and in my prayers always.

I am closing my fifty-two years of military service. When I joined the Army, even before the turn of the century, it was the fulfillment of all of my boyish hopes and dreams. The world has turned over many times since I took the oath on the plain at West Point, and the hopes and dreams have long since vanished, but I still remember the refrain of one of the most popular barracks ballads of that day which proclaimed most proudly that old soldiers never die; they just fade away. And like the old soldier of that ballad, I now close my military career and just fade away, an old soldier who tried to do his duty as God gave him the light to see that duty.

Good-bye.

"Not only have I met him, Ma'am; I studied dramatics under him for five years in Washington and four years in the Philippines."

Dwight D. Eisenhower, when asked if he'd ever met MacArthur

"MacArthur's face is grim, his voice deep and intense. His hands tremble slightly as he reads a brief statement. . . ."

Frank Tremaine, *Stanford Magazine*, September 2, 1945, "In the Wake of the War: A young newsman from the Class of '36 reflects on World War II while covering the Japanese surrender"

American general Douglas MacArthur salutes.

"Could I have but a line a century hence crediting a contribution to the advance of peace, I would yield every honor which has been accorded by war."

General MacArthur on his role as Supreme Commander of the Occupation of Japan

"The best adjective for MacArthur's attitude toward this peace is 'Olympian.' He is thinking in centuries and populations."

Shelley Mydans, *Time*, September 2, 1945

"Duty, Honor, Country"

Excerpts from Speech on Receiving West Point's Sylvanus Thayer Award, May 1962

No human being could fail to be deeply moved by such a tribute as this.... But this award is not intended primarily for a personality, but to symbolize a great moral code—a code of conduct and chivalry. ...

"Duty," "honor," "country"—those three hallowed words reverently dictate what you want to be, what you can be, what you will be. They are your rallying point to build courage when courage seems to fail, to regain faith when there seems to be little cause for faith, to create hope when hope becomes forlorn. ...

The unbelievers will say they are but words, but a slogan, but a flamboyant phrase. Every pedant, every demagogue, every cynic, every hypocrite, every troublemaker, and, I am sorry to say, some others of an entirely different character, will try to downgrade them. ...

But these are some of the things they build. They build your basic character. They mold you for your future roles as the custodians of the nation's defense. They make you strong enough to know when you are weak, and brave enough to face yourself when you are afraid.

They teach you to be proud and unbending in honest failure, but humble and gentle in success; not to substitute words for action; not to seek the path of comfort, but to face the stress and spur of difficulty and challenge; to learn to stand up in the storm, but to have compassion on those who fall; to master yourself before you seek to master others; to have a heart that is clean, a goal that is high; to learn to laugh, yet never forget how to weep; to reach into the future, yet never neglect the past; to be serious, yet never take yourself too seriously; to be modest so that you will remember the simplicity of true greatness, the open mind of true wisdom, the meekness of true strength.

They give you a temperate will, a quality of imagination, a vigor of the emotions, a freshness of the deep springs of life, a temperamental predominance of courage over timidity, an appetite for adventure over love of ease.

They create in your heart the sense of wonder, the unfailing hope of what next, and the joy and inspiration of life. They teach you in this way to be an officer and a gentleman.

And what sort of soldiers are those you are to lead? Are they reliable? Are they brave? Are they capable of victory?

Their story is known to all of you. It is the story of the American man at arms....

His name and fame are the birthright of every American citizen. In his youth and strength, his love and loyalty, he gave all that mortality can give. He needs no eulogy from me, or from any other man. He has written his own history and written it in red on his enemy's breast.

In 20 campaigns, on a hundred battlefields, around a thousand campfires, I have witnessed that enduring fortitude, that patriotic self-abnegation, and that invincible determination which have carved his statue in the hearts of his people. ...

I do not know the dignity of their birth, but I do know the glory of their death. They died unquestioning, uncomplaining, with faith in their hearts, and on their lips the hope that we would go on to victory.

Always for them: duty, honor, country. ...

Their resolute and determined defense, their swift and sure attack, their indomitable purpose, their complete and decisive victory—always through the bloody haze of their last reverberating shot, the vision of gaunt, ghastly men, reverently following your password of duty, honor, country.

You now face a new world, a world of change. The thrust into outer space of the satellite, spheres, and missiles marks a beginning of another epoch in the long story of mankind.... And through all this welter of change and development your mission remains fixed, determined, inviolable. It is to win our wars....

Yours is the profession of arms, the will to win, the sure knowledge that in war there is no substitute for victory, that if you lose, the Nation will be destroyed, that the very obsession of your public service must be duty, honor, country.

Others will debate the controversial issues, national and international, which divide men's minds. But serene, calm, aloof, you stand as the Nation's war guardians, as its lifeguards from the raging tides of international conflict, as its gladiators in the arena of battle....

Let civilian voices argue the merits or demerits of our processes of government....

These great national problems are not for your professional participation or military solution. Your guidepost stands out like a tenfold beacon in the night: duty, honor, country....

From your ranks come the great captains who hold the Nation's destiny in their hands the moment the war tocsin sounds.

The long, gray line has never failed us. Were you to do so, a million ghosts in olive drab, in brown khaki, in blue and gray, would rise from their white crosses, thundering those magic words: duty, honor, country.

This does not mean that you are warmongers. On the contrary, the soldier above all other people prays for peace, for he must suffer and bear the deepest wounds and scars of war. But always in our ears ring the ominous words of Plato...: "Only the dead have seen the end of war."

The shadows are lengthening for me. The twilight is here. My days of old have vanished—tone and tints. They have gone glimmering through the dreams of things that were. Their memory is one of wondrous beauty, watered by tears and coaxed and caressed by the smiles of yesterday. I listen then, but with thirsty ear, for the witching melody of faint bugles blowing reveille, of far drums beating the long roll.

In my dreams I hear again the crash of guns, the rattle of musketry, the strange, mournful mutter of the battlefield. But in the evening of my memory I come back to West Point. Always there echoes and re-echoes: duty, honor, country.

Today marks my final roll call with you. But I want you to know that when I cross the river, my last conscious thoughts will be of the corps, and the corps, and the corps.

I bid you farewell.

General of the Army Douglas MacArthur after the review held in his honor at U.S. Military Academy, West Point, New York.

"[MacArthur] is a sovereign power in his own right, with stubborn confidence in his own judgment. Diplomacy and a vast concern for the opinions and sensitivities of others are the political qualities essential to this new assignment, and these are precisely the qualities General MacArthur has been accused of lacking in the past."

James Reston, *The New York Times*, July 9, 1950, on MacArthur's appointment as the first commander of the United Nation's army in Korea

"The entire world is quietly at peace."

Surrender Ceremony on the USS *Missouri*

September 2, 1945

On this momentous day, General Douglas MacArthur steps up to the microphone aboard the battleship USS *Missouri* anchored 35 miles outside of the ravaged Japanese capital of Tokyo. "His face," according to reports, "is grim, his voice deep and intense. His hands tremble slightly...." The Japanese are about to sign the documents of formal surrender. General MacArthur will make two speeches that early September morning—the first, to accept the surrender of Japan; the second, to address the world.

"... a better world shall emerge out of the blood and carnage of the past"

Speech Preceding the Formal Surrender of Japan

After three years, eight months, and twenty-five days and the deaths of more than 50 million military personnel and civilians on all sides, MacArthur, in only 169 words, sums up the past, deals with the present, and shares his hopes for the future. Yet with these 169 words, MacArthur accomplishes everything one would hope to achieve on such an occasion: solemnity, eloquence, and grace —not a word wasted, not a word missing.

He creates this profound effect by the use of perfectly timed phrasing. Every sentence has an almost identical rhythm—a short phrase (for example, we are gathered here) followed by an explanation or refinement of that phrase (representatives of the warring powers) followed by a concluding phrase that continues, after the pause created by the second, the rhythm of the first (to conclude a solemn agreement…).

ANALYSIS

Notice how effectively MacArthur uses that precise three-part pattern in each of the four sentences in this paragraph. The power of this phrasing comes from the descriptive second phrase. If you were to read only the first and third phrases, omitting the second phrase, the speech would lose its lift, its elegance, and even its solemnity. It would be almost pedestrian, something the flamboyant General clearly would never allow!

As Lincoln did in the Gettysburg Address, MacArthur saves his longest sentence for last. The reason for this is simple: Short sentences can be powerful but they do not allow emotions to flow and soar and, used at the end, can be anticlimactic. MacArthur builds the momentum and emotion of this short speech with increasingly long sentences (20, then 25, then 28, then 44, and finally 52 words) to achieve his desired effect.

SPEECH

We are gathered here, representatives of the major warring powers, to conclude a solemn agreement whereby peace may be restored. The issues, involving divergent ideals and ideologies, have been determined on the battlefields of the world and hence are not for our discussion or debate. Nor is it for us here to meet, representing as we do a majority of the people of the earth, in a spirit of distrust, malice or hatred. But rather it is for us, both victors and vanquished, to rise to that higher dignity which alone befits the sacred purposes we are about to serve, committing all our people unreservedly to faithful compliance with the understanding they are here formally to assume.

It is my earnest hope, and indeed the hope of all mankind, that from this solemn occasion a better world shall emerge out of the blood and carnage of the past—a world dedicated to the dignity of man and the fulfillment of his most cherished wish for freedom, tolerance and justice.

"...to preserve in peace what we won in war."

Radio Address to the World After the Surrender

After the surrender documents were signed, the Japanese delegation departed. General MacArthur then walked to another set of microphones, assumed a very different oratorical voice, and broadcast the following radio message to his "fellow countrymen" and to the world.

Like the speech before it, this one is precise and well thought out, but it has an added dimension—a spiritual and prophetic vision. Clearly, MacArthur approached his oratory as carefully as he did his military maneuvers.

SPEECH	ANALYSIS
My fellow countrymen, today the guns are silent. A great tragedy has ended. A great victory has been won. The skies no longer rain death—the seas bear only commerce—men everywhere walk upright in the sunlight. The entire world is quietly at peace. The holy mission has been completed,	Accomplishing a revival of the momentum, if not the style, of the first speech, notice the nine short phrases or sentences that start this historic address.
and in reporting this to you, the people, I speak for the thousands of silent lips, forever stilled among the jungles and the beaches and in the deep waters of the Pacific which marked the way. I speak for the unnamed brave millions homeward bound to take up the challenge of that future which they did so much to salvage from the brink of disaster.	Now, with the drama built by the short phrases, he instantly makes the transition to longer, rhythmic sentences.
As I look back upon the long, tortuous trail from those grim days of Bataan and Corregidor, when an entire world lived in fear, when democracy was on the defensive everywhere, when modern civilization trembled in the balance, I thank a merciful God that He has given us the faith, the courage and the power from which to mold victory. We have known the bitterness of defeat and the exultation of triumph, and from both we have learned there can be no turning back.	Shifting again, MacArthur continues the momentum with a series of triplets each starting with the word *when*, and then shifts again, this time with *thanks* to God, as he moves to painful memories of the past—drawn both from his own experience and the world's.
We must go forward to preserve in peace what we won in war. A new era is upon us. Even the lesson of victory itself brings with it profound concern, both for our future security and the survival of civilization. The destructiveness of the war potential, through progressive advances in scientific discovery, has in fact now reached a point which revises the traditional concepts of war.	His visual imagery and use of juxtaposition is perfectly planned—look how he moves from *no turning back* of the preceding sentence to *go forward* in this one. Note, too, how in just one sentence, he sounds his theme for the rest of the speech and sets the agenda for a post-war world.
Men since the beginning of time have sought peace. . . . Military alliances, balances of power, leagues of nations,	Another triplet.
all in turn failed, leaving the only path to be by way of the crucible of war. We have had our last chance.	Obviously referring to the introduction of the atom bomb, MacArthur looks back at the just concluded war as *our last chance* and warns of the consequences.
If we do not now devise some greater and more equitable system, Armageddon will be at our door.	He turns now, from general to prophet.

MacArthur signs as Supreme Commander of Allied Powers as Generals Wainright and Percival look on.

And then moves even further into the spiritual realm.	The problem basically is theological and involves a spiritual recrudescence and improvement of human character that will synchronize with our almost matchless advances in science, art, literature and all material and cultural developments of the past two thousand years.
Sounding even more like a priest than a general, MacArthur hammers his theological theme home in this profound sentence as he offers his stinging prescription on how to save the world.	It must be of the spirit if we are to save the flesh.
From lofty spiritual heights, he descends to earth to address the very concrete issue of the day—the rebuilding of Japan.	We stand in Tokyo today reminiscent of our countryman, Commodore Perry, ninety-two years ago. His purpose was to bring to Japan an era of enlightenment and progress, by lifting the veil of isolation to the friendship, trade, and commerce of the world. But alas the knowledge thereby gained of western science was forged into an instrument of oppression and human enslavement. Freedom of expression, freedom of action, even freedom of thought were denied through appeal to superstition, and through the appli-

cation of force. We are committed by the Potsdam Declaration of principles to see that the Japanese people are liberated from this condition of slavery. It is my purpose to implement this commitment just as rapidly as the armed forces are demobilized and other essential steps taken to neutralize the war potential.

The energy of the Japanese race, if properly directed, will enable expansion vertically rather than horizontally. If the talents of the race are turned into constructive channels, the country can lift itself from its present deplorable state into a position of dignity.

In a display of statesmanship, MacArthur turns to the future with hope, compliments the vanquished, and uses a word *dignity*, which has great meaning to the people of Japan.

To the Pacific basin has come the vista of a new emancipated world. Today, freedom is on the offensive, democracy is on the march. Today, in Asia as well as in Europe, unshackled peoples are tasting the full sweetness of liberty, the relief from fear.

In the Philippines, America has evolved a model for this new free world of Asia. In the Philippines, America has demonstrated that peoples of the East and peoples of the West may walk side by side in mutual respect and with mutual benefit. The history of our sovereignty there has now the full confidence of the East.

With business taken care of, MacArthur again becomes poetic and turns to broader, more philosophical themes.

And so, my fellow countrymen, today I report to you that your sons and daughters have served you well and faithfully with the calm, deliberate, determined fighting spirit of the American soldier and sailor, based upon a tradition of historical truth as against the fanaticism of an enemy supported only by mythological fiction. Their spiritual strength and power has brought us through to victory.

And, as he signs off, MacArthur adopts a fatherly tone, masterfully playing the role of general, patriot, historian, and philosopher affirming, yet again, the dominant role of spirituality.

They are homeward bound—take care of them.

He ends (as he often does) with a short phrase and a flourish that perhaps only great actors and flamboyant generals can carry off.

Douglas MacArthur

THE SPEECH—WHAT TO LOOK FOR: The precise and strategic phrasing, the poetry of the language, and the spirituality of the message make this (and other MacArthur speeches) some of the most brilliantly written speeches of the century.

THE DELIVERY—WHAT TO LISTEN FOR: The drama in his voice, the depth of his voice, and the extraordinarily well-timed pauses give these already powerful speeches an even greater feeling of history in the making and impact.

THE PERSON—QUALITIES OF GREATNESS: Determination, patriotism, and strength. A man of war with the soul of a poet.

ALBERT EINSTEIN

"The war is won, but the peace is not."

A CLARION CALL TO CONSCIENCE

He didn't speak at all until he was three years old, but as an adult, his words—on a wide range of topics—had an enormous impact. Searching for "God's design," Einstein said, was "the source of all true art and science," and in his 76 years of searching, he left his indelible "fingerprints" on what *Time* magazine called "the scientific touchstones of our age—the Bomb, space travel, electronics."

Born in Ulm, Germany, in 1879, he was hardly the perfect student. Making plans to quit school at age 15 because he was bored, young Albert was formally expelled at age 16 because he was disruptive to other students. Without having finished high school, Einstein tried to enroll in the Swiss Federal Institute of Technology, but failed the entrance exam. He finally obtained his secondary school degree and was accepted into the Institute, graduating with a math and science teaching degree. He then spent seven years at the Swiss Patent Office where, in his

"In a hundred years, as we turn to another new century—nay, ten times a hundred years, when we turn to another new millennium —the name that will prove most enduring from our own amazing era will be that of Albert Einstein: genius, political refugee, humanitarian, locksmith of the mysteries of the atom and the universe."

Walter Isaakson, Managing Editor, *Time* magazine's Person of the Century, January 3, 2000

1913	Becomes a professor of theoretical physics at the University of Berlin and director of Kaiser Wilhelm Institute of Physics	**1939**	Sends letter to President Franklin Roosevelt urging atomic bomb research
1914	Completes the general theory of relativity	**1940**	Becomes an American citizen; retains Swiss citizenship
1920	Meets Niels Bohr; first visit to the United States	**1946**	Assumes chairmanship of Emergency Committee of Atomic Scientists
1922	Awarded the Nobel Prize in physics for 1921		
1932	Presents "My Credo" to the German League of Human Rights in Berlin	**1952**	Offered and refuses presidency of Israel
1933	Emigrates to the United States	**1955**	Dies of heart failure on April 18

spare time, he published three scientific papers (known as "The 1905 Papers") that earned him his Ph.D. and, ultimately, transformed the world of physics.

The first paper on the photoelectric effect provided the theoretical foundation for quantum physics and paved the way for television, lasers, and semiconductors. It earned him the Nobel Prize for Physics in 1921. In his second paper, he proposed what is now called "the special theory of relativity," which includes what is probably science's most famous equation, $E=mc^2$ (energy equals mass times the velocity of light squared), one of the building blocks leading to the development of nuclear power.

(above) Four Nobel Prize Winners, Sinclair Lewis, Frank Kellogg, Albert Einstein, and Irving Langmuir stand together at the Hotel Roosevelt on December 18, 1933, at a celebration of the 100th anniversary of the birth of Alfred Nobel.

(left) Dr. Albert Einstein in his studio in Berlin in the early 1920s.

In the third paper, which dealt with statistical mechanics, he provided proof of the existence of molecules and atoms. Among other things, the last two theories paved the way for the development of the atomic bomb as well as the peaceful uses of atomic energy.

(top) Albert Einstein dictates a scientific paper to his secretary in his attic flat in Berlin (ca. 1930).

(above) Albert Einstein, right, and his daughter, Margot, with her future husband, Dimitri Marianoff, the noted Russian scientist.

Ten years later, in 1915, building on the special theory that he had developed at the age of 26, Einstein went on to create his "general theory of relativity." *Time* magazine describes its effect: "Just as Einstein's earlier work paved the way to harnessing the smallest subatomic forces, the general theory opened up an understanding of the largest of all things, from the formative Big Bang of the universe to its mysterious black holes." When his theory was proved by astronomers three years later, a leading scientist declared, "Our conceptions of the fabric of the universe must be fundamentally altered."

As his fame and status grew, Einstein passionately embraced nonscientific topics—social justice, war, religion, and the purpose and nature of life. Despite his role in the creation of the atomic bomb, he was a pacifist, and therefore a very reluctant contributor to its development. In the end, the discovery of nuclear fission made him fear that the Nazis, from whom he had escaped when he left Germany in 1933, would develop and use the bomb, which caused him to abandon his opposition to the development of the bomb by the United States.

The Purpose of Life

"Brief is this existence, like a brief visit in a strange house. The path to be pursued is poorly lit by a flickering consciousness whose center is the limiting and separating 'I.'… When a group of individuals becomes a 'we,' a harmonious whole, they have reached as high as humans can reach."

"My Credo"
Excerpts from Speech to the German League of Human Rights, Fall, 1932

Our situation on this earth seems strange. Every one of us appears here involuntarily and uninvited for a short stay, without knowing the whys and the wherefore….

I never coveted affluence and luxury and even despise them a good deal….

I always have a high regard for the individual and have an insuperable distaste for violence and clubmanship. All these motives made me into a passionate pacifist and anti-militarist. I am against any nationalism, even in the guise of mere patriotism. Privileges based on position and property have always seemed to me unjust and pernicious, as did any exaggerated personality cult. I am an adherent of the ideal of democracy, although I well know the weaknesses of the democratic form of government. Social equality and economic protection of the individual appeared to me always as the important communal aims of the state.

Although I am a typical loner in daily life, my consciousness of belonging to the invisible community of those who strive for truth, beauty, and justice has preserved me from feeling isolated.

The most beautiful and deepest experience a man can have is the sense of the mysterious. It is the underlying principle of religion as well as all serious endeavour in art and science. He who never had this experience seems to me, if not dead, then at least blind. To sense that behind anything that can be experienced there is a something that our mind cannot grasp and whose beauty and sublimity reaches us only indirectly and as a feeble reflection, this is religiousness. In this sense I am religious. To me it suffices to wonder at these secrets and to attempt humbly to grasp with my mind a mere image of the lofty structure of all that there is.

In 1939, Einstein—in a now famous letter—warned President Roosevelt of the possible consequences. "It may become possible," he said, "to set up nuclear chain reactions [and] this new phenomenon would also lead to the construction of bombs." For a variety of reasons, the U.S. did not launch its atomic weapons project until 1941. In August 1942, it became "The Manhattan Project," which did in fact create the world's first atomic bomb.

(top) Albert Einstein and Chaim Weizman, both proponents of Zionism, arrive in the United States on the SS *Rotterdam* to discuss Jewish settlement in Palestine with the leaders of the American Jewish community (1921).

(above) Albert Einstein with the astronomer Dr J A Miller at Spoul de Swartmore Observatory.

"The masses of mankind … grew to know him not as a universe-maker whose theories they could not hope to understand but as a world citizen, one of the outstanding spiritual leaders of his generation, a symbol of the human spirit and its highest aspirations."

The New York Times obituary, April 19, 1955

Excerpts from Speech at Nobel Prize Anniversary Dinner, December 10, 1945

Speaking in New York in 1945 at the end of WWII, on the fifth anniversary of the Nobel Peace Prize, Einstein sounds a clarion call to conscience and points a finger at the world's political establishment, challenging them to do what is right to safeguard the atomic bomb and the future of humanity itself. The simple idealism of Einstein's message gives it great impact and poignancy.

ANALYSIS

Einstein was not a flowery speaker; he got right to the point, wasting few words. I love the precision with which he speaks: Each sentence is clean; each is exact. He opens this talk by comparing physicists (in general), but by implication himself, with the prize's benefactor, Alfred Nobel, the inventor of dynamite. By doing so, he immediately connects the peace prize to the critical modern-day issue of nuclear arms control.

Einstein, a long-time pacifist himself, segues into feelings of responsibility and guilt. While he talks about physicists in general, we know that he would later say his participation in the creation of the atomic bomb was the biggest mistake of his life.

Notice the passion and sense of urgency he conveys simply by doubling up on his words.

Again he acknowledges the role he and other scientists played, but this time instead of talking about guilt, he offers an explanation for it, and then the zinger—what the Allies, particularly the U.S. and U.K., were supposed to provide in return.

Now, Einstein pulls no punches, and points a finger of accusation toward the Allies for their failure to live up to the bargain they had made. (The Atlantic Charter was an eight-point document signed by FDR and Winston Churchill in 1941. Among other things it expressed the goal that all nations "must come to the abandonment of the use of force.")

By repeating the phrases *the world was promised* or *the nations were promised* three times in quick succession, Einstein drums home his case. By the contrast between the promises unkept and the actuality, he forcefully demonstrates that the results were exactly opposite to what was promised.

SPEECH

Physicists find themselves in a position not unlike that of Alfred Nobel. Alfred Nobel invented the most powerful explosive (dynamite) ever known up to his time, a means of destruction par excellence. In order to atone for this, in order to relieve his human conscience he instituted his awards for the promotion of peace and for achievements of peace.

Today, the physicists who participated in forging the most formidable and dangerous weapon of all times are harassed by an equal feeling of responsibility, not to say guilt.

And we cannot desist from warning, and warning again, we cannot and should not slacken in our efforts to make the nations of the world, and especially their governments, aware of the unspeakable disaster they are certain to provoke unless they change their attitude toward each other and toward the task of shaping the future.

We helped in creating this new weapon in order to prevent the enemies of mankind from achieving it ahead of us, which, given the mentality of the Nazis, would have meant inconceivable destruction and the enslavement of the rest of the world. We delivered this weapon into the hands of the American and the British people as trustees of the whole of mankind, as fighters for peace and liberty.

But so far we fail to see any guarantee of peace, we do not see any guarantee of the freedoms that were promised to the nations in the Atlantic Charter. The war is won, but the peace is not.

The great powers, united in fighting, are now divided over the peace settlements. The world was promised freedom from fear, but in fact fear has increased tremendously since the termination of the war. The world was promised freedom from want, but large parts of the world are faced with starvation while others are living in abundance. The nations were promised liberation and justice. But we have witnessed, and are witnessing even now, the sad spectacle of "liberating" armies firing into populations who want their independence and social equality, and supporting in those countries,

49

The noted scientist, Dr. Albert Einstein, director of the Kaiser Wilhelm Institute of Physics, addressing a group of fellow scientists in Harnackhaus, Berlin-Dahlem.

by force of arms, such parties and personalities as appear to be most suited to serve vested interests. Territorial questions and arguments of power, obsolete though they are, still prevail over the essential demands of common welfare and justice.

Allow me to be more specific about just one case, which is but a symptom of the general situation: the case of my own people, the Jewish people.

He goes now from the general promises to the more specific and personalizes the problem.

As long as Nazi violence was unleashed only, or mainly, against the Jews the rest of the world looked on passively, and even treaties and agreements were made with the patently criminal government of the Third Reich. Later, when Hitler was on the point of taking over Rumania and Hungary, at the time when Maidanek and Oswiecim were in Allied hands, and the methods of the gas chambers were well known all over the world, all attempts to rescue the Rumanian and Hungarian Jews came to naught because the doors of Palestine were closed to Jewish immigrants by the British government, and no country could be found that would admit those forsaken people. They were left to perish like their brothers and sisters in the occupied countries.

In this paragraph, we see Einstein at his most passionate and personal (remember, he himself was forced to flee Nazi persecution). Notice how boldly he criticizes the British and, although not named, it is clear that his next reference is to the United States, in particular, and the rest of the world, in general.

We shall never forget the heroic efforts of the small countries, of the Scandinavian, the Dutch, the Swiss nations, and of individuals in the occupied parts of Europe who did all in their power to protect Jewish lives. We do not forget the humane attitude of the Soviet Union who was the only one among the big powers to open her doors to hundreds of thousands of Jews when the Nazi armies were advancing in Poland.

He makes the attack even more direct as he acknowledges the efforts of the few countries that did come to the aid of the Jews. By commending the Soviet Union, he offers a direct slap in the face to Britain and the United States.

Albert Einstein at home in New York.

Rhetorical questions instantly engage the audience and focus attention on what follows, which, in this case, is another stinging condemnation.

But after all that has happened, and was not prevented from happening, how is it today?

Note the words he uses: *denied access to their haven, left to hunger and cold and persisting hostility, many . . . still kept in the degrading conditions of concentration camps, shamefulness and hopelessness of the situation.* His tone has decidedly changed. Now it is angry, purposefully angry.

While in Europe territories are being distributed without any qualms about the wishes of the people concerned, the remainders of European Jewry, one fifth of its pre-war population, are again denied access to their haven in Palestine and left to hunger and cold and persisting hostility.

There is no country, even today, that would be willing or able to offer them a place where they could live in peace and security. And the fact that many of them are still kept in the degrading conditions of concentration camps by the Allies gives sufficient evidence of the shamefulness and hopelessness of the situation.

The "White Paper" effectively stopped Jewish immigration into Palestine at a time when many European Jews had no other place to go.

These people are forbidden to enter Palestine with reference to the principle of democracy, but actually the Western powers, in upholding the ban of the White Paper, are yielding to the threats and the external pressure of five vast and under-populated Arab States.

It is sheer irony when the British Foreign Minister tells the poor lot of European Jews they should remain in Europe because their genius is needed there, and, on the other hand, advises them not to try to get at the head of the queue lest they might incur new hatred and persecution.

Words That Shook the World

Well, I am afraid, they cannot help it; with their six million dead they have been pushed at the head of the queue, of the queue of Nazi victims, much against their will.

You can almost feel Einstein's blood boil as he indicts the Allied powers. His tone has shifted, from more formal to more colloquial, from longer to shorter, punchier phrases. Note the effective use of the word *queue* in the preceding paragraph and then in this one to demonstrate the tragic irony of the situation for the European Jews.

The picture of our postwar world is not bright.

His assessment of the situation is not good, and he now offers the real challenge to the world.

As far as we, the physicists, are concerned, we are no politicians and it has never been our wish to meddle in politics. But we know a few things that the politicians do not know.

He first pulls back and deliberately understates his understanding of politics. Whenever one admits a weakness or lack of experience, this seeming candor lends credibility to what one does know.

And we feel the duty to speak up and to remind those responsible that there is no escape into easy comforts, there is no distance ahead for proceeding little by little and delaying the necessary changes into an indefinite future, there is no time left for petty bargaining.

This allows him now to show what he *does* know, and he states it with rare force as he rapidly repeats the words *there is no* in three successive phrases.

The situation calls for a courageous effort, for a radical change in our whole attitude, in the entire political concept.

Now Einstein, the man who revolutionized science, calls for an equivalent revolution in world politics.

May the spirit that prompted Alfred Nobel to create his great institution, the spirit of trust and confidence, of generosity and brotherhood among men, prevail in the minds of those upon whose decisions our destiny rests. Otherwise human civilization will be doomed.

In this last paragraph, we see Einstein as both humanist and Old Testament prophet, foretelling of impending Armageddon with stunning, matter-of-fact directness.

Albert Einstein

THE SPEECH—WHAT TO LOOK FOR: His anger and determination to ensure that his scientific efforts do not help destroy the world, but rather improve it and his deeply felt humanism, all expressed with great clarity and precision.

THE DELIVERY—WHAT TO LISTEN FOR: The accent is challenging but beneath it there is wonderful warmth and sweetness.

THE PERSON—QUALITIES OF GREATNESS: Unabated intellectual curiosity, his social activism in so many areas, and his endless quest to see "God's handiwork" in all things.

ELEANOR ROOSEVELT

"... the international Magna Carta of all men everywhere."

"FIRST LADY OF THE WORLD" WINS BATTLE FOR HUMAN RIGHTS

What would you do if, as a child, you were painfully shy, lacked self-esteem, were uncomfortable about your looks, and, as an adult, you were frequently depressed and horrified of speaking in public? If you were Eleanor Roosevelt, you'd become one of the most powerful women of the century, entertain at the White House, and travel the world as one of its most dominant voices for social change. You'd also become ambassador to the United Nations and work tirelessly for those causes and you would facilitate the birth of one of the twentieth century's most profound documents—the Universal Declaration of Human Rights.

How did she do it? She focused on her passions and, luckily for the world, her overwhelming passion was for making a contribution to others.

Born into one of America's oldest and most prominent families, Eleanor Roosevelt grew up in the midst of wealth, prestige, and power. Her uncle Teddy was the 26th President of the United States. Despite all this, life was not easy for Eleanor. Her parents separated when she was young. Her mother, an unemotional woman, whom some regarded as the most beautiful woman in New York, died when Eleanor was only eight. Her father, an alcoholic whom Eleanor adored, died only two years later. She married her distant cousin, Franklin Delano Roosevelt, in 1905, bore him six children (the first of whom died in infancy), struggled against a domineering mother-in-law, faced her husband's infidelity, and—after Franklin was stricken with poliomyelitis and was unable to get around easily—became his eyes and ears. Throughout their marriage, she remained his political partner and helpmate—

1928 Her article "Women Must Learn to Play the Game as Men Do" published in *Redbook* magazine; FDR elected governor of New York	by President Truman; joins NAACP board of directors
1933 FDR inaugurated; Eleanor becomes the first First Lady to hold press conference	**1947** Elected chairperson of the 18-nation UN Human Rights Commission; begins drafting the Universal Declaration of Human Rights
1936 Begins writing syndicated column "My Day"	**1948** Universal Declaration of Human Rights approved
1939 Resigns from DAR to protest their refusal to allow Marian Anderson, a black singer, to perform at Constitution Hall	**1952** Resigns from UN after Eisenhower wins election
1940 Addresses Democratic National Convention—the first woman to do so	**1961** Reappointed to the UN by President Kennedy
1945 FDR dies on April 12; Eleanor appointed U.S. delegate to the UN	**1962** Chairs President's Commission on the Status of Women and Commission of Inquiry into the Administration of Justice in the Freedom Struggle; dies November 7 and is buried next to FDR at Hyde Park on November 10

some might even say his conscience. After his death, she continued her work on behalf of the world.

Eleanor was not your typical First Lady. She used her position to influence Franklin, the people around him, and the nation. She was the first woman to speak before a national convention, to write a syndicated column ("My Day," which she wrote for 27 years), to work as a lecturer, to become a radio commentator. In addition she wrote more than 150 letters a day and held more than 300 regular press conferences (where, in order to help women journalists, she refused to allow any men, since women at that time were not allowed to cover the President).

As a young woman, Eleanor taught calisthenics to immigrants in the slums, joined the Consumer's League to better conditions in garment factories, taught history and government at a girl's school; during WWI, she worked with the Red Cross and visited shell-shocked veterans at St. Elizabeth Hospital. After the war, her activities increased: She volunteered as a translator for the International Congress of Working Women; joined the League of Women Voters and the Women's Division of the Democratic Party (she was later named Director of Women's Activities of the Democratic National Committee) as well as the Women's Trade Union League. As the First Lady, she worked to create Arthursdale, an experimental homestead project for West Virginia coal miners; helped to found the National Youth Administration, which employed young Americans; fought for anti-lynching legislation; served as Assistant Director of Civilian Defense; and toured the South Pacific during WWII.

After Franklin's death, she served as a member of the NAACP Board of Directors; a U.S. delegate to the United Nations; chairperson of the 18-nation UN Human Rights Commission, where she was instrumental in the drafting and

Franklin D. Roosevelt and Eleanor Roosevelt (top right) in Campobello Island, where they vacationed.

"You gain strength, courage and confidence by every experience in which you really stop to look fear in the face…. You must do the thing you think you cannot do."

Eleanor Roosevelt, *You Learn by Living*, 1960

(above) Eleanor Roosevelt in Campous, France visiting camp for Jewish emigres for Israel.

(above left) King George VI, Eleanor Roosevelt, and Queen Elizabeth in London.

"About the only value that the story of my life may have is to show that one can, even without any particular gifts, overcome obstacles that seem insurmountable if one is willing to face the fact that they must be overcome; that in spite of timidity and fear, in spite of lack of special talents one can find a way to live widely and fully."

Eleanor Roosevelt, *The Autobiography of Eleanor Roosevelt*

passage of the Universal Declaration of Human Rights by the UN General Assembly; pushed President Truman to recognize and support the new state of Israel; and served as the first chairperson of the President's Commission on the Status of Women and Chairwoman of the Commission of Inquiry into the Administration of Justice in the Freedom Struggle, a leading-edge civil rights effort.

In everything she did, she remained true to her ideals, demonstrating both pragmatism and enormous courage and determination. Attending the Southern Conference for Human Welfare meeting in Birmingham, Alabama in 1936, the First Lady openly defied local segregation laws by sitting in the center aisle, between whites and blacks, after she was told by the police that she could not sit with black people.

Although she was Harry Truman's personal choice as delegate to the United Nations, she threatened to embarrass him and quit if he did not reconsider and grant official recognition to the newly created State of Israel in 1948.

General Gomes, Bishop of Natal, and Eleanor Roosevelt in Natal, Brazil.

The Preamble to the Universal Declaration of Human Rights

Adopted by the General Assembly of the United Nations, December 10, 1948

Whereas recognition of the inherent dignity and of the equal and inalienable rights of all members of the human family is the foundation of freedom, justice and peace in the world,

Whereas disregard and contempt for human rights have resulted in barbarous acts which have outraged the conscience of mankind, and the advent of a world in which human beings shall enjoy freedom of speech and belief and freedom from fear and want has been proclaimed as the highest aspiration of the common people,

Whereas it is essential, if man is not to be compelled to have recourse, as a last resort, to rebellion against tyranny and oppression, that human rights should be protected by the rule of law,

Whereas it is essential to promote the development of friendly relations between nations,

Whereas the peoples of the United Nations have in the Charter reaffirmed their faith in fundamental human rights, in the dignity and worth of the human person and in the equal rights of men and women and have determined to promote social progress and better standards of life in larger freedom,

Whereas Member States have pledged themselves to achieve, in cooperation with the United Nations, the promotion of universal respect for and observance of human rights and fundamental freedoms,

Whereas a common understanding of these rights and freedoms is of the greatest importance for the full realization of this pledge,

Now, therefore, The General Assembly proclaims This Universal Declaration of Human Rights.

She was unstoppable when she believed in something. Despite death threats, a bounty placed on her head by the Ku Klux Klan, and FBI investigations into her life, she continued to fight for what she believed.

Eleanor Roosevelt's crowning achievement and greatest legacy, however, was her role in passing the Universal Declaration of Human Rights, a document that has served as a model for countries around the globe. Her long history of passionate work on behalf of civil rights, the impoverished, workers' and women's rights, and so many other issues made her the perfect advocate for the Declaration. The delegates, recognizing her conviction and moral stature, elected her chairperson of the Commission on Human Rights. There, the qualities—common sense, optimism, energy, and conviction—that helped her through earlier challenges allowed her to bring together people who might in other circumstances not have supported one another.

As she had throughout her life, Eleanor Roosevelt triumphed by staying true to her personal motto—"Do the thing you think you cannot do"—and became one of the century's most powerful and effective advocates for social justice and an inspiration to millions around the world.

"The Russians seem to have met their match in Mrs. Roosevelt. The proceedings sometimes turn into a long vitriolic attack on the U.S. when she is not present. These attacks, however, generally denigrate into flurries in the face of her calm and undisturbed but often pointed replies."

The New York Times

"... the international Magna Carta of all men everywhere."

Statement on the Adoption of the Universal Declaration of Human Rights, December 9, 1948

Eleanor Roosevelt was not a natural orator. Her speeches, mostly delivered without notes, sometimes rambled, and her high, somewhat "squeaky" voice may have distracted some from the seriousness of her subjects. Nevertheless, driven by necessity and passion, she persisted and became a tremendous voice for women's rights, workers' rights, civil rights, and, ultimately, for human rights.

She called the passage of the Universal Declaration of Human Rights her most important accomplishment, and in this speech presented at the United Nations, the once-shy Eleanor Roosevelt sets the tone for the adoption of the document she believes will benefit the disadvantaged of the world. Although simple, this is a very elegant speech. Mrs. Roosevelt was not a flowery speaker, yet despite its serious, straightforward manner, we can sense the excitement and passion she undoubtedly felt.

A fascinating sidelight of this speech is the glimpse it gives us into the person Eleanor Roosevelt was. She never grandstanded or sought credit for what she had done to bring about the document. As you will see, she even used the words of others to express the grander emotions, and, in doing so, made certain the focus stayed on the event and not on her.

ANALYSIS

Interestingly, and very diplomatically, Mrs. Roosevelt begins by addressing some of her personal disappointments as well as those of the United States. She points out that the final document did not contain everything she or the government she represented would have liked, but she does it in such an affirmative way that it does not detract from the positive message she wants to convey.

Mindful that this is a diplomatic speech in support of ratification of a document that will affect the United States— and that she is speaking not for herself, but in her capacity as a delegate to the United Nations—she goes on to discuss key points on which she must make the United States' position clear.

SPEECH

The long and meticulous study and debate of which this Universal Declaration of Human Rights is the product means that it reflects the composite views of the many men and governments who have contributed to its formulation. Not every man nor every government can have what he wants in a document of this kind. There are of course particular provisions in the declaration before us with which we are not fully satisfied. I have no doubt this is true of other delegations, but taken as a whole the Delegation of the United States believes that this [is] a good document—even a great document—and we propose to give it our full support. The position of the United States on the various parts of the declaration is a matter of record in the Third Committee. I shall not burden the Assembly, and particularly my colleagues of the Third Committee, with a restatement of that position here.

Certain provisions of the declaration are stated in such broad terms as to be acceptable only because of the limitations in article 29 providing for limitation on the exercise of the rights for the purpose of meeting the requirements of morality, public order, and the general welfare. An example of this is the provision that everyone has the right of equal access to the public service in his country. The basic principle of equality and of nondiscrimination as to public employment is sound, but it cannot be accepted without limitations. My government, for example, would consider that this is unquestionably subject to limitation in the interest of public order and the general welfare. It would not consider that the exclusion from public employment of persons holding subversive political beliefs and not loyal to the basic principles and practices of the constitution and laws of the country would in any way infringe upon this right.

Likewise, my Government has made it clear in the course of the development of the declaration that it does not consider that the economic and social and cultural rights stated in the declaration imply an obligation on governmental action. This was made quite clear in the Human Rights Commission text of article 23 which served as a so-called "umbrella" article

Eleanor Roosevelt and United Nations Universal Declaration of Human Rights in Spanish text.

to the articles on economic and social rights. We consider that the principle has not been affected by the fact that this article no longer contains a reference to the articles which follow it. This in no way affects our whole-hearted support for the basic principles of economic, social, and cultural rights set forth in these articles.

In giving our approval to the declaration today it is of primary importance that we keep clearly in mind the basic character of the document. It is not a treaty; it is not an international agreement. It is not and does not purport to be a statement of basic principles of law or legal obligation. It is a declaration of basic principles of human rights and freedoms, to be stamped with the approval of the General Assembly by formal vote of its members, and to serve as a common standard of achievement for all peoples of all nations.

In the language of diplomacy, she then summarizes the precise scope and intent of the document as the United States sees it.

We stand today at the threshold of a great event both in the life of the United Nations and in the life of mankind, that is the approval by the General Assembly of the Universal Declaration of Human Rights recommended by the Third Committee. This declaration may well become the international Magna Carta of all men everywhere.

We hope its proclamation by the General Assembly will be an event comparable to the proclamation of the Declaration of the Rights of Man by the

With the diplomatic "housekeeping" now out of the way, she begins to say what is in her heart—the things that motivated her to work so hard for the passage of this Declaration.

By comparing this Declaration to some of the greatest documents in history—*The Magna Carta, The Declaration of the Rights of Man,* and *The Bill of Rights*—Mrs. Roosevelt sets expectations very high for this new document.

Eleanor Roosevelt at Reverend Hayes Housing Project in Newark, New Jersey.

French people in 1789, the adoption of the Bill of Rights by the people of the United States, and the adoption of comparable declarations at different times in other countries. At a time when there are so many issues on which we find it difficult to reach a common basis of agreement, it is a significant fact that 58 states have found such a large measure of agreement in the complex field of human rights. This must be taken as testimony of our common aspiration first voiced in the Charter of the United Nations to lift men everywhere to a higher standard of life and to a greater enjoyment of freedom.

What follows is a powerful but simple sentence, which summarizes the document and justifies expectations.

Man's desire for peace lies behind this declaration.

She follows it with a very compelling argument—perhaps the most compelling for a world still reeling from World War II.

The realization that the flagrant violation of human rights by Nazi and Fascist countries sowed the seeds of the last world war has supplied the impetus for the work which brings us to the moment of achievement here today.

In a recent speech in Canada, Gladstone Murray said: "The central fact is that man is fundamentally a moral being, that the light we have is imperfect does not matter so long as we are always trying to improve it . . . we are equal in sharing the moral freedom that distinguishes us as men. Man's status makes each individual an end in himself. No man is by nature simply the servant of the state or of another man . . . the ideal and fact of freedom—and not technology—are the true distinguishing marks of our civilization."

Now, either because she is more comfortable using someone else's flowery words or because she genuinely admires the words and wants to share them, Mrs. Roosevelt hits her loftiest tone quoting a famous Canadian, the first general manager of the Canadian Broadcasting Company.

This declaration is based upon the spiritual fact that man must have freedom in which to develop his full stature and through common effort to raise the level of human dignity.

Notice next how beautifully she rolls out of this poetic statement to summarize her own profoundly humanistic argument.

We have much to do to fully achieve and to assure the rights set forth in this declaration. But having them put before us with the moral backing of 58 nations will be a great step forward.

As we here bring to fruition our labors on this Declaration of Human Rights, we must at the same time rededicate ourselves to the unfinished task which lies before us. We can now move on with new courage and inspiration to the completion of an international covenant on human rights and of measures for the implementation of human rights.

And then, ever the pragmatist, she returns to what is still to be done.

In conclusion I feel that I cannot do better than to repeat the call to action by Secretary Marshall in his opening statement to this Assembly:

"Let this third regular session of the General Assembly approve by an overwhelming majority the Declaration of Human Rights as a statement of conduct for all; and let us, as Members of the United Nations, conscious of our own short-comings and imperfections, join our effort in all faith to live up to this high standard."

In a very effective and moving finale, she again uses someone else's words to express the uplifting message of her speech.

Eleanor Roosevelt

THE SPEECH—WHAT TO LOOK FOR: Mrs. Roosevelt is serious and to the point, yet so modest that she allows other voices to make the passionate and emotional points rather than draw attention to herself.

THE DELIVERY—WHAT TO LISTEN FOR: Although lacking in "performance qualities," the steadfast earnestness of purpose shines through in every word.

THE PERSON—QUALITIES OF GREATNESS: Unrelenting passion, compassion, vision, and purpose that pushed her to "do the thing you think you cannot do" throughout her public and personal life.

Eleanor Roosevelt / "... the international Magna Carta of all men everywhere."

60

JOHN F. KENNEDY

"Ich bin ein Berliner."

PRESIDENT BUOYS SPIRITS OF BELEAGUERED BERLINERS

The second of Rose and Joseph P. Kennedy's ten children, John Fitzgerald Kennedy was born into one of America's most ambitious families and named in honor of his mother's father (John Francis Fitzgerald, the popular Boston mayor everybody knew as Honey Fitz). JFK's father was an energetic businessman whose ambition led him, in the opinion of some, to play a little "fast and loose" with the law on his way to amassing a fortune. Because of his wealth and significant political influence, Joe Kennedy was named Ambassador to England in 1937 by President Franklin Roosevelt.

John was a somewhat sickly child. In fact, a family joke had it that even mosquitoes took great risks in biting him. Jack, as he was called, was not a stellar student, preferring tennis, basketball, football, and golf to studying, but he did well in his favorite subjects, history and English. At Choate, the boarding school for boys he attended, he revealed a passion for current events—he even had a daily subscription to *The New York Times*.

In 1936, he enrolled in Harvard, where his older brother Joe Jr. was already a student. It was there, while playing football, that he ruptured a disk in his spine, an injury that would bother him for the rest of his life. It was also at this time that his father became ambassador to England, allowing him and his brother Joe to visit England and Europe where their father would brief them on the German and Italian war build-up. As a result, JFK wrote his senior thesis on why Great Britain was unprepared for war with Germany—an opinion, it seems, he shared with Winston Churchill. The thesis was later published in the book *Why England Slept*.

Following in brother Joe's footsteps, after graduating from Harvard in 1940, Kennedy became a Lieutenant and commanded Patrol Torpedo (PT) boat 109 in the South Pacific, with a crew of twelve men. On the night of August 2, 1943, a Japanese destroyer traveling at full speed rammed PT109, splitting it in half and killing two crew members instantly. JFK was slammed hard against the cockpit, again injuring his back. Despite the injury, in the dark, Kennedy hauled badly burned crew members to safety. They were marooned on an island for seven days before being rescued. When he returned home, Jack was awarded the Navy and Marine Corps Medal for his leadership and courage. Sadly, one year later, Jack's brother Joe was not as fortunate. He died when his plane exploded on a mission in Europe.

Joe, Jr. had been groomed for politics by his father. On his eldest son's death, Joe, Sr. convinced Jack that he should run for Congress. JFK's political career was launched in 1946 when he was elected to Congress to represent Massachusetts' eleventh district. After three terms in the House, he won a Senate seat in 1952.

In 1960, in one of the closest elections in history, JFK defeated Richard Nixon to become, at the age of 43, the youngest man and the first Catholic elected President. His stirring inaugural address established the "New Frontier" and ignited a new attitude in Washington and across America.

Brought to a tragic end by his assassination in Dallas on November 22, 1963, the country and the world mourned the loss of a leader whose style, charm, and oratory inspired millions.

(left) Lt. John F. Kennedy aboard PT109, 1943.

(above) John F. Kennedy, Jr., Jacqueline Bouvier Kennedy, Caroline Kennedy, John F. Kennedy, Hyannis Port, Massachusetts, August 4, 1962.

"I am asking each of you to be new pioneers on that New Frontier."

JFK, acceptance speech, Democratic Convention, 1960

President and Mrs. Kennedy arrive for Inaugural Ball. President Kennedy, Mrs. Kennedy, others. National Guard Armory, Washington, DC (January 20, 1961).

"Ask not what your country can do for you ..."
Excerpts from Inaugural Address, January 20, 1961

... [W]e observe today not a victory of party, but a celebration of freedom—symbolizing an end, as well as a beginning—signifying renewal, as well as change. For I have sworn before you and Almighty God the same solemn oath our forebears prescribed nearly a century and three quarters ago.

The world is very different now. For man holds in his mortal hands the power to abolish all forms of human poverty and all forms of human life. And yet the same revolutionary beliefs for which our forebears fought are still at issue around the globe—the belief that the rights of man come not from the generosity of the state, but from the hand of God.

We dare not forget today that we are the heirs of that first revolution. Let the word go forth from this time and place, to friend and foe alike, that the torch has been passed to a new generation of Americans—born in this century, tempered by war, disciplined by a hard and bitter peace, proud of our ancient heritage—and unwilling to witness or permit the slow undoing of those human rights to which this Nation has always been committed, and to which we are committed today at home and around the world.

Let every nation know, whether it wishes us well or ill, that we shall pay any price, bear any burden, meet any hardship, support any friend, oppose any foe, in order to assure the survival and the success of liberty....

To those old allies whose cultural and spiritual origins we share, we pledge the loyalty of faithful friends. United, there is little we cannot do. ... Divided there is little we can do—for we dare not meet a powerful challenge at odds and split asunder....

To those people in the huts and villages across the globe struggling to break the bonds of mass misery, we pledge our best efforts to help them help themselves,... not because we seek their votes, but because it is right. If a free society cannot help the many who are poor, it cannot save the few who are rich.

To our sister republics south of our border, ... know that we shall join with them to oppose aggression or subversion anywhere in the Americas. And let every other power know that this Hemisphere intends to remain the master of its own house....

Finally, to those nations who would make themselves our adversary, we offer not a pledge but a request: that both sides begin anew the quest for peace, before the dark powers of destruction unleashed by science engulf all humanity in planned or accidental self-destruction.

We dare not tempt them with weakness. For only when our arms are sufficient beyond doubt can we be certain beyond doubt that they will never be employed....

So let us begin anew—remembering on both sides that civility is not a sign of weakness, and sincerity is always subject to proof. Let us never negotiate out of fear. But let us never fear to negotiate.

Let both sides explore what problems unite us instead of belaboring those problems which divide us....

Let both sides seek to invoke the wonders of science instead of its terrors. Together let us explore the stars, conquer the deserts, eradicate disease, tap the ocean depths, and encourage the arts and commerce.

Let both sides unite to heed in all corners of the earth the command of Isaiah—to "undo the heavy burdens … and to let the oppressed go free."

And if a beachhead of cooperation may push back the jungle of suspicion, let both sides join in creating a new endeavor, not a new balance of power, but a new world of law, where the strong are just and the weak secure and the peace preserved.

All this will not be finished in the first 100 days. Nor will it be finished in the first 1,000 days, nor in the life of this Administration, nor even perhaps in our lifetime on this planet. But let us begin.

In your hands, my fellow citizens, more than mine, will rest the final success or failure of our course. Since this country was founded, each generation of Americans has been summoned to give testimony to its national loyalty. The graves of young Americans who answered the call to service surround the globe.

Now the trumpet summons us again—not as a call to bear arms, though arms we need; not as a call to battle, though embattled we are—but a call to bear the burden of a long twilight struggle, year in and year out, "rejoicing in hope, patient in tribulation"—a struggle against the common enemies of man: tyranny, poverty, disease, and war itself....

In the long history of the world, only a few generations have been granted the role of defending freedom in its hour of maximum danger. I do not shrink from this responsibility—I welcome it. I do not believe that any of us would exchange places with any other people or any other generation. The energy, the faith, the devotion which we bring to this endeavor will light our country and all who serve it—and the glow from that fire can truly light the world.

And so, my fellow Americans: ask not what your country can do for you—ask what you can do for your country.

My fellow citizens of the world: ask not what America will do for you, but what together we can do for the freedom of man.

Finally, whether you are citizens of America or citizens of the world, ask of us the same high standards of strength and sacrifice which we ask of you. With a good conscience our only sure reward, with history the final judge of our deeds, let us go forth to lead the land we love, asking His blessing and His help, but knowing that here on earth, God's work must truly be our own.

American president John F Kennedy making a point during a press conference in the new State Department Auditorium in Washington.

(above) President Kennedy's Motorcade The motorcade of President Kennedy, Chancellor Konrad Adenauer, and West Berlin Mayor Willy Brandt makes its way through cheering crowds after the three leaders visited the Berlin Wall.

(left) President Kennedy goes to the Berlin Wall in June 1963 on his visit to West Berlin. The Wall, erected in August 1961, quickly became a stark Cold War symbol of the impasse between the Communist World and the Free World, and it perpetuated the division of Germany in the heart of Europe.

"All in a Day's Work": The Berlin Airlift

For eleven months during the 1948 Berlin blockade, planes landed and unloaded goods every three minutes, twenty-four hours a day! The Allies flew food, medicine, and essential staples into West Berlin daily across "enemy" lines, flying a hair's breadth over the tops of apartment buildings bordering the landing fields. The Allies intended to keep their pledge to the people of West Berlin that they could live in their city in freedom.

Compassionate airmen, affectionately known as "Sweet Bombers," personally sewed tiny handmade "parachutes" and filled them with chocolate for the children. As they flew low over the city, they slid open their windows and gently floated the parachutes down. They also "bombed" the gleeful kids who ran alongside their planes by throwing out full sacks of Mars® bars, candy, and chewing gum. This inadvertently may have been one of the most successful branding campaigns for a chocolate bar!

"He has strengthened European confidence in American leadership."

Arthur J. Olsen, "President's Trip to Europe as Seen from Abroad," *The New York Times*, June 30, 1963

In what may have been his most emotional—even inspired—public moment, John Kennedy stood in front of one million wildly enthusiastic West Germans at the Berlin Wall and forged a bond that continues to this day.

To understand the impact of Kennedy's speech, we need to go back to 1948 and the Berlin blockade. After WWII, Germany had been divided into four sectors, each governed by one of the Allies. Berlin fell within the Russian sector, but for a number of reasons it, too, was divided into four parts. In 1948, the Soviet Union cut off its section of the city from the rest in an attempt to force the city into political submission. The result was economic devastation and starvation. The other Allies, led by the United States, responded aggressively with an innovative—and successful—airlift of goods.

By 1961, enormous Cold War tension existed between the U.S. and the USSR. Both Soviet Premier Nikita Khrushchev and President Kennedy jockeyed for political position. Khrushchev took the offensive, announcing his intention to make Berlin a single, unified city that, naturally, would fall under the administration of Communist East Germany. West Berliners were afraid, and the world took notice.

Kennedy and Krushchev began a slow dance to the uneven rhythm of different ideologies. As the metaphoric music got faster, the dance became more dangerous. On July 25, 1961, Kennedy addressed the American people about the Berlin Crisis, as he called it. He told them that the United States would defend the rights of the people of West Berlin and would do whatever was necessary to accomplish that. He linked the fate of the people of West Berlin to the fate of free people everywhere.

U.S. Army Checkpoint, Berlin, 1961.

The President on Tour

The New York Times, June 30, 1963

For John F. Kennedy the man it was a week of extraordinary personal achievement.... More than a million Rhinelanders lined the route, chanting "Ken-ned-DEE" and wildly applauding. In Cologne itself he drew a crowd of 350,000 ... Mr. Kennedy got a roar when he ended a speech with "Kolle Alaaf!" meaning "Hooray for Cologne!" In Bonn he got another cheer when he said Chicago has more ethnic Germans than the West German capital. All this as about 20,000,000 West Germans watched on TV.... Tuesday came another motorcade, another million cheering Germans and another show of "Willkommen" signs....

...The emotional climax came Wednesday when the President flew to Berlin. Still another million, at least, screamed "Ken-ned-DEE" in the streets. One placard held up for him to read said: "John. You our best friend."... The TV cameras were on Mr. Kennedy for most of the eight hours he was in the city, and especially at the dramatic moments which he gazed in silence over The Wall at the Brandenburg Gate, where the Communists had hung great banners between the pillars to block his view; and at Checkpoint Charlie....

Less than three weeks later, at exactly midnight on August 13th, the Communist government sealed off the remaining east–west borders, drawing the Iron Curtain closed. Construction of the Berlin Wall began. Rising seemingly overnight, it actually took four days to build this high, thick wall of ugly concrete topped by razor wire and sentry posts, stationed with armed guards who shot to kill.

In the blink of an eye, families found themselves separated forever, with children and parents, and husbands and wives, sometimes on opposite sides of the wall simply because of where they were at the time it went up. Actually, anyone who desired to could *return* to East Germany, but armed guards, barbed wire, and dogs prevented anyone inside from getting out.

In June 1963, as part of a controversial European tour, John Kennedy traveled to Germany to see the Berlin Wall for himself. It is said that nearly 90 percent of Berlin turned out to greet the President as his motorcade traversed almost 30 miles from the airport into town. That day, the city stood still, as millions of people waited along the route to catch a glimpse of the young president.

From his motorcade, Kennedy could see the devastation of East Berlin—its dilapidated buildings and boarded-up windows that made it seem frozen in time since WWII. He was visibly shaken by what he saw, so shaken that he ignored the urgings of his aides who argued for a more conciliatory tone, a tone he had used in a much lauded speech on June 10 at American University ("The United States, as the world knows, will never start a war. We do not want a war."). In fact, as he rode in his limousine, he inserted stronger, more emotional, more defiant language

The Truth About the Jelly Doughnut

There has been much written about the four famous words "Ich bin ein Berliner." Kennedy clearly meant to say, "I am a Berliner," to express his solidarity with the people of Berlin. Some people say he got it wrong and ended up saying, "I am a jelly doughnut."

The truth? Kennedy had carefully crafted his remarks, but at the last minute asked his translator how to say, "I am a Berliner." The translator correctly told him "Ich bin ein Berliner." Neither knew a native Berliner would say "Ich bin Berliner." No *"ein."* To confuse matters further, "ein Berliner" is indeed the name of a popular Berlin pastry—a jelly-filled doughnut.

Of course, it doesn't matter. No one really cared. The crowd went wild and the world was inspired. Still, the story of the "mistake" persists and will as long at the words ring in our ears.

Leaving the American Sector of Berlin, 1961.

into his speech. Its defiance and personal charm, however, were exactly what the huge crowd wanted. Today, because of that extraordinary moment in history, the square in which he spoke is known as "Kennedyplatz."

A crowd of over 1,000,000 people had assembled to listen to the President speak at the Rudolf Wilde Platz, situated directly opposite the majestic, and now unused, Brandenburg Gate. The Communists had placed heavy red material across its arches to prevent East Berliners from seeing the president, but Kennedy knew his words would carry beyond the people standing in the plaza to the many East Berliners on the other side of the Wall, who would hear his words through the blaring speakers positioned throughout the plaza, or, surreptitiously, over the radio. As it turned out, Kennedy's speech was the first major multi-media event of its kind—the very first time that a speech was ever broadcast on radio and television at the same time. In all, nearly 20 million people in twelve countries saw or heard this speech simultaneously.

From the platform outside City Hall, Kennedy could see the gigantic square awash in a sea of human faces. The noise was overwhelming as the people chanted, "Ken-ned-dee," "Ken-ned-DEE." The leader of the free world issued bold remarks that day, and his brilliant use of two simple phrases ensured its place in history. The speech was quite brief, but it delivered a deeply moving and powerful message that reverberated globally.

Twenty-three years later, President Ronald Reagan stood in front of the same barrier and uttered his famous words... "Mr. Gorbachev, tear down this wall." In 1989 the Berlin Wall, finally, came tumbling down!

Remarks Delivered in the Rudolph-Wilde-Platz, Berlin Wall, June 26, 1963

Ask anyone to name John F. Kennedy's best speech and you get a different answer. Some people remember his 1960 acceptance speech at the Democratic Convention in Los Angeles. Others regard his 1961 inaugural address as one of the most inspirational of all time. Of all his speeches, however, Kennedy's provocative address to over one million people at the Rudolf-Wilde-Platz in West Berlin on June 26, 1963 was perhaps his most emotional. Spoken to the largest live audience of his career, what makes it so spine-tingling is how he worked the huge crowd and the way in which he addressed timeless themes of freedom.

SPEECH

I am proud to come to this city as the guest of your distinguished Mayor, who has symbolized throughout the world the fighting spirit of West Berlin. And I am proud to visit the Federal Republic with your distinguished Chancellor who, for so many years, has committed Germany to democracy and freedom and progress, and to come here in the company of my fellow American, General Clay, who has been in this city during its great moments of crisis and will come again if ever needed.

Two thousand years ago the proudest boast was "civis Romanus sum." Today, in the world of freedom, the proudest boast is "Ich bin ein Berliner."

I appreciate my interpreter translating my German!

There are many people in the world who really don't understand, or say they don't, what is the great issue between the free world and the Communist world. Let them come to Berlin. There are some who say that communism is the wave of the future. Let them come to Berlin. And there are some who say in Europe and elsewhere we can work with the Communists. Let them come to Berlin. And there are even a few who say that it is true that communism is an evil system, but it permits us to make economic progress. "*Laßt sie nach Berlin kommen*." Let them come to Berlin.

ANALYSIS

Kennedy does three things in his dynamic opening statement: First, by his repeated use of the word *proud*, he is setting the tone of the speech. Second, he reinforces the theme by repeating the word *proud* and, at the same time, makes it even more personal by complimenting his hosts and acknowledging General Clay, the commander of the Berlin airlift and a true hero to Berliners. Third, promising to send the general back, he sends a subtle message to the Soviet Union that he has no intentions of abandoning Berlin. (Listen to the thunderous cheers on the CD.) He continues to send that double message with words like: *fighting spirit, democracy, freedom,* and *progress*—all included in just the first two sentences!

Having jump-started the crowd, he launches into the theme of the speech. *Civis Romanus sum* means "I am a Roman citizen." To put Berlin on the same level as one of the world's great civilizations with the words *Ich bin ein Berliner* made the crowd ecstatic, especially because Kennedy said them in German. They would have loved it in English, but for the president to say it in *their* language was a masterful stroke, since it reinforced his "oneness" with them.

And here is Kennedy, again, at his most charming, commenting playfully on his translator's perhaps automatic translation of his German phrase back into English.

Most speakers are lucky if their speeches include one strong rallying cry like *Ich bin ein Berliner*, but here, as in a truly complex symphony, Kennedy almost immediately introduces another strong and emotionally compelling theme—*Let them come to Berlin*. Notice how he builds on the emotion he has already generated by repeating this phrase four times in six short, punchy sentences. (As Kennedy delivered these lines, he uses his voice to play each phrase differently—almost like sounding the same note on five different instruments.) The first time, it sounds like a suggestion; the second, a stronger suggestion; in the third, a taunt; the fourth time, it is delivered in a stunning, crowd-pleasing German; and the fifth time, a fist pounding English reiteration—a virtual demand.

President John F. Kennedy delivering his "Ich bin ein Berliner" speech in Rudolph-Wilde-Platz, now called John-F.-Kennedy-Platz.

Then, having brought the audience to a climax, he brings them back, momentarily, to the substance of the speech. A powerful and stinging indictment of communism in one sentence, made stronger, in part, because of his candor in describing democracy. Admitting your shortcomings before you launch into a repudiation of someone else's *always* strengthens your argument.

Freedom has many difficulties and democracy is not perfect, but we have never had to put a wall up to keep our people in, to prevent them from leaving us.

Before continuing, he flatters them (which when said well, as it is here, can be a very effective tool; but, when said badly, seems insincere and can backfire terribly) in a very successful effort to pump up their spirits (no one knew when it would end, and, in fact, it took another 26 years until the Wall finally did come down).

I want to say, on behalf of my countrymen, who live many miles away on the other side of the Atlantic, who are far distant from you, that they take the greatest pride that they have been able to share with you, even from a distance, the story of the last 18 years. I know of no town, no city that has been besieged for 18 years that still lives with the vitality and the force, and the hope and the determination of the city of West Berlin.

This speech has many audiences: those in the Plaza, as well as all Germans (East and West); the Soviet leadership, the Europeans, and, of course, the American audience at home. Here Kennedy is extending an emotional message of compassion and understanding for the West Berliners, at the same time as he is offering emotional support to the East Berliners listening on the other side of the wall.

While the wall is the most obvious and vivid demonstration of the failures of the Communist system, for all the world to see, we take no satisfaction in it, for it is, as your Mayor has said, an offense not only against history but an offense against humanity, separating families, dividing husbands and wives and brothers and sisters, and dividing a people who wish to be joined together.

What is true of this city is true of Germany—real, lasting peace in Europe can never be assured as long as one German out of four is denied the elementary right of free men, and that is to make a free choice. In 18 years of peace and good faith, this generation of Germans has earned the right to be free, including the right to unite their families and their nation in lasting peace, with good will to all people. You live in a defended island of freedom, but your life is part of the main.

To reinforce his message, Kennedy uses the words, *free* or *freedom* four times in this paragraph. The metaphor of Berlin—particularly West Berlin—as a beleaguered (but defended) island surrounded by a hostile East Germany is as apt as it is poetic.

So let me ask you as I close, to lift your eyes beyond the dangers of today, to the hopes of tomorrow, beyond the freedom merely of this city of Berlin, or your country of Germany, to the advance of freedom everywhere, beyond the wall to the day of peace with justice, beyond yourselves and ourselves to all mankind.

Kennedy sets a a kind of chant: four times beginning a phrase with the word *beyond* followed by something immediate and concrete and then skillfully taking us to something spiritual and idealistic.

Freedom is indivisible, …

Translation: No wall can ever work.

and when one man is enslaved, all are not free.

Beautiful use of opposition to stress a point.

When all are free, then we can look forward to that day when this city will be joined as one and this country and this great Continent of Europe in a peaceful and hopeful globe. When that day finally comes, as it will, …

The confidence Kennedy exudes when he says *as it will* make these perhaps the most important three words in the entire speech.

… the people of West Berlin can take sober satisfaction in the fact that they were in the front lines for almost two decades. All free men, wherever they may live, are citizens of Berlin, and, therefore, as a free man, I take pride in the words "Ich bin ein Berliner."

A beautiful way to end: Kennedy has come full circle, returning to the theme of pride with which he began the speech and tying it directly to the "Ich bin ein Berliner" theme; this time, making it even more personal by saying "I take pride in the words. . . ." Not only were all free men Berliners, but JFK was himself a proud Berliner. Judging by the overwhelming emotional reaction of the massive crowd, they were more than happy to include him as one of their own.

John Fitzgerald Kennedy

THE SPEECH—WHAT TO LOOK FOR: Playing the two themes—"Ich bin ein Berliner" and "Let them come to Berlin"—throughout the speech like a hypnotic mantra induced a euphoria in the huge and adoring crowd. Short in length but strong on emotion and pointed in its attack, this speech did what it was supposed to do: Boost the morale of the German people when they needed it most.

THE DELIVERY—WHAT TO LISTEN FOR: JFK was at his most emotionally ebullient. He allowed the emotion of the crowd to fill him and drive him. You can hear it in his cadence and in how much "fun" he was having as he becomes a cheerleader for a million adoring fans.

THE PERSON—QUALITIES OF GREATNESS: The compelling combination of grace, vision, integrity, and, of course, youth and style make JFK—as well as his speeches—something rare and special.

MARTIN LUTHER KING, JR.

"I have a dream. . ."

HIGHLIGHTS

1929 Born on January 15 and named Michael Luther King, Jr., later renamed Martin

1954 Moves to Montgomery to preach at Dexter Avenue Baptist Church

1955 Finishes his Ph.D. in systematic theology; December 1 Rosa Parks arrested for violating segregation laws; bus boycott launched in Montgomery; December 5, elected head of newly formed protest group, the Montgomery Improvement Association

1956 January 30, home bombed; December 21, Montgomery buses desegregate

1957 Southern Christian Leadership Conference formed; King is named first president

LEADER OF A GENTLE ARMY CALLS FOR PAYMENT ON "A DREAM DEFERRED"

Martin Luther King, Jr., is one of the twentieth century's most inspiring leaders and one of its most gifted orators. The son and grandson of pastors and civil rights activists, he, too, became a pastor, and, upon receiving his doctorate in Systematic Theology, he accepted a post at Dexter Avenue Baptist Church in Montgomery, Alabama.

At that time, in Alabama as well as in other parts of the south, a black person had to give up his or her seat on a bus if a white person wanted it. In December 1955, a black woman in Montgomery—Rosa Parks—didn't get up and she was thrown in jail for saying "no." It was the law. This time, though, the people of Montgomery joined together in protest and determined to boycott the buses.

After Rosa Parks was arrested, King, an ardent student of Mahatma Gandhi and nonviolent strategies, was chosen president of the Montgomery Improvement Association, the organization responsible for coordinating the bus boycott. The boycott continued through 1956, and although he was arrested and his home bombed, King remained steadfast. His leadership, strength, and oratorical abilities began to bring him national prominence. One year later, the United States Supreme Court declared the law unconstitutional.

That was just the beginning of the struggle for King. In Alabama and elsewhere throughout the southern United States, blacks were kept from voting, they couldn't serve on juries, they couldn't drink from certain water fountains or swim in certain swimming pools. Although integration of public schools was ordered by the

Supreme Court in its landmark 1954 *Brown v. Board of Education* decision, the reality was that black children still didn't safely go to the same schools as white children and the Court's ruling did not apply to state-run colleges and universities.

What's more, black people couldn't eat at certain restaurants, or rent or buy homes in certain neighborhoods. In some areas, they had to step off the sidewalk into the street when a white person walked by. It wasn't the law, but they knew what might happen if they didn't "show proper respect."

Building on the success of the Montgomery bus boycott, King—along with other black southern ministers—created the Southern Christian Leadership Conference (SCLC) in 1957. In the beginning, the SCLC, with King as its president, concentrated on voting rights and legal remedies to obtain them. By the 1960s, student sit-ins, Freedom Rides, and other mass protests for voting rights and against all forms of segregation had multiplied. Challenges to King's nonviolent cautious approach began to surface in the late 1960s from younger black militants, particularly the Student Nonviolent Coordinating Committee (SNCC) and charismatic leader Malcolm X who declared, "There is no such thing as a nonviolent revolution."

After an unsuccessful campaign in Albany, Georgia, King determined to step up his efforts and, in 1963, was invited to Birmingham, Alabama to lead a campaign to unseat the segregationist three-man city commission. Birmingham voters had turned them out of office, but, led by "Bull" Connor, the Commissioner of Public Safety, they refused to step aside and allow the newly elected mayor and

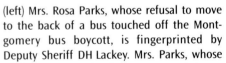

(left) Mrs. Rosa Parks, whose refusal to move to the back of a bus touched off the Montgomery bus boycott, is fingerprinted by Deputy Sheriff DH Lackey. Mrs. Parks, whose appeal on a $14 fine for violating segregation laws was turned down, was among the 100 or so indicted by a Grand Jury on anti-boycott charges.

(above) Students at Florida A&M College, protesting segregation on the bus lines, jeer at the driver of a city bus as he drives his empty vehicle across the school campus (1956).

"The Negro's great stumbling block is not the White Citizen's Council or the Ku Klux Klan, but the white moderate who is more devoted to order than to justice."

Letter from Birmingham Jail, April 16, 1963

(above) Black students at North Carolina A&T College participate in a sit-in at a F. W. Woolworth's lunch counter reserved for white customers in Greensboro, North Carolina (1960).

(below) Dr. King being arrested in Birmingham, Alabama, April 12, 1963.

"Many people thought he was out of his mind when he led an army, not armed with guns or bricks or stones, 50,000 strong in Montgomery, Alabama, in 1955, and said to his followers: 'Love your enemies, pray for them that curse and spitefully use you.'"

Ralph Abernathy, at the Commemoration service for Martin Luther King, Jr., January 15, 1969

commissioners to assume control. Sit-ins met with arrests, but little media attention. King, too, would be arrested. In his weeks in prison he wrote what would become his *Letter from Birmingham Jail,* which outlined his goal of eliminating segregation from all spheres, including job discrimination.

Upon his release, he dramatically changed tactics, deciding to put children in the forefront of his campaign. Nearly one thousand children were arrested. There was no more room left in the jails. Still more children demonstrated. Connor ordered the firemen to hose them. Confirming King's strategy, this caught the attention of the media and shocked the nation. Birmingham capitulated and public facilities were integrated. At least partly in response to King's activities, that June, President Kennedy submitted to Congress the legislation that would eventually become the Civil Rights Act of 1964.

It was the March on Washington for Jobs and Freedom later that year, with its estimated 250,000–400,000 people, black and white, crammed between the Lincoln Memorial and the Washington Monument, that was to be Martin Luther King, Jr.'s defining moment. Today it is King's "I have a dream" speech that is most remembered, but the goals of the actual march were broad and diverse in an attempt to unite various factions of the civil rights movement with labor unions and other activists.

Ten months later, the Civil Rights Act of 1964, the most extensive civil rights legislation since the Civil War, was finally passed. Martin Luther King, Jr., was awarded the Nobel Prize for Peace on December 10, 1964.

As his stature grew, so did his interests expand. On April 4, 1967, King spoke out vehemently against the war in Vietnam. Making the connection between con-

Dr. Martin Luther King Jr., head of the Southern Christian Leadership Conference, addresses marchers during his "I Have a Dream" speech at the Lincoln Memorial in Washington, D.C., August 28, 1963.

"Beyond Vietnam: A Time to Break Silence"

Excerpts from Speech to Meeting of Clergy and Laity Concerned, April 4, 1967

... As I have walked among the desperate, rejected and angry young men I have told them that Molotov cocktails and rifles would not solve their problems. I have tried to offer them my deepest compassion while maintaining my conviction that social change comes most meaningfully through nonviolent action. But they asked—and rightly so—what about Vietnam? They asked if our own nation wasn't using massive doses of violence to solve its problems, to bring about the changes it wanted. ... For the sake of those boys, for the sake of this government, for the sake of the hundreds of thousands trembling under our violence, I cannot be silent. ...

"King was a preacher who spoke in biblical cadences ideally suited to leading a stride toward freedom that found its inspiration in the Old Testament story of the Israelites and the New Testament gospel of Jesus Christ."

Jack E. White, *Time 100*, "Leaders & Revolutionaries: Twenty people who helped define the political and social fabric of our times," June 14, 1999

"A magnificent blend of eloquence and raw fact, of searing denunciation and tender wooing, of political sagacity and Christian insight, of tough realism and infinite compassion."

Christian Century, April 19, 1967, commenting on King's April 4, 1967 speech denouncing America's role in Vietnam

ditions in the slums and military spending, he spoke at churches and anti-war rallies warning of dire consequences at home and abroad if the war continued.

In his last speech, the day before he was assassinated, King told the sanitation workers in whose support he was speaking that the time had come to expand the struggle. He called for an economic boycott of companies whose hiring practices were unfair and for support of black-owned banks and insurance companies. Sadly, what that speech will be most remembered for is King's poignant assessment of his life, and the hauntingly chilling premonition of his own death.

Martin Luther King, Jr., was murdered on April 4, 1968. His vision and work continue through the Civil Rights Act of 1964, the Voting Rights Act of 1965, and especially the example he set for countless millions around the world.

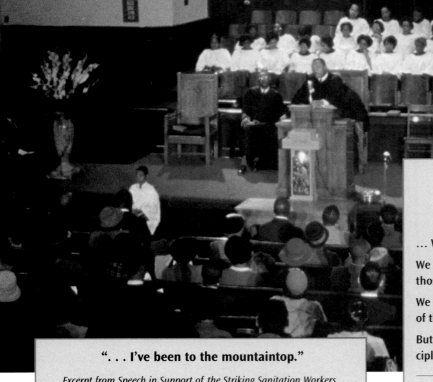

"... I've been to the mountaintop."

Excerpt from Speech in Support of the Striking Sanitation Workers, April 3, 1968

... Well, I don't know what will happen now. We've got some difficult days ahead. But it doesn't matter with me now. Because I've been to the mountaintop. And I don't mind. Like anybody, I would like to live a long life. Longevity has its place. But I'm not concerned about that now. I just want to do God's will. And He's allowed me to go up to the mountain. And I've looked over. And I've seen the promised land. I may not get there with you. But I want you to know tonight, that we, as a people, will get to the promised land. And I'm happy, tonight. I'm not worried about anything. I'm not fearing any man. Mine eyes have seen the glory of the coming of the Lord. ...

"As I sat on the stone steps looking out on the vast throng I was fully conscious that this was one of the great moments in the history of blacks in America. Never had so many black Americans come together from all sections of the country to strike a blow for first-class citizenship…"

Louis Martin, former advisor to President John F. Kennedy (from *Walking with Presidents: Louis Martin and the Rise of Black Political Power* by Alex Poinsett)

Lyndon B. Johnson on Voting Rights
"Our Constitution … forbids it."

Radio and Television Remarks Upon Signing the Civil Rights Bill, July 2, 1964

… We believe that all men are created equal. Yet many are denied equal treatment.

We believe that all men have certain unalienable rights. Yet many Americans do not enjoy those rights.

We believe that all men are entitled to the blessings of liberty. Yet millions are being deprived of those blessings—not because of their own failures, but because of the color of their skin. …

But it cannot continue. Our Constitution, the foundation of our Republic, forbids it. The principles of our freedom forbid it. Morality forbids it. And the law I will sign tonight forbids it. …

"The American Promise"

Special Message to the Congress, March 15, 1965

Mr. Speaker, Mr. President, Members of Congress:

I speak tonight for the dignity of man and the destiny of democracy.…

This was the first nation in the history of the world to be founded with a purpose. The great phrases of that purpose still sound in every American heart, North and South: "All men are created equal"—"government by consent of the governed"—"give me liberty or give me death."…

Those words are a promise to every citizen that he shall share in the dignity of man. This dignity … says that he shall share in freedom, he shall choose his leaders, educate his children, provide for his family according to his ability and his merits as a human being.… There is no constitutional issue here. The command of the Constitution is plain.

There is no moral issue. It is wrong—deadly wrong—to deny any of your fellow Americans the right to vote in this country.

There is no issue of States rights or national rights. There is only the struggle for human rights.…

It is the effort of American Negroes to secure for themselves the full blessings of American life. Their cause must be our cause too. Because it is not just Negroes, but really it is all of us, who must overcome the crippling legacy of bigotry and injustice.

And we shall overcome.

… [A] century has passed, more than a hundred years, since the Negro was freed. And he is not fully free tonight.…

A century has passed, more than a hundred years, since equality was promised. And yet the Negro is not equal.…

The real hero of this struggle is the American Negro. His actions and protests, his courage to risk safety and even to risk his life, have awakened the conscience of this Nation.…

He has called upon us to make good the promise of America.…

"I have a dream. . ."

Speech Delivered at the March on Washington for Jobs and Freedom, August 28, 1963

This speech is perfect In every way. The use of language, the emotional build-up, the penetrating message and the flawless delivery are, plain and simple, perfection. It's all the more amazing when you discover that King disregarded his prepared remarks and spoke largely extemporaneously, which only demonstrates that great speeches come from the heart, not just the pen.

To accomplish Dr. King's aims, this speech required three key elements working perfectly together: First, it had to be strong. No one could be the leader of this movement unless the people could feel his passion, anger, and conviction. Second, it had to be taken seriously by the Establishment. Even if all those on the Mall that day were ecstatic, the speech would not have worked if King or the movement he represented were seen as fringe or extremist. Third, it had to come from the heart and be emotionally uplifting, even spiritual. Dr. King knew that words are simply sounds floating in the air unless they carry with them the energy of human emotion.

By using strong visual images—seventy in all—King accomplished all of these things, and more. To this day, the emotional impact of this speech reverberates to those who heard it then as well as to those who first hear it now. Like the Gettysburg Address, it is a speech with lasting impact.

ANALYSIS

In 1963, and to this day, many people believe that Abraham Lincoln's Gettysburg Address was the greatest speech of the nineteenth century, if not the greatest speech ever given. Notice how Dr. King begins what many believe is the greatest speech of the twentieth century as Lincoln did by setting the speech in time. Using Lincoln's life and work as the foundation for his speech gives it immediate credibility. Note, too, the extraordinary and vivid use of visual imagery. In this paragraph alone you'll find six such images: a *symbolic shadow, a beacon light, seared in flames, withering injustice, joyous daybreak,* and *long night of captivity.*

Here, the words *in the corners of American society* add visual dimension to our idea of languishing. The phrase *an exile in his own land* is a direct and poignant allusion to the biblical "stranger in a strange land," while the repetition of the phrase *one hundred years later* hammers home just how critical the situation is.

We come now to the metaphor—that of an unpaid debt—that drives one of the basic themes of this speech.

Having cleverly put the Founding Fathers in the role of debtors and aroused our sympathies for the holders of that debt, King—by inserting the simple word *sacred*—has elevated the Founding Fathers' promissory note to a spiritual, not just a legal, obligation.

SPEECH

I am happy to join with you today in what will go down in history as the greatest demonstration for freedom in the history of our nation.

Five score years ago, a great American, in whose symbolic shadow we stand signed the Emancipation Proclamation. This momentous decree came as a great beacon light of hope to millions of Negro slaves who had been seared in the flames of withering injustice. It came as a joyous daybreak to end the long night of captivity.

But one hundred years later, we must face the tragic fact that the Negro is still not free. One hundred years later, the life of the Negro is still sadly crippled by the manacles of segregation and the chains of discrimination. One hundred years later, the Negro lives on a lonely island of poverty in the midst of a vast ocean of material prosperity. One hundred years later, the Negro is still languishing in the corners of American society and finds himself an exile in his own land. So we have come here today to dramatize an appalling condition.

In a sense we have come to our nation's capital to cash a check. When the architects of our republic wrote the magnificent words of the Constitution and the Declaration of Independence, they were signing a promissory note to which every American was to fall heir. This note was a promise that all men would be guaranteed the inalienable rights of life, liberty, and the pursuit of happiness.

It is obvious today that America has defaulted on this promissory note insofar as her citizens of color are concerned. Instead of honoring this sacred obligation,

King now takes this imagery a step further. Not only is it a debt; it's a debt that has been more than defaulted on. America has tried to pull the wool over the eyes of blacks, and passed a bad check. To anyone who ever struggled over money—and no doubt there were some in his audience—the image of an "NSF" check hit home.

America has given the Negro people a bad check which has come back marked "insufficient funds."

Look how he rips the carpet out from under the two most obvious objections to his point (always better to answer critics before they can attack) and notice how elegantly he uses strong visual imagery to diminish their argument.

But we refuse to believe that the bank of justice is bankrupt. We refuse to believe that there are insufficient funds in the great vaults of opportunity of this nation. So we have come to cash this check—a check that will give us upon demand the riches of freedom and the security of justice.

The counterpoint of *the fierce urgency of now* with the *luxury of cooling off* and *the tranquilizing drug of gradualism* makes both a visual and ironic statement.

We have also come to this hallowed spot to remind America of the fierce urgency of now. This is no time to engage in the luxury of cooling off or to take the tranquilizing drug of gradualism.

The strong visual imagery continues—five vivid word pictures in this paragraph alone.

Now is the time to rise from the dark and desolate valley of segregation to the sunlit path of racial justice. Now is the time to open the doors of opportunity to all of God's children. Now is the time to lift our nation from the quicksands of racial injustice to the solid rock of brotherhood.

As King continues, along with Shakespearean allusions, he makes the most of the images of heat with nuanced references to the violence of earlier summers and the potential for future eruptions.

It would be fatal for the nation to overlook the urgency of the moment and to underestimate the determination of the Negro. This sweltering summer of the Negro's legitimate discontent will not pass until there is an invigorating autumn of freedom and equality. Nineteen sixty-three is not an end, but a beginning. Those who hope that the Negro needed to blow off steam and will now be content will have a rude awakening if the nation returns to business as usual. There will be neither rest nor tranquility in America until the Negro is granted his citizenship rights.

The whirlwinds of revolt will continue to shake the foundations of our nation until the bright day of justice emerges.

But there is something that I must say to my people who stand on the warm threshold which leads into the palace of justice. In the process of gaining our rightful place we must not be guilty of wrongful deeds. Let us not seek to satisfy our thirst for freedom by drinking from the cup of bitterness and hatred.

We must forever conduct our struggle on the high plane of dignity and discipline. We must not allow our creative protest to degenerate into physical violence. Again and again we must rise to the majestic heights of meeting physical force with soul force.

The marvelous new militancy which has engulfed the Negro community must not lead us to distrust of all white people, for many of our white brothers, as evidenced by their presence here today, have come to realize that their destiny is tied up with our destiny and their freedom is inextricably bound to our freedom.

Invoking *soul force* instead of *physical force,* Dr. King now addresses those among them who have been calling for violence. He compliments them on their marvelous new militancy, and, true to the spirit of the March, reminds them that all white people are not their enemy and that both communities' destinies are intertwined.

We cannot walk alone. And as we walk, we must make the pledge that we shall march ahead. We cannot turn back. There are those who are asking the devotees of civil rights, "When will you be satisfied?"

We can never be satisfied as long as our bodies, heavy with the fatigue of travel, cannot gain lodging in the motels of the highways and the hotels of the cities. We cannot be satisfied as long as the Negro's basic mobility is from a smaller ghetto to a larger one. We can never be satisfied as long as a Negro in Mississippi cannot vote and a Negro in New York believes he has nothing for which to vote.

Using the age-old and very effective technique of asking a question, Dr. King answers it with specific demands, providing a counterpoint to the more general imagery that precedes it. Nevertheless, he never lets go of the rhythm that builds the emotion in this speech. Notice how he uses six parallel sentences in a row (*never be satisfied* or *cannot be satisfied*) to hammer the point home.

No, no, we are not satisfied, and we will not be satisfied until justice rolls down like waters and righteousness like a mighty stream.

Remarkably, this was the very last line that came from Dr. King's prepared text. From this point on, he did not look at his speech, but—master orator that he was—allowed the emotion and inspiration of the moment to carry him as he delivers the rest of this speech extemporaneously. Read the following paragraphs carefully and you will see that the tone becomes more personal and less intellectual, more heartfelt and less academic and, yes, vastly more spiritual.

I am not unmindful that some of you have come here out of great trials and tribulations. Some of you have come fresh from narrow cells. Some of you have come from areas where your quest for freedom left you battered by the storms of persecution and staggered by the winds of police brutality. You have been the veterans of creative suffering. Continue to work with the faith that unearned suffering is redemptive.

One of the most important parts of any speech is the moment where the speaker "identifies" with the audience and shows either that he is one of them or that he truly understands them and speaks for them. Usually this comes toward the beginning of the speech, but Reverend King didn't need to do that; his audience already identified with him. Instead, he uses this device toward the end of his speech to launch his "call to action."

Unearned suffering may be redemptive, but King knows he must bring his audience back to their earthly goals. Using short phrases and repeating them, he builds to a crescendo (the shorter the phrase, the easier it is to build rhythm; the more the repetition, the greater the emotion). Interestingly, Dr. King, in his prepared text, had planned to say, "And so today, let us go back to our communities as members of the international association for the advancement of creative dissatisfaction," but decided instead to go with this much more positive call to action. Six times he repeats the phrase *go back*.

Go back to Mississippi, go back to Alabama, go back to South Carolina, go back to Georgia, go back to Louisiana, go back to the slums and ghettos of our northern cities, knowing that somehow this situation can and will be changed. Let us not wallow in the valley of despair.

Amazingly, as he explains in his autobiography, the word *dream* and the entire *I have a dream* theme were not in his prepared text. Spontaneously, he says, he decided to go back to a theme he had used in Detroit two months earlier, and, without notes, went where it took him. Without the *I have a dream* theme, the speech, as written, was terrific, but the repetition of this theme—a theme that everyone could immediately relate to—gave the speech a dimension that transcended time and place.

I say to you today, my friends, that in spite of the difficulties and frustrations of the moment, I still have a dream.

Here, in the very first sentence after announcing the theme, Dr. King continues to broaden the appeal of the speech to include all people, not only the blacks in the audience. With this single sentence he tells the rest of America that he and his followers believe in the same things as they do, and that there is no reason to fear.

It is a dream deeply rooted in the American dream.

Repeating one of the most inspirational themes of any speech eight times, the speech really starts to sing.

I have a dream that one day this nation will rise up and live out the true meaning of its creed: "We hold these truths to be self-evident, that all men are created equal." I have a dream that one day on the red hills of Georgia the sons of former slaves and the sons of former slave owners will be able to sit down together at a table of brotherhood. I have a dream that one day even the state of Mississippi, a desert state sweltering with the heat of injustice and oppression, will be transformed into an oasis of freedom and justice. I have a dream that my four little children will one day live in a nation where they will not be judged by the color of their skin but by the content of their character. I have a dream today. I have a dream that one day the state of Alabama, whose governor's lips are presently dripping with the words of interposition and nullification, will be transformed into a situation where little black boys and black girls will be able to join hands with little white boys and white girls and walk together as sisters and brothers. I have a dream today.

I have a dream that one day every valley shall be exalted, every hill and mountain shall be made low, the rough places will be made plain, and the crooked places will be made straight, and the glory of the Lord shall be revealed, and all flesh shall see it together.

His years as a preacher came to the forefront here. How can anyone not be moved by such perfect cadence, imagery, and power?

This is our hope. This is the faith with which I return to the South. With this faith we will be able to hew out of the mountain of despair a stone of hope. With this faith we will be able to transform the jangling discords of our nation into a beautiful symphony of brotherhood. With this faith we will be able to work together, to pray together, to struggle together, to go to jail together, to stand up for freedom together, knowing that we will be free one day.

King now steps back a bit, perhaps to rest before building to another, even higher crescendo. Although he still uses repetition, the sentences are longer, less rhythmic, but the imagery is still strong. Reinforcing the spiritual tone, he repeats the word *faith* to add momentum, and in the last sentence, pulls out the stops with five successive uses of the word *together* that kick the speech into virtual overdrive.

This will be the day when all of God's children will be able to sing with a new meaning, "My country, 'tis of thee, sweet land of liberty, of thee I sing. Land where my fathers died, land of the pilgrim's pride, from every mountainside, let freedom ring."

As he moves toward the final crescendo, he brilliantly pulls at our patriotic heartstrings, evoking the very foundations of the country to make his point. No one, no matter how jaded, could argue with the hope of these two sentences.

And if America is to be a great nation this must become true. So let freedom ring from the prodigious hilltops of New Hampshire. Let freedom ring from the mighty mountains of New York. Let freedom ring from the heightening Alleghenies of Pennsylvania! Let freedom ring from the snowcapped Rockies of Colorado! Let freedom ring from the curvaceous peaks of California! But not only that; let freedom ring from Stone Mountain of Georgia! Let freedom ring from Lookout Mountain of Tennessee! Let freedom ring from every hill and every molehill of Mississippi. From every mountainside, let freedom ring.

When we let freedom ring, when we let it ring from every village and every hamlet, from every state and every city, we will be able to speed up that day when all of God's children, black men and white men, Jews and Gentiles, Protestants and Catholics, will be able to join hands and sing in the words of the old Negro spiritual, "Free at last! Free at last! Thank God Almighty, we are free at last!"

Having grabbed our minds and touched our souls, Martin Luther King, Jr., takes us step by step through America in a second crescendo that, I believe, is unmatched in the history of public oratory!

Martin Luther King, Jr.

THE SPEECH—WHAT TO LOOK FOR: This is a veritable symphony in words. While staying true to his hard-hitting message to the world, the seventy concrete visual images that brought every paragraph to life, the rhythm of his phrasing, and the flawless establishment of memorable themes lift the audience to a climax that is probably unmatched.

THE DELIVERY—WHAT TO LISTEN FOR: Here is a 100 percent commitment to the words, the emotion, and the spirit underneath the words. You feel Dr. King in every syllable, in every richly voiced sound, in every perfectly timed pause, and every perfectly enunciated variation. He owns every millisecond of the speech and it comes not from his head, but from his heart and soul.

THE PERSON—QUALITIES OF GREATNESS: His unequivocal commitment to nonviolent change in the face of great pressure, his intellect, integrity, passion, and his extraordinary gift for words allowed all people, black and white, to be moved by the wisdom of his message.

BARRY GOLDWATER

"...extremism in the defense of liberty is no vice!"

"MR. CONSERVATIVE" LAUNCHES MODERN CONSERVATIVE MOVEMENT

Often considered conservatism's political founder; sometimes called a "Republican's Republican"; other times, "Mr. Conservative," Barry Goldwater was one of its most vivid personalities.

Goldwater was born on January 1, 1909, in the Arizona Territory, three years before it became a state. Before starting the successful department store chain, Goldwater's, his grandfather, Michel Goldwasser, a Jewish immigrant from Poland, ran a saloon below a bordello. His grandson never finished college, dropping out to run the family business. During World War II, Goldwater served in the Army Air Force as a pilot. He became group commander of the 90th Air Base Squadron and chief of staff of the Fourth Air Force. In 1947, he was onboard the first flight of P-47s across the North Atlantic. An avid aviator, he was the first nonrated test pilot to fly the U-2, SR-71, and B-1. He retired from the U.S. Air Force Reserve in 1967 with the rank of major general.

After WWII, his raw personality and refreshing candor put him on the fast track to national prominence in American politics. He entered politics in 1949 when he became a Phoenix City Councilman. In 1952, he won a seat in the United States Senate, where he fought for conservative causes, quickly becoming an outspoken leader of that movement.

In 1964, just 12 years after assuming his first Senate seat, U.S. Senator Barry Goldwater was standing in front of the Republican Convention in San Francisco and the nation as their nominee for president. Although he lost the election in a landslide to Lyndon Johnson, Goldwater did not give up. He was reelected to the

Senate in 1968 and served until 1986, a prominent fighter for the causes in which he believed.

The movement his candidacy stirred still continues, although he did not always agree with everything his followers said. Its once-revolutionary ideas still resonating with conservatives almost forty year later. This movement, which Robert Alan Goldberg referred to as "the Woodstock of American Conservatism," involved and inspired a diverse group that included future presidential candidate Pat Buchanan, "Goldwater Girl" Hillary Rodham Clinton (the former First Lady, now United States Senator); and, perhaps most important, Ronald Reagan, whose national reputation was launched during that campaign. As a result, many people today see Goldwater's defeat as the beginning rather than the end of the conservative movement in America.

Reagan's nationally televised appeal for Goldwater, the famous "A time for choosing" speech (dubbed "*The* Speech" by conservatives), just one week before the 1964 election, created a platform for the former actor from California. It also raised over $8 million for Goldwater's campaign. Along with Goldwater's acceptance speech, it provided the foundation for conservative ideology for the remainder of the century.

Twenty years later, in an ironic turn, Barry Goldwater was asked to speak at the Republican National Convention in support of the man who supported him in 1964, now President Ronald Reagan. A month earlier at the Democratic National

(left) Mr. and Mrs. Barry Goldwater after the 1964 election.

(right) Barry Goldwater was 30 when he took up photography—about the time this photo was taken; he became one of the best photographers of the Southwest.

Barry Goldwater / "…extremism in the defense of liberty is no vice!"

82

Supporters of Barry Goldwater hold up signs at the Republican National Convention. Goldwater went on to lose the general election to Democrat Lyndon B. Johnson.

"He went to Washington in 1953, a freshman Senator from the desert obscurity of Arizona. Over the next decade, Barry Goldwater became a political folk hero of sorts: a hip-shooting Arizonan with cowboy candor and confidence, a virile Western repudiation of the liberalism and decadence of the East."

Jerry Kammer, *The Arizona Republic,* January 18, 1987

Convention, at the very same San Francisco Cow Palace at which Goldwater had given his acceptance speech, Mario Cuomo attacked the Republican Party, conservatism, and Reagan. Now, Goldwater jumped to the defense of all three.

> A month ago I sat in my den and watched the Democratic National Convention. Speaker after speaker promised the moon to every narrow, selfish interest group in the country. But they ignored the hopes and aspirations of the largest special interest group of all, free men and free women.

> ... [T]onight I want to speak about freedom. And let me remind you that extremism in the defense of liberty is no vice. ... Members of the convention, we have a leader, a real leader, a great Commander in Chief: President Ronald Reagan. And in your hearts, you know he's right.

In May 1986, President Reagan presented Goldwater with the Presidential Medal of Freedom—the nation's highest civilian award—during a ceremony at the White House.

Goldwater's acceptance speech at the 1964 Republican National Convention overflows with hard-hitting attacks on the Democratic party and even on moderates in his own party. This was a raucous convention, deeply split on whether Barry Goldwater was the right man to lead the party and whether or not he could defeat Lyndon Johnson.

Just two days before Goldwater won the nomination, New York's liberal Republican Governor Nelson Rockefeller made a stinging attack on the senator from Arizona, arguing that he was too extreme to lead the party or the country. Rockefeller's speech was so inflammatory that his speech was interrupted—mainly with booing—22 times.

In his acceptance speech, Goldwater memorably challenged Rockefeller's attack with the words: "extremism in defense of liberty is no vice! . . . Moderation in the pursuit of justice is no virtue."

In victory and defeat, Goldwater was his own man. Despite his support of Reagan and other conservatives, Goldwater continued speaking out for what he believed, even when it meant disagreeing with his friends and supporters. He espoused his own brand of "frontier libertarianism"—vociferously criticizing Nixon and calling for his resignation and attacking the religious right on issues of abortion and homosexual rights. Those who opposed him on those issues, he said, were ignoring the conservative movement's core principle, "That government should stay out of people's private lives."

Until he died at the age of 89, Goldwater remained true to his principles and will forever be remembered for his integrity, his fiery personality, and for the generations of conservatives he spawned and the impact that they had on the twentieth century and beyond.

(left) Senator Barry Goldwater and his running-mate William Miller raise their hands after making their acceptance speeches at the 1964 Republican National Convention.

(above) Goldwater speaks with Vice President Richard Nixon about the nomination of Henry Cabot Lodge, Jr. as Nixon's running mate for the 1960 Presidential elections.

"I've often said that if I didn't know the Goldwater of 1964—and had to depend on the press, I'd have voted against the son-of-a-bitch myself."

Barry Goldwater, looking back on his loss, by 16 million votes, to Lyndon Johnson

Republican Presidential Nomination Acceptance Speech, July 16, 1964

Bold, honest, controversial, and clearly deeply felt, this is a speech that demonstrates the strong power that conviction exerts on the success of a speech. Goldwater's greatest vulnerability—his unrestrained vehemence and "loose cannon" candor—are also his greatest strengths and are what make this speech, and most of his speeches, stirring and unpredictable.

ANALYSIS

Goldwater's opening is interesting. In all such speeches, the candidate must acknowledge the party's leaders, but here Goldwater, knowing that he is facing a divided party, calls upon past leaders—Hoover and Eisenhower—in an effort to establish a connection to his own candidacy. Yet, he doesn't refer to Hoover as President Hoover, but as Mr., perhaps because his presidency was too closely linked with the Great Depression, and he calls Eisenhower, whose reputation as president was somewhat tarnished at the time, general, where his star shone bright.

The party is anything but united, but by forcefully stating a unity that is not there, he hopes to begin creating one behind his candidacy—if nothing else.

Notice the similarity to Churchill's offer of his own "blood, toil, tears and sweat" and Goldwater's *every fiber of my being* and his *enthusiasm, devotion,* and *hard work.*

With very rich images, he creates a vivid portrait of two totally opposite societies: one free and flourishing; the other, a swampland. Notice, also, the first of many religious references, and the contrast between *false prophets* and *proven ways.*

After a bruising and divisive fight for the nomination, Goldwater subtly attempts to heal the rifts by trumpeting a patriotic theme with which few would disagree. But, again, it is his unabated, all-out fervor that dominates. The *every action, every word, every breath, and every heartbeat* phrase, again, is reminiscent of a resolute Churchill pumping up the British people to stand tall against the imminent German invasion. To Goldwater, this "war" for freedom is just as real and just as threatening. Using *freedom* in a

SPEECH

To my good friend and great Republican, Dick Nixon, and your charming wife, Pat; my running mate and that wonderful Republican who has served us so well for so long, Bill Miller and his wife, Stephanie; to Thurston Morton, who's done such a commendable job in chairmaning this convention; to Mr. Herbert Hoover, who I hope is watching, and to that great American and his wife, General and Mrs. Eisenhower; to my own wife, my family, and to all of my fellow Republicans here assembled, and Americans across this great nation.

From this moment, united and determined, we will go forward together, dedicated to the ultimate and undeniable greatness of the whole man. Together we will win.

I accept your nomination with a deep sense of humility. I accept, too, the responsibility that goes with it, and I seek your continued help and your continued guidance. My fellow Republicans, our cause is too great for any man to feel worthy of it. Our task would be too great for any man, did he not have with him the heart and the hands of this great Republican party.

And I promise you tonight that every fiber of my being is consecrated to our cause, that nothing shall be lacking from the struggle that can be brought to it by enthusiasm, by devotion, and plain hard work.

In this world no person, no party can guarantee anything, but what we can do and what we shall do is to deserve victory, and victory will be ours.

The good Lord raised this mighty Republic to be a home for the brave and to flourish as the land of the free—not to stagnate in the swampland of collectivism, not to cringe before the bully of communism.

Now, my fellow Americans, the tide has been running against freedom. Our people have followed false prophets. We must, and we shall, return to proven ways—not because they are old, but because they are true.

We must, and we shall, set the tide running again in the cause of freedom. And this party, with its every action, every word, every breath, and every heartbeat, has but a single resolve, and that is freedom.

Freedom made orderly for this nation by our constitutional government; freedom under a government limited by laws of nature and of nature's God; freedom—balanced so that liberty lacking order will not become the slavery of the prison cell; balanced so that liberty lacking order will not become the license of the mob and of the jungle.

triplet—and then repeating *liberty lacking order* twice—builds great momentum here.

Now, we Americans understand freedom; we have earned it, we have lived for it, and we have died for it. This nation and its people are freedom's models in a searching world. We can be freedom's missionaries in a doubting world.

This last sentence is very revealing. Goldwater sees himself as *freedom's missionary* and, in effect, uses this speech to proselytize first to his party so that they will join him in his holy campaign.

But, ladies and gentlemen, first we must renew freedom's mission in our own hearts and in our own homes.

During four, futile years the administration which we shall replace has distorted and lost that faith.

Like a born-again minister, he is calling the strays back to the fold.

It has talked and talked and talked and talked the words of freedom, but it has failed and failed and failed in the works of freedom.

Rarely will you see a word repeated three or more times consecutively in a speech, but notice how he does it twice here. It works because it is part and parcel of the vehement tone he has established throughout.

Now failure cements the wall of shame in Berlin; failures blot the sands of shame at the Bay of Pigs; failures marked the slow death of freedom in Laos; failures infest the jungles of Vietnam; and failures haunt the houses of our once great alliances and undermine the greatest bulwark ever erected by free nations, the NATO community.

Failures proclaim lost leadership, obscure purpose, weakening wills, and the risk of inciting our sworn enemies to new aggressions and to new excesses.

But Goldwater is not satisfied in playing solely on emotions. He backs up his claims with specific assertions of Kennedy/Johnson failures, using the word itself six times. Note here the vivid way by which he refers to each catastrophe—not the Berlin Wall, but the *wall of shame*; not just the Bay of Pigs, but the *sands of shame. Failure* creates *slow death, infests the jungles, haunt(s) the houses.* Could anything be worse?

And because of this administration we are tonight a world divided. We are a nation becalmed. We have lost the brisk pace of diversity and the genius of individual creativity. We are plodding at a pace set by centralized planning, red tape, rules without responsibility, and regimentation without recourse.

Political convention speeches are akin to throwing red meat to the lions; they are designed to rally the troops. Therefore, they almost always lay out long lists of the horrible things the opposition has done. As Goldwater's sweeping criticism of the Kennedy/Johnson administration continues, they may stretch the credulity of nonsupporters, but they succeed in solidifying party activists to the cause, which is what an acceptance speech is intended to do. In this case, Goldwater's strong conviction and passion make these claims even more believable to his followers. His use of imagery, like Mario Cuomo's convention speech twenty years later, is central to its effectiveness. A man on a mission, his words convey how upset he is (and his audience should be) by anything that slows the mission. Look at the words he uses: *becalmed* and *plodding* instead of moving at a *brisk pace.*

Rather than useful jobs in our country, people have been offered bureaucratic make-work; rather than moral leadership, they have been given bread and circuses; they have been given spectacles, and, yes, they've even been given scandals.

Note, too, the nice use of contrast in the last sentence.

Barry Goldwater / "...extremism in the defense of liberty is no vice!"

86

His attacks on the Democrats get stronger and more specific as he enumerates the problems he sees.

Tonight there is violence in our streets, corruption in our highest offices, aimlessness among our youth, anxiety among our elderly; and there's a virtual despair among the many who look beyond material success toward the inner meaning of their lives. And where examples of morality should be set, the opposite is seen. Small men seeking great wealth or power have too often and too long turned even the highest levels of public service into mere personal opportunity.

Now, certainly simple honesty is not too much to demand of men in government. We find it in most. Republicans demand it from everyone. They demand it from everyone no matter how exalted or protected his position might be.

The growing menace in our country tonight, to personal safety, to life, to limb and property, in homes, in churches, on the playgrounds and places of business, particularly in our great cities, is the mounting concern—or should be—of every thoughtful citizen in the United States. Security from domestic violence, no less than from foreign aggression, is the most elementary and fundamental purpose of any government, and a government that cannot fulfill this purpose is one that cannot long command the loyalty of its citizens.

History shows us, demonstrates that nothing, nothing prepares the way for tyranny more than the failure of public officials to keep the streets from bullies and marauders.

Using a classic technique—demonizing the enemy—here he attacks the deepest, most core values of the Democrats and, essentially, portrays them as godless heathens.

Now, we Republicans see all this as more, much more, than the result of mere political differences or mere political mistakes. We see this as the result of a fundamentally and absolutely wrong view of man, his nature and his destiny.

Those who seek to live your lives for you, to take your liberty in return for relieving you of yours, those who elevate the state and downgrade the citizen, must see ultimately a world in which earthly power can be substituted for divine will. And this nation was founded upon the rejection of that notion and upon the acceptance of God as the author of freedom.

Here he makes use of a well-known adage—Power tends to corrupt; absolute power corrupts absolutely— to reinforce his message.

Now, those who seek absolute power, even though they seek it to do what they regard as good, are simply demanding the right to enforce their own version of heaven on earth, and let me remind you they are the very ones who always create the most hellish tyranny. Absolute power does corrupt, and those who seek it must be suspect and must be opposed.

A fascinating discussion of the word *equality*, a word that continues to generate much legislation and debate, and one that at the time would have resonated well with his conservative audience because many disapproved of recent civil rights and other legislation and were fearful of where it would lead.

Their mistaken course stems from false notions, ladies and gentlemen, of equality. Equality, rightly understood as our founding fathers understood it, leads to liberty and to the emancipation of creative differences; wrongly understood, as it has been so tragically in our time, it leads first to conformity and then to despotism.

Fellow Republicans, it is the cause of Republicanism to resist concentrations of power, private or public, which enforce such conformity and inflict such despotism.

It is the cause of Republicanism to ensure that power remains in the hands of the people—and, so help us God, that is exactly what a Republican president will do with the help of a Republican Congress.

It is further the cause of Republicanism to restore a clear understanding of the tyranny of man over man in the world at large. It is our cause to dispel the foggy thinking which avoids hard decisions in the delusion that a world of conflict will somehow resolve itself into a world of harmony, if we just don't rock the boat or irritate the forces of aggression—and this is hogwash.

It is further the cause of Republicanism to remind ourselves, and the world, that only the strong can remain free: that only the strong can keep the peace.

Goldwater was well known for his colorful language, so *hogwash* probably was a very sanitized version of what he would have preferred to say!

Now, I needn't remind you, or my fellow Americans regardless of party, that Republicans have shouldered this hard responsibility and marched in this cause before. It was Republican leadership under Dwight Eisenhower that kept the peace, and passed along to this administration the mightiest arsenal for defense the world has ever known.

And I needn't remind you that it was the strength and the unbelievable will of the Eisenhower years that kept the peace by using our strength, by using it in the Formosa Strait, and in Lebanon, and by showing it courageously at all times.

It was during those Republican years that the thrust of Communist imperialism was blunted. It was during those years of Republican leadership that this world moved closer not to war, but closer to peace than at any other time in the last three decades.

And I needn't remind you—but I will—that it's been during Democratic years that our strength to deter war has been stilled and even gone into a planned decline.

In these next paragraphs, Goldwater attempts to do two very important things: First, he makes the link between *strength* and *peace* in order to demonstrate that he is not the "war monger" many had called him. Paradoxically, he argues, being strong and ready to fight brings peace, not war. Second, he wants to ally himself and his image to the warm and secure feelings that his party and the country had for Eisenhower and equates Eisenhower's actions with his own plans.

It has been during Democratic years that we have weakly stumbled into conflicts, timidly refusing to draw our own lines against aggression, deceitfully refusing to tell even our people of our full participation and tragically letting our finest men die on battlefields unmarked by purpose, unmarked by pride or the prospect of victory.

Yesterday it was Korea; tonight it is Vietnam. Make no bones of this. Don't try to sweep this under the rug. We are at war in Vietnam. And yet the President, who is the commander in chief of our forces, refuses to say—refuses to say, mind you—whether or not the objective over there is victory, and his Secretary of Defense continues to mislead and misinform the American people, and enough of it has gone by.

Notice how in this sentence he builds a powerful rhythm mainly through his use of adverbs—those -*ly* words—which lead directly to an emotional close.

And I needn't remind you—but I will—it has been during Democratic years that a billion persons were cast into Communist captivity and their fate cynically sealed.

Today, today in our beloved country, we have an administration which seems eager to deal with communism in every coin known—from gold to wheat, from consulates to confidence, and even human freedom itself.

Here his fervent anti-communist rhetoric is designed to appeal to his core supporters. It does this successfully, but it also sets the seeds for his defeat since this fervent rhetoric scared many other voters and handed an issue to Lyndon Johnson, who successfully exploited it.

Barry Goldwater / "...extremism in the defense of liberty is no vice!"

88

Now, the Republican cause demands that we brand communism as the principal disturber of peace in the world today. Indeed, we should brand it as the only significant disturber of the peace. And we must make clear that until its goals of conquest are absolutely renounced and its rejections with all nations tempered, communism and the governments it now controls are enemies of every man on earth who is or wants to be free.

Now, we here in America can keep the peace only if we remain strong. Only if we keep our eyes open and keep our guard up can we prevent war. And I want to make this abundantly clear—I don't intend to let peace or freedom be torn from our grasp because of lack of strength, or lack of will—and that I promise you Americans.

With the repetition of the phrase *I can see* over the next six paragraphs, he signals a change in tone and turns visionary here, a poetic contrast to the "pit bull" aggressive qualities that precede it. In a strange way, it almost echoes Martin Luther King, Jr.'s "one day" imagery in his "I have a dream" speech.

I believe that we must look beyond the defense of freedom today to its extension tomorrow. I believe that the communism which boasts it will bury us will instead give way to the forces of freedom. And I can see in the distant and yet recognizable future the outlines of a world worthy of our dedication, our every risk, our every effort, our every sacrifice along the way. Yes, a world that will redeem the suffering of those who will be liberated from tyranny.

I can see, and I suggest that all thoughtful men must contemplate, the flowering of an Atlantic civilization, the whole world of Europe reunified and free, trading openly across its borders, communicating openly across the world.

In contrast to—and in direct attack on—John Kennedy's famous promise to land a man on the moon by 1970, Goldwater sets what he believes to be a loftier goal for America and Americans to aspire to.

It is a goal far, far more meaningful than a moon shot. It's a truly inspiring goal for all free men to set for themselves during the latter half of the twentieth century. I can also see, and all free men must thrill to, the events of this Atlantic civilization joined by a straight ocean highway to the United States. What a destiny! What a destiny can be ours to stand as a great central pillar linking Europe, the Americans, and the venerable and vital peoples and cultures of the Pacific!

I can see a day when all the Americas, North and South, will be linked in a mighty system—a system in which the errors and misunderstandings of the past will be submerged one by one in a rising tide of prosperity and interdependence.

We know that the misunderstandings of centuries are not to be wiped away in a day or wiped away in an hour. But we pledge, we pledge, that human sympathy—what our neighbors to the south call an attitude of simpatico—no less than enlightened self-interest will be our guide.

And I can see this Atlantic civilization galvanizing and guiding emergent nations everywhere. Now, I know this freedom is not the fruit of every soil. I know that our own freedom was achieved through centuries of unremitting efforts by brave and wise men. And I know that the road to freedom is a long and a challenging road, and I know also that some men may walk away from it, that some men resist challenge, accepting the false security of governmental paternalism.

A group of Republican Party leaders at a press conference at the White House during the Watergate crisis, (from left) Deputy Press Secretary Gerald Warren, Senate Minority Leader Hugh Scott, Senator Barry Goldwater, and John Rhodes, the House Minority Leader. It was at this meeting that Barry Goldwater informed President Nixon that impeachment could not be avoided. Subsequently, Nixon resigned.

And I pledge that the America I envision in the years ahead will extend its hand in help in teaching and in cultivation so that all new nations will be at least encouraged to go our way, so that they will not wander down the dark alleys of tyranny or to the dead-end streets of collectivism.

My fellow Republicans, we do no man a service by hiding freedom's light under a bushel of mistaken humility. I seek an America proud of its past, proud of its ways, proud of its dreams, and determined actively to proclaim them. But our examples to the world must, like charity, begin at home.

To achieve the goals he *sees*, Goldwater makes a promise about what America under his leadership will do to make those goals a reality.

In our vision of a good and decent future, free and peaceful, there must be room, room for the liberation of the energy and the talent of the individual, otherwise our vision is blind at the outset.

We must assure a society here which, while never abandoning the needy, or forsaking the helpless, nurtures incentives and opportunity for the creative and the productive.

We must know the whole good is the product of many single contributions.

This "frontier individualism" that focuses on *the liberation of the energy and the talent of the individual* defines Barry Goldwater and is at the core of most of his political beliefs, including his belief that communism or "collectivism" is one of the great evils in the world.

And I cherish the day when our children once again will restore as heroes the sort of men and women who, unafraid and undaunted, pursue the truth, strive to cure disease, subdue and make fruitful our natural environment, and produce the inventive engines of production, science and technology.

This nation, whose creative people have enhanced this entire span of history, should again thrive upon the greatness of all those things which we—we as individual citizens—can and should do.

During Republican years, this again will be a nation of men and women, of families proud of their role, jealous of their responsibilities, unlimited in their aspirations—a nation where all who can will be self-reliant.

In his focus on the power of the individual, he sounds a theme similar to the one Robert Kennedy invoked in his 1966 speech to students in South Africa, while in talking of *the whole man,* he lays the philosophical foundation for the small government argument.

Barry Goldwater / "…extremism in the defense of liberty is no vice!"

90

We Republicans see in our constitutional form of government the great framework which assures the orderly but dynamic fulfillment of the whole man as the great reason for instituting orderly government in the first place.

We see in private property and in economy based upon and fostering private property the one way to make government a durable ally of the whole man rather than his determined enemy. We see in the sanctity of private property the only durable foundation for constitutional government in a free society.

And beyond all that we see and cherish diversity of ways, diversity of thoughts, of motives, and accomplishments. We don't seek to live anyone's life for him.

Goldwater sums up the essence of his political philosophy in one sentence: The purpose of democracy and freedom is the development and fulfillment and protection of the individual—and the best government is therefore the least government necessary to secure those things.

We only seek to secure his rights, guarantee him opportunity, guarantee him opportunity to strive, with government performing only those needed and constitutionally sanctioned tasks which cannot otherwise be performed.

We Republicans seek a government that attends to its inherent responsibilities of maintaining a stable monetary and fiscal climate, encouraging a free and a competitive economy, and enforcing law and order.

Thus do we seek inventiveness, diversity, and creative difference within a stable order, for we Republicans define government's role where needed at many, many levels—preferably, though, the one closest to the people involved: our towns and our cities, then our counties, then our states, then our regional contacts, and only then the national government.

That, let me remind you, is the land of liberty built by decentralized power. On it also we must have balance between the branches of government at every level.

Balance, diversity, creative difference—these are the elements of Republican equation. Republicans agree, Republicans agree heartily to disagree on many, many of their applications. But we have never disagreed on the basic fundamental issues of why you and I are Republicans.

Goldwater now moves away from almost exclusively addressing his core audience or attempting to convert the larger audience hearing his speech and, instead, tries to pull the fractured convention and party together by trumpeting those values all Republicans deeply share. Quoting Abraham Lincoln, perhaps America's most revered president and also a Republican, would please both segments of this audience.

This is a party— this Republican Party is a party for free men. Not for blind followers and not for conformists. Back in 1858 Abraham Lincoln said this of the Republican party—and I quote him because he probably could have said it during the last week or so—it was composed of strained, discordant, and even hostile elements. End of the quote, in 1958 [sic].

Yet all of these elements agreed on one paramount objective: to arrest the progress of slavery, and place it in the course of ultimate extinction.

Today, as then, but more urgently and more broadly than then, the task of preserving and enlarging freedom at home and safeguarding it from the forces of tyranny abroad is great enough to challenge all our resources and to require all our strength.

Next he addresses Rockefeller supporters and other moderates who had challenged his candidacy, and takes an unusual stance in an acceptance speech. Instead of asking them to join for the good of the party, he lays down the gauntlet, and says, in essence, accept what we say or go away—we are looking for "true believers."

Anyone who joins us in all sincerity, we welcome. Those, those who do not care for our cause, we don't expect to enter our ranks, in any case. And let our Republicanism so focused and so dedicated not be made fuzzy and futile by unthinking and stupid labels.

I would remind you that extremism in the defense of liberty is no vice!

And here in the line we all remember he provides the rationale for his fervent passion and summarizes his entire speech.

And let me remind you also that moderation in the pursuit of justice is no virtue!

The beauty of the very system we Republicans are pledged to restore and revitalize, the beauty of this federal system of ours, is in its reconciliation of diversity with unity. We must not see malice in honest differences of opinion, and no matter how great, so long as they are not inconsistent with the pledges we have given to each other in and through our Constitution.

And he reinforces it with its complement. Together these two sentences are classics. They say almost everything he wants to say in a high-impact, unforgettable way. Like Kennedy's "Ask not," MacArthur's "Old soldiers," Churchill's "Blood, toil, tears, and sweat," Martin Luther King, Jr.'s "I have a dream," and so many others, short, punchy phrases or sentences—"sound bites"—are what we remember.

Our Republican cause is not to level out the world or make its people conform in computer-regimented sameness. Our Republican cause is to free our people and light the way for liberty throughout the world. Ours is a very human cause for very humane goals. This party, its good people, and its unquestionable devotion to freedom will not fulfill the purposes of this campaign which we launch here now until our cause has won the day, inspired the world, and shown the way to a tomorrow worthy of all our yesteryears.

Summarizing the *cause* (repeated four times) and the themes he has propounded throughout the speech, Goldwater ends with a rhythmic, poetic triplet.

I repeat, I accept your nomination with humbleness, with pride, and you and I are going to fight for the goodness of our land. Thank you.

So focused is he on the goal that even as he comes to the finale, he can't accept the nomination with a simple thank-you, and instead must end this powerful speech with a call to arms.

Barry Goldwater

THE SPEECH—WHAT TO LOOK FOR: Rarely does a politician, or any speaker, have the courage to say what he believes without spinning or finessing the message. This speech is a great example of oratorical courage—a bold, "in your face," no-holds-barred exposition of a visionary thinker's inner thoughts and feelings.

THE DELIVERY—WHAT TO LISTEN FOR: The lack of warmth and richness in his voice is made up for with abundant amounts of certainty and conviction. You can hear that this man "owns" and believes every word he utters.

THE PERSON—QUALITIES OF GREATNESS: Vision, conviction, candor, and an almost unheard of willingness to stand up for his beliefs without regard to the opinion of others.

Barry Goldwater / "…extremism in the defense of liberty is no vice!"

92

ROBERT F. KENNEDY

as remembered by Edward M. Kennedy

"Some men see things as they are and say why. I dream things that never were and say why not."

HIGHLIGHTS

1925   Born on November 20 in Brookline, Massachusetts

1946   Works on older brother John's congressional primary

1951   Graduates Virginia Law School; appointed assistant U.S. attorney

1952–1959   Serves as assistant counsel to Permanent Investigations Subcommittee, Chaired by Senator Joe McCarthy; appointed minority (Democratic) counsel to Senate Investigations Subcommittee; appointed chief counsel to Senate Investigations Subcommittee; chief counsel, Senate Select Committee on Improper Activities in the Labor and/or Management Field (Rackets Committee), headed by Senator John McClellan

POLITICS OF THE SOUL:
COMPASSIONATE, VISIONARY, AND DARING

Who knows what history would have held for America and the world if an assassin's bullet had not snuffed out the life of Robert F. Kennedy on June 6, 1968, just minutes after winning the California Democratic Primary.

Robert Francis Kennedy, the seventh of the ten children born to Joseph and Rose Kennedy, had distinguished himself in the 42 years he lived. The successful manager of his brother John F. Kennedy's 1952 campaign for the United States Senate, he became counsel to the Senate Subcommittee chaired by Senator Joseph R. McCarthy, in 1953, but resigned after six months, disturbed by McCarthy's tactics. Later, working as chief counsel of the Senate Labor Rackets Committee investigating corruption in trade unions, he earned a national reputation. He left that position in 1959 in order to manage his brother's 1960 presidential campaign.

As Attorney General, RFK's Justice Department is remembered for its investigation and prosecution of members of the organized crime syndicates; its commitment to enforce the laws guaranteeing the right of all Americans to vote, to attend school, and to use public accommodations; and its determination to use the full force of the federal government to confront those who would deny them. According to historian William Manchester, Robert Kennedy "was the last Attorney General to preside over a Justice Department devoted to the pursuit of justice." In recognition of his contributions, the Justice Department building was officially renamed "The Robert F. Kennedy Building" on November 20, 2001.

More important perhaps than his official role as Attorney General was Robert Kennedy's place as the closest adviser to his brother, the President. In that capacity,

1960	Brother John announces candidacy for presidency and names Robert campaign manager	**1965**	Sworn in as senator from New York; brother Ted sworn in as senator from Massachussetts
1961	January 20, John inaugurated; Robert sworn in as attorney general	**1966**	In January, supports President Johnson's decision to resume bombing of North Vietnam, but calls for nonmilitary solution to conflict; in June, visits South Africa and speaks out against apartheid
1961	In May, sends U.S. Marshals to protect Freedom Riders in Alabama		
1962	Cuban Missile Crisis (October 16–28)		
1963	November 22, brother John assassinated	**1968**	Announces candidacy for president on March 16; wins primaries in Indiana and Nebraska in April; loses in Oregon; June 4, wins Democratic presidential primary in South Dakota and California; June 6, dies of gunshot wounds after winning the California Democratic Primary
1964	July 29, President Johnson rejects Robert for vice president; August 22, enters U.S. Senate race in New York; September 3, resigns as attorney general		

he is widely credited for helping to develop and implement the administration's successful strategy to blockade Cuba during the Cuban Missile Crisis, thus avoiding direct military action and minimizing the risk of nuclear war.

Devastated by the assassination of his brother on November 22, 1963, Robert Kennedy briefly continued to serve as Attorney General in President Johnson's cabinet. He resigned the post and, in 1964, he ran for, and won, the seat to represent New York State in the United States Senate.

Although he was only a junior senator from New York, his every action and initiative received national attention from a nation still badly shaken by JFK's death. As the "heir" to the Kennedy political dynasty, observers of Robert in public and in private closely watched his political and social conscience evolve. His emerging passions and priorities were clear: To focus on problems stemming from poverty and injustice and to give voice to the concerns of the powerless, at home and abroad. He traveled to South Africa and to Latin America and was ahead of his time in calling attention to the challenges posed by the dire situations in those areas.

As senator, he was heavily involved in the Senate subcommittee to investigate the conditions facing agricultural workers in California. In early 1966, Robert met with Cesar Chavez, the founder and leader of the United Farm Workers (the first successful farm workers' union in United States history), who had spearheaded a strike of itinerant grape pickers, calling for a

(top) The Kennedy brothers, August 28, 1963.

(above) Robert F. Kennedy (second from left), counsel to the McClellan Committee, questions an unidentified witness during a committee hearing as his brother, Senator John F. Kennedy, listens (1957).

(above) Sen. Robert F. Kennedy speaks to campaign workers minutes before he was shot in Los Angeles early in the morning of June 5, 1968. At his side are his wife, Ethel, and his California campaign manager, Jesse Unruh, speaker of the California Assembly. After making a short speech, Kennedy left the platform and was shot in an adjacent room.

(left) RFK in the Mississippi Delta (1967).

national boycott of grapes picked by nonunion workers. Robert would soon become a friend and supporter of Chavez, calling him "one of the heroic figures of our time." In March 1968, as an affirmation of his firm belief in nonviolent protest, Chavez embarked on a 25-day fast. Robert Kennedy flew to be with him when he ended the fast.

Kennedy was, at one time, a supporter of President Johnson's conduct of the Vietnam war, but, by February 1966, as the American role increased and the war widened, he publicly dissented from the administration's position. In a speech on March 18, 1968, before Johnson had withdrawn from the upcoming presidential race, Robert Kennedy made it very clear that, if he were president, he would institute a very different Vietnam policy.

> The cost is in our young men, the tens-of-thousands of their lives cut off forever. The cost is in our world position, in neutrals and allies alike, every day more baffled by and estranged from a policy they cannot understand. Higher yet, is the price we pay in our own innermost lives, and in the spirit of our country. ... But the costs of the war's present course far outweigh anything we can reasonably hope to gain by it, for ourselves or for the people of Vietnam. It must be ended, and it can be ended in a peace of brave men ... now is the time to stop.

By June 1968, the country was reeling: The January Tet Offensive in Vietnam unnerved those who had been optimistic about the war's outcome. In March

"Anyone who saw him … through the 1968 campaign, redeeming his brother, challenging his party, opposing the war, his hair flying, those hands cut and scraped, those eyes prophetic, knows they are not likely to see such a candidacy again. But in a monotonous world of polls and packaging, he still reminds us of the alternative: the politics of soul."

Tom Hayden, a leader of the anti-war movement in the 1960s

Words That Shook the World

"... wisdom through the awful grace of God."

Remarks on the Death of Martin Luther King, Jr., April 4, 1968

I have bad news for you, for all of our fellow citizens, and people who love peace all over the world, and that is that Martin Luther King was shot and killed tonight.

Martin Luther King dedicated his life to love and to justice for his fellow human beings, and he died because of that effort.

In this difficult day, in this difficult time for the United States, it is perhaps well to ask what kind of a nation we are and what direction we want to move in. For those of you who are black—considering the evidence there evidently is that there were white people who were responsible—you can be filled with bitterness, with hatred, and a desire for revenge. We can move in that direction as a country, in great polarization—black people amongst black, white people amongst white, filled with hatred toward one another.

Or we can make an effort, as Martin Luther King did, to understand and to comprehend, and to replace that violence, that stain of bloodshed that has spread across our land, with an effort to understand with compassion and love.

For those of you who are black and are tempted to be filled with hatred and distrust at the injustice of such an act, against all white people, I can only say that I feel in my own heart the same kind of feeling. I had a member of my family killed, but he was killed by a white man. But we have to make an effort in the United States, we have to make an effort to understand, to go beyond these rather difficult times.

My favorite poet was Aeschylus. He wrote: "In our sleep, pain which cannot forget falls drop by drop upon the heart until, in our own despair, against our will, comes wisdom through the awful grace of God."

What we need in the United States is not division; what we need in the United States is not hatred; what we need in the United States is not violence or lawlessness; but love and wisdom, and compassion toward one another, and a feeling of justice toward those who still suffer within our country, whether they be white or they be black.

So I shall ask you tonight to return home, to say a prayer for the family of Martin Luther King, that's true, but more importantly to say a prayer for our own country, which all of us love—a prayer for understanding and that compassion of which I spoke.

We can do well in this country. We will have difficult times; we've had difficult times in the past; we will have difficult times in the future. It is not the end of violence; it is not the end of lawlessness; it is not the end of disorder.

But the vast majority of white people and the vast majority of black people in this country want to live together, want to improve the quality of our life, and want justice for all human beings who abide in our land.

Let us dedicate ourselves to what the Greeks wrote so many years ago: to tame the savageness of man and make gentle the life of this world.

Let us dedicate ourselves to that, and say a prayer for our country and for our people.

(top) Rev. Dr. Martin Luther King, Jr., and Attorney General Robert F. Kennedy in the White House Rose Garden following President Kennedy's meeting with leaders of the civil rights movement, 1963.

(above) RFK touring a riot-scarred Washington, D.C. in the aftermath of Rev. Dr. Martin Luther King, Jr.'s assassination, 1968.

"He was a fearless and prescient leader, a rich man who became the tribune of the poor, and hoisted the flag of defiance outside the citadels of privilege and prejudice. He was a man of compassion and vision, the very best we had."

William Manchester, historian and biographer

(above) Members of the Kennedy family visit the grave of Sen. Robert F. Kennedy at Arlington National Cemetery, June 6, 1975, the anniversary of his assassination. Standing from left are: Mrs. Ethel Kennedy; Joseph, son; Robert, son; Mrs. Joan Kennedy, sister-in-law; Sen. Edward Kennedy, D-MS. Kneeling are: Patrick, son of Sen. Edward Kennedy; Christopher, Rory, and Matthew, children of Sen. Robert Kennedy.

(top right) The casket of Robert F. Kennedy is carried to the gravesite at Arlington National Cemetery, June 8, 1968. The pallbearers are led by Kennedy's oldest son, Joseph. Ted Kennedy is second from left.

"The heartbreak which the Kennedys, old and young, gallantly strove to hide from public gaze broke through to the surface in a brief but moving eulogy delivered at the requiem mass in New York by Sen. Edward Kennedy, last of the fours sons who now inherits the mantle of family leadership."

San Francisco Examiner, June 9, 1968

Senator Eugene McCarthy had a surprisingly good showing (42 percent to Johnson's 49 percent) when he challenged President Johnson in the New Hampshire Democratic primary. Days later, Robert Kennedy, who had earlier said he would not run, decided to enter the race. President Johnson shocked the nation on March 31 by announcing that he would not run for another term as president. Hubert Humphrey, the vice president, now free to run, decided to throw his hat into the ring.

Then on April 4, Martin Luther King, Jr., was assassinated in Memphis, triggering riots and acts of violence in many American cities. Robert Kennedy's genuine courage was vividly demonstrated that night. As it happened, he was on a campaign tour in Indianapolis, Indiana, in the middle of his bid for the nomination, when he heard that Martin Luther King, Jr., had been fatally shot. Kennedy had been scheduled to speak to a black crowd at an outdoor rally that evening. Although Indianapolis police urged him to cancel the event, Kennedy refused. His frantic aides rushed to change Kennedy's speech to incorporate references to King, but their car became separated from the flatbed truck carrying the candidate. By the time they arrived, he was standing alone in the freezing cold, on the back of the truck, without his speech, extemporaneously calming this crowd of 1,000. After the speech, the crowd—to the amazement of all—quietly dispersed. (Those close to Bobby Kennedy talk about this speech as the first, and only, time he mentioned John Kennedy's death in public, so devastated had he been by it.)

Kennedy won the Indiana and Nebraska primaries against Senator Eugene McCarthy, but lost the Oregon primary. On June 4, 1968, he defeated McCarthy in two key elections in South Dakota and in California. After his victory speech in Los Angeles, he was shot at point-blank range by Sirhan Sirhan as he exited the ballroom through the kitchen of the Ambassador Hotel. He was 42 years old when he died in the early morning hours of June 6, 1968.

(above) The Kennedy family at Hickory Hill, Virginia (1966). Left to right: Maxwell Taylor Kennedy, Christopher Kennedy, Kerry Kennedy, Michael Kennedy, Courtney Kennedy, David Kennedy, Robert Kennedy Jr., Joseph P. Kennedy II, Kathleen Kennedy, Ethel Kennedy, Senator Robert F. Kennedy.

(right) EMK delivers speech

The nation, still in a state of shock from the King murder, still raw from JFK's assassination in 1963, was stunned and shattered. People waited to pay their respects, creating lines that extended over 25 city blocks beyond St. Patrick's Cathedral in New York. After the funeral service on June 8, the entourage continued to Pennsylvania Station where a 21-car funeral train left New York for Union Station in Washington, D.C. Along the way throngs of mourners waited patiently for hours to pay their last respects. The train arrived several hours behind schedule and Robert Kennedy was buried after dark, in a rare evening ceremony at Arlington National Cemetery.

Faced with the daunting task of putting this life into full perspective, Edward (Ted) M. Kennedy looked to Bobby's own words, and found the perfect vehicle in Robert Kennedy's address to 18,000 students in South Africa on June 6, 1966, delivered, coincidentally, two years to the day before his death.

"An emotional highlight of the funeral was an unannounced eulogy by Ted Kennedy. With a heroic effort at self control that verged on breaking at the end of his address, Kennedy spoke of his brother's qualities as a man and as a leader of his generation."

The Washington Post, June 9, 1968

Senator Edward M. Kennedy's Eulogy for Senator Robert F. Kennedy, June 8, 1968

Ted Kennedy's eulogy to his brother Robert is, as emotional speeches should be, about love and life-affirming values. The way in which he brought his father, brothers, and sister into the eulogy—at the very beginning—and left himself out, accomplished what a eulogy should—truly honored the loved one. On a personal level, what is most touching is the sense we get of the immense love Ted felt for his big brother and his apparent willingness to open his heart and show his vulnerability, which is demonstrated by the repeated cracking of his voice.

Ted Kennedy does something highly unusual in this tribute: Most of it is drawn verbatim from Bobby's own words, first, eulogizing their father and, then from his 1966 speech in Cape Town, South Africa. Ted could not have chosen a better way for Bobby to be remembered than with this speech, which was one of RFK's finest oratorical moments and contains some of the most beautiful passages ever delivered about the human condition.

ANALYSIS

SPEECH

After he acknowledges the family, Ted, his voice cracking, quickly enunciates the theme of the eulogy—*love*.

On behalf of Mrs. Robert Kennedy, her children and the parents and sisters of Robert Kennedy, I want to express what we feel to those who mourn with us today in this Cathedral and around the world. We loved him as a brother and father and son. From his parents, and from his older brothers and sisters—Joe, Kathleen and Jack—he received inspiration which he passed on to all of us. He gave us strength in time of trouble, wisdom in time of uncertainty, and sharing in time of happiness. He was always by our side.

He defers to his brother's eloquent words about their father, Joseph P. Kennedy, who could not attend his son's funeral because of his own failing health—and shares Bobby's very personal description of the meaning of love.

Love is not an easy feeling to put into words. Nor is loyalty, or trust or joy. But he was all of these. He loved life completely and lived it intensely.

A few years back, Robert Kennedy wrote some words about his own father and they expressed the way we in his family feel about him. He said of what his father meant to him: "What it really all adds up to is love—not love as it is described with such facility in popular magazines, but the kind of love that is affection and respect, order, encouragement, and support. Our awareness of this was an incalculable source of strength, and because real love is something unselfish and involves sacrifice and giving, we could not help but profit from it.

"Beneath it all, he has tried to engender a social conscience. There were wrongs which needed attention. There were people who were poor and who needed help. And we have a responsibility to them and to this country. Through no virtues and accomplishments of our own, we have been fortunate enough to be born in the United States under the most comfortable conditions. We, therefore, have a responsibility to others who are less well off."

This is what Robert Kennedy was given. What he leaves us is what he said, what he did and what he stood for. A speech he made to the young people of South Africa on their Day of Affirmation in 1966 sums it up the best, and I would read it now:

99

"In our sleep, pain which cannot forget falls drop by drop upon the heart until, in our own despair, against our will, comes wisdom through the awful grace of God."

Robert had had to talk many times about tragic events. Often he turned to poetry to express his feelings. In his famous speech in Indianapolis just minutes after Martin Luther King, Jr., was assassinated, he quoted from memory his favorite poet Aeschylus ("the father of tragedy"):

"There is discrimination in this world and slavery and slaughter and starvation. Governments repress their people; and millions are trapped in poverty while the nation grows rich; and wealth is lavished on armaments everywhere.

"These are differing evils, but they are common works of man. They reflect the imperfection of human justice, the inadequacy of human compassion, our lack of sensibility toward the sufferings of our fellows.

Notice how Robert mirrors these words in the next two paragraphs, starting with the despair and then moving into wisdom.

"But we can perhaps remember—even if only for a time—that those who live with us are our brothers; that they share with us the same short moment of life; that they seek—as we do—nothing but the chance to live out their lives in purpose and happiness, winning what satisfaction and fulfillment they can.

"Surely this bond of common faith, this bond of common goal, can begin to teach us something. Surely, we can learn, at least, to look at those around us as fellow men. And surely we can begin to work a little harder to bind up the wounds among us and to become in our own hearts brothers and countrymen once again.

And now Robert's optimism begins to surface as he draws his audiences to a higher place, a place where there is hope and common dreams and brotherhood.

"Our answer is to rely on youth—not a time of life but a state of mind, a temper of the will, a quality of imagination, a predominance of courage over timidity, of the appetite for adventure over the love of ease.

After lifting the audience up, he flatters them.

"The cruelties and obstacles of this swiftly changing planet will not yield to obsolete dogmas and outworn slogans. They cannot be moved by those who cling to a present that is already dying, who prefer the illusion of security to the excitement and danger that come with even the most peaceful progress. It is a revolutionary world we live in; and this generation at home and around the world, has had thrust upon it a greater burden of responsibility than any generation that has ever lived.

Notice how, with strong arguments and poetic imagery, he gives his audience no choice but to embrace and fight for change in this tremendously powerful motivational paragraph. You can hear the echoes—in ideas as well as words—of John F. Kennedy's inaugural address. This is especially true in the last sentence.

"Some believe there is nothing one man or one woman can do against the enormous array of the world's ills. Yet many of the world's great movements, of thought and action, have flowed from the work of a single man. A young monk began the Protestant reformation, a young general extended an empire from Macedonia to the borders of the earth, and a young woman reclaimed the territory of France. It was a young Italian explorer who discovered the New World, and the thirty-two-year-old Thomas Jefferson who proclaimed that all men are created equal.

And in what was clearly a statement of Robert Kennedy's belief about his own mission in life, he eloquently argues for the importance of taking personal responsibility and the accomplishments that flow from it. (The unidentified references are to Martin Luther, Alexander the Great, Joan of Arc, and Christopher Columbus.)

Senator Edward M. Kennedy waves from the rear platform of the observation car bearing the remains of his slain brother, Senator Robert F. Kennedy, as the funeral train passed through North Philadelphia Station, June 8, 1968. Others on platform are unidentified.

To underscore his point, Robert Kennedy tells his listeners what each and every one of them, individually, can do to make a difference in the world.

"These men moved the world, and so can we all. Few will have the greatness to bend history itself, but each of us can work to change a small portion of events, and in the total of all those acts will be written the history of this generation. It is from numberless diverse acts of courage and belief that human history is shaped.

This sentence includes the phrase that would be inscribed on the marker at Robert Kennedy's grave. It is also, in my opinion, one of the most beautiful sentences in the history of political oratory because of the way in which the idea is communicated through a flood of concrete images that dance and splash until they reach a crescendo of emotional inspiration.

"Each time a man stands up for an ideal, or acts to improve the lot of others, or strikes out against injustice, he sends forth a tiny ripple of hope, and crossing each other from a million different centers of energy and daring, those ripples build a current that can sweep down the mightiest walls of oppression and resistance.

RFK was also a pragmatist, and here he demonstrates to his audience that he understands the obstacles they face, but again, ends on a positive note.

"Few are willing to brave the disapproval of their fellows, the censure of their colleagues, the wrath of their society. Moral courage is a rarer commodity than bravery in battle or great intelligence. Yet it is the one essential, vital quality for those who seek to change a world that yields most painfully to change. And I believe that in this generation those with the courage to enter the moral conflict will find themselves with companions in every corner of the globe.

Forging a bond between himself (a wealthy white man) and the students, who were privileged because they were educated, he challenges them not to use that privilege, that education, for personal gain, but, by implication, like him, for the good of all. This is important as he gives them a new, and challenging, way to evaluate the whole of their very lives.

"For the fortunate among us, there is the temptation to follow the easy and familiar paths of personal ambition and financial success so grandly spread before those who enjoy the privilege of education. But that is not the road history has marked out for us. Like it or not, we live in times of danger and uncertainty. But they are also more open to the creative energy of men than

---

Words That Shook the World

any other time in history. All of us will ultimately be judged and as the years pass we will surely judge ourselves, on the effort we have contributed to building a new world society and the extent to which our ideals and goals have shaped that effort."

"The future does not belong to those who are content with today, apathetic toward common problems and their fellow man alike, timid and fearful in the face of new ideas and bold projects. Rather it will belong to those who can blend vision, reason and courage in a personal commitment to the ideals and great enterprises of American Society.

   "Our future may lie beyond our vision, but it is not completely beyond our control. It is the shaping impulse of America that neither fate nor nature nor the irresistible tides of history, but the work of our own hands, matched to reason and principle, that will determine our destiny. There is pride in that, even arrogance, but there is also experience and truth. In any event, it is the only way we can live."

And, using his brother's words from another of Robert Kennedy's speech, one RFK had given to students at the University of California in Berkeley on October 22, 1966, Ted Kennedy brings the message and the vision back to America.

This is the way he lived. My brother need not be idealized, or enlarged in death beyond what he was in life, to be remembered simply as a good and decent man, who saw wrong and tried to right it, saw suffering and tried to heal it, saw war and tried to stop it.

Here Ted smoothly rolls out of his brother's words and into his own to extol (but modestly) his brother. Ted's use of the triplet gives this paragraph momentum, but it is the simplicity of message that makes it so very touching. (It is interesting to see how this point is repeated in Charles, Earl Spencer's eulogy to his sister, Princess Diana.)

Those of us who loved him and who take him to his rest today, pray that what he was to us and what he wished for others will some day come to pass for all the world.

   As he said many times, in many parts of this nation, to those he touched and who sought to touch him:

   "Some men see things as they are and say why.

   I dream things that never were and say why not."

Now he leads us to Robert's legacy—his vision of the future.

   And he concludes this very emotional tribute by again using his brother's words, this time from his most famous saying, paraphrasing from George Bernard Shaw.

The Eulogy and Robert Kennedy

THE SPEECH—WHAT TO LOOK FOR: Robert's poetic words reveal a reflective soulfulness that cuts through to the core of what it means to be human. It is impossible to read these words and not be touched. In the eulogy, Ted allowed his brother's words to speak for the man—a loving and wise decision, since the words were so eloquent.

THE DELIVERY—WHAT TO LISTEN FOR: Robert's sincerity, thoughtfulness, and lack of pretense shine through. Ted Kennedy's voice cracking four separate times with authentic, heartfelt emotion show us the power of allowing oneself to be vulnerable.

THE PERSON—QUALITIES OF GREATNESS: RFK's passion and compassion; you can't help but notice how driven by his ideals he had become. At the same time you can't fail to be impressed with Ted Kennedy's sensitivity and grace under what could have only been excruciating pressure.

BARBARA JORDAN

"My faith in the Constitution is whole, it is complete, it is total."

HIGHLIGHTS

1936	Born on February 21 in Houston, Texas
1952	Wins National United Ushers Association Oratorical Contest
1956	Graduates magna cum laude, Texas Southern University
1959	Graduates Boston University Law School
1962	Runs for the Texas House of Representatives; loses election
1964	Loses second campaign for the Texas legislature
1966	Elected to the Texas State Senate, becoming the state's first woman senator and first black senator since 1883
1968	Wins second term in Texas Senate

"THE VOICE" SPOKE FOR AMERICA

Barbara Charline Jordan was undoubtedly America's greatest woman orator of the twentieth century. With fastidious preparation, dazzling logic, stunning articulation, and a mastery of voice and tone that held her audiences spellbound, she was an inspiration to all who heard her—boys and girls, men and women, blacks and whites.

Born in Houston in 1936, this was not a time of great opportunity for black people in the United States, and particularly not for black women. Barbara Jordan had to pave the way herself. And she did. After losing her bid for the Texas Assembly in 1962 and 1964, in 1966 she won her bid for the Texas Senate, becoming the first woman to serve there and the first African American since 1883. In 1972 she became the first black woman elected to Congress from the Deep South. Later she became the first black woman to serve on corporate boards in America. In just a few years, Barbara Jordan broke some of America's biggest and most important color and gender barriers.

It wasn't always easy. When she was first elected to the Texas Senate, it was reported by Molly Ivins, a political columnist for the *Fort Worth Star-Telegram*, that one senator would refer to her as "that old nigamammy washer woman." But, it didn't take long for the slurs to stop because, when Barbara Jordan spoke, Texas State Senators and everyone else within earshot simply had to sit up and take notice. So powerful was she that in just eight years, Barbara Jordan was elected president pro-tem of the Texas Senate—the first African-American elected to preside over a legislative body anywhere in the country. Appropriately, because of the extraordinary depth and richness of her speaking, they called her "The Voice."

1972	Elected to U.S. House of Representatives, the first black woman elected to Congress from the Deep South; assigned to House Judiciary Committee	1979	Retires from public life; becomes professor of public affairs at University of Texas, Austin
1973	Begins to suffer from neurological impairment that will eventually confine her to a wheelchair	1992	Keynote speaker at Democratic National Convention
1974	Gains national recognition with televised speech during impeachment hearings of President Richard M. Nixon; elected to second term in Congress	1993	Appointed by President Clinton to Chair the U.S. Commission on Immigration Reform
		1994	Receives the Presidential Medal of Freedom
1976	Delivers keynote speech at Democratic National Convention; wins third congressional term	1996	Dies on January 17 in Austin, Texas

Shortly after Richard Nixon won reelection in 1972, defeating George McGovern, revelations—which began to seep out prior to the election—about a break-in at the Democratic National Committee's headquarters at the Watergate intensified. Stories of cover-ups, lies, bizarre personalities, and secret tapes dominated the media, the country, and the world. Committees to investigate the allegations were established in the Senate and the House of Representatives. In July of 1974, the House Judiciary Committee began hearings to consider the need for the impeachment of President Nixon for his role in the Watergate break-in and "cover-up." Barbara Jordan—lawyer, professor, and first-term Congresswoman—was one of the thirty-eight members of that committee charged with this enormous responsibility.

The issues were very straightforward. The Judiciary Committee was charged with investigating and then voting on three articles of impeachment. They were:

Congresswoman Barbara Jordan delivers her opening remarks on July 25, 1974, during the House Judiciary Committee's hearings on the issue of the impeachment of President Richard Nixon.

1. *Obstruction of Justice* (Approved by a vote of 27–11 by the House Judiciary Committee on Saturday, July 27, 1974): Members of Nixon's reelection committee unlawfully entered the headquarters of the Democratic National Committee in Washington, D.C., for the purpose of stealing political intelligence. Following this break-in, Nixon used the powers of his office to obstruct the investigation of this unlawful entry; to cover up, conceal, and protect those responsible; and to conceal the existence and scope of unlawful activities.

2. *Abuse of Power* (Approved 28–10 by the House Judiciary Committee on Monday, July 29, 1974): Nixon was accused of repeatedly violating the

"Her great baritone voice was so impressive that her colleagues in the Legislature used to joke that if Hollywood ever needed someone to be the voice of the Lord Almighty, only Jordan would do."

Molly Ivins, "Barbara Jordan: A Great Spirit," Creators Syndicate Inc., January 19, 1996

(above) Rep. Peter Rodino, Chairman of the House Judiciary Committee, talks to newsmen following the committee's afternoon session of their impeachment inquiry, May 16. Rodino is flanked by committee member Barbara Jordan, and Chief Counsel for the committee's impeachment inquiry John Doar.

(left) After resigning, President Nixon leaves the White House with his family, Vice President Ford and his wife.

"Her start in politics was quite humble…. But Barbara Jordan was not underestimated for long. Her most enduring talents—the power of her voice and the strength of her words—were quickly discovered."

Senator Barbara Boxer, speaking before the U.S. Senate, January 22, 1996

"Barbara Jordan's life was a monument to the three great threads that run throughout the fabric of American history: our love of liberty, a belief in progress, and our search for common ground….

"Whenever she stood to speak, she jolted the nation's attention with her artful and articulate defense of the Constitution and the American Dream and the common heritage and destiny we share whether we like it or not."

President Bill Clinton, speaking at Barbara Jordan's funeral

Constitutional rights of citizens, hindering the administration of justice, and disregarding the law governing agencies of the executive branch.

3. *Contempt of Congress* (Approved 21–17 by the House Judiciary Committee on Tuesday, July 30, 1974): Nixon willfully disobeyed subpoenas issued by the House Judiciary Committee on April 11, 1974; May 15, 1974; May 30, 1974; and June 24, 1974. [He also] unlawfully failed to produce evidence as directed by the subpoenas.

Before the panel would vote on the articles of impeachment, each member was given the opportunity to make an opening statement—with the nation and the world watching the televised proceedings of this highly charged congressional investigation.

Having been elected only a year and one half before, Congresswoman Jordan had the least seniority on the committee and was, therefore, the very last speaker. Finally, after the other 37 congresspersons had spoken, late in the evening on July 25, 1974 it was Barbara Jordan's turn. From her first word to her last, the audience and the nation were spellbound.

After that speech, people would say that Jordan so loved the U.S. Constitution that she always carried a copy of it with her. Using a precise, point-by-point, lawyerly argument, her passion for the Constitution was plainly evident in every paragraph as she made an eloquent, but emotional case for impeachment.

The reaction was overwhelming. After years of fighting to improve the lives of minorities, the poor, and the disenfranchised, Barbara Jordan was an "overnight

Excerpts from "Who Then Will Speak for the Common Good?"
Democratic Convention Keynote Address, July 12, 1976

One hundred and forty-four years ago, members of the Democratic Party first met in convention to select a Presidential candidate. Since that time, Democrats have continued to convene once every four years and draft a party platform and nominate a Presidential candidate. And our meeting this week is a continuation of that tradition.

But there is something different about tonight. There is something special about tonight. What is different? What is special? I, Barbara Jordan, am a keynote speaker. . . .

And now we must look to the future. Let us heed the voice of the people and recognize their common sense. If we do not, we not only blaspheme our political heritage, we ignore the common ties that bind all Americans.

Many fear the future. Many are distrustful of their leaders, and believe that their voices are never heard. Many seek only to satisfy their private wants. To satisfy private interests.

But this is the great danger America faces. That we will cease to be one nation and become instead a collection of interest groups: city against suburb, region against region, individual against individual. Each seeking to satisfy private wants.

If that happens, who then will speak for America?

Who then will speak for the common good?

This is the question which must be answered in 1976. . . .

Now, I began this speech by commenting to you on the uniqueness of a Barbara Jordan making the keynote address. Well I am going to close my speech by quoting a Republican President and I ask you that as you listen to these words of Abraham Lincoln, relate them to the concept of national community in which every last one of us participates:

As I would not be a slave, so I would not be a master. This expresses my idea of Democracy. Whatever differs from this, to the extent of the difference is no Democracy.

Representative Barbara Jordan tells a House Judiciary subcommittee that she favors extension of the ratification period for the proposed Equal Rights Amendment.

"What the people want is simple. They want an America as good as its promise."

Barbara Jordan, Harvard University Commencement Address, June 16, 1977

"If the society today allows wrongs to go unchallenged, the impression is created that those wrongs have the approval of the majority."

Barbara Jordan, remarks at a symposium, "The Johnson Years: LBJ: The Differences He Made," sponsored by the University of Texas at Austin and the Lyndon Baines Johnson Library, May 3–5, 1990

"Justice of right is always to take precedence over might."

Barbara Jordan, remarks at a symposium, "The Great Society: A Twenty-Year Critique," sponsored by the Lyndon Baines Johnson Library and the Lyndon B. Johnson School of Public Affairs, April 1985

celebrity." Two years later the Democratic Party gave her the ultimate honor when they invited her to be the keynote speaker at their next convention. On July 12, 1976, she became the first black woman (yet again!) to give a keynote address to either party's convention. Few who heard it will forget its impact.

She was reelected to Congress in 1976, and retired from public life in 1979, after completing the term. Fighting both multiple sclerosis (from which she had suffered since 1974) and leukemia, Barbara Jordan died of pneumonia in January 1996, but not before being given America's highest civilian honor, the Presidential Medal of Freedom, by President Clinton in 1994. She was buried at Texas State Cemetery, an honor reserved for Texas heroes—the first African-American woman, yet again, even in death, to receive the honor of being buried there.

Opening Statement to the House Judiciary Committee Proceedings on the Impeachment of Richard Nixon, July 25, 1974

While the words in this speech are powerful, this is one of those speeches that you have to listen to in order to feel its full impact.
Barbara Jordan knew how to use the cadence and inflection of her voice to impress and even hypnotize her audience.
So, you may want to listen to the portion on the CD before you read the speech so you can hear her unique tone and cadence
as you read the following words.

ANALYSIS

For this woman, for this black American, for this voracious student of American history, this was, indeed, a *glorious opportunity.*

One of the most subtly elegant and stinging indictments of America's past ever delivered. From this powerful paragraph, she takes us from being *left out* of *we, the people* and leads us to the next where she is now the *inquisitor*, sitting in judgment on the most powerful man on earth, the President of the United States. See how smoothly she handles this transition.

One of Barbara Jordan's gifts as a communicator is her ability to turn complicated concepts into clear, simple language without losing any of the meaning. This skill is enhanced by her ability to provide a rock-solid foundation for her arguments—in this case, her frequent references to the Founding Fathers and the Constitution itself. Listening to her you get the impression that it is not just one Texas Congresswoman making these arguments, but that the whole history of the nation is standing behind her.

SPEECH

Mr. Chairman, I join my colleague Mr. Rangel in thanking you for giving the junior members of this committee the glorious opportunity of sharing the pain of this inquiry. Mr. Chairman, you are a strong man, and it has not been easy but we have tried as best we can to give you as much assistance as possible.

Earlier today we heard the beginning of the Preamble to the Constitution of the United States, "We, the people." It is a very eloquent beginning. But when that document was completed, on the seventeenth of September in 1787, I was not included in that "We, the people." I felt somehow for many years that George Washington and Alexander Hamilton just left me out by mistake. But through the process of amendment, interpretation, and court decision I have finally been included in "We, the people."

Today I am an inquisitor. I believe hyperbole would not be fictional and would not overstate the solemnness that I feel right now. My faith in the Constitution is whole, it is complete, it is total. I am not going to sit here and be an idle spectator to the diminution, the subversion, the destruction of the Constitution.

"Who can so properly be the inquisitors for the nation as the representatives of the nation themselves?" (Federalist, no. 65). The subject of its jurisdiction are those offenses which proceed from the misconduct of public men. That is what we are talking about. In other words, the jurisdiction comes from the abuse of violation of some public trust. It is wrong, I suggest, it is a misreading of the Constitution for any member here to assert that for a member to vote for an article of impeachment means that that member must be convinced that the president should be removed from office. The Constitution doesn't say that. The powers relating to impeachment are an essential check in the hands of this body, the legislature, against and upon the encroachment of the executive. In establishing the division between the two branches of the legislature, the House and the Senate, assigning to the one the right to accuse and to the other the right to judge, the framers of this Constitution were very astute. They did not make the accusers and the judges the same person.

We know the nature of impeachment. We have been talking about it awhile now. "It is chiefly designed for the president and his high ministers" to somehow be called into account. It is designed to "bridle" the executive if he engages in excesses. "It is designed as a method of national inquest into the public men." (Hamilton, Federalist, no. 65.) The framers confined in the congress the power if need be, to remove the president in order to strike a delicate balance between a president swollen with power and grown tyrannical, and preservation of the independence of the executive. The nature of impeachment is a narrowly channeled exception to the separation-of-powers maxim; the federal convention of 1787 said that. It limited impeachment to high crimes and misdemeanors and discounted and opposed the term "mal-administration." "It is to be used only for great misdemeanors," so it was said in the North Carolina ratification convention. And in the Virginia ratification convention: "We do not trust our liberty to a particular branch. We need one branch to check the others."

The North Carolina ratification convention: "No one need be afraid that officers who commit oppression will pass with immunity."

"Prosecutions of impeachments will seldom fail to agitate the passions of the whole community," said Hamilton in the Federalist Papers, no. 65. "And to divide it into parties more or less friendly or inimical to the accused." I do not mean political parties in that sense.

The drawing of political lines goes to the motivation behind impeachment; but impeachment must proceed within the confines of the constitutional term "high crimes and misdemeanors."

Of the impeachment process, it was Woodrow Wilson who said that "nothing short of the grossest offenses against the plain law of the land will suffice to give them speed and effectiveness. Indignation so great as to overgrow party interest may secure a conviction; but nothing else can."

Jordan's very direct, no-nonsense delivery—no hyperbole, no "spin," just the facts—gives her tremendous credibility when she draws a conclusion or gives an opinion. In the next few paragraphs she lays out the historical basis for impeachment and the extent of the crimes that must be committed in order for it to be invoked. She continues to cite the Founding Fathers as she meticulously constructs her case.

Common sense would be revolted if we engaged upon this process for insurance, campaign finance reform, housing, environmental protection, energy sufficiency, mass transportation. Pettiness cannot be allowed to stand in the face of such overwhelming problems. So today we are not being petty. We are trying to be big because the task we have before us is a big one.

Having summarized the legal case for impeachment, she does not ignore commenting on the uniqueness of the Committee's action in considering impeachment.

This morning, in a discussion of the evidence, we were told that the evidence which purports to support the allegations of misuse of the CIA by the president is thin. We are told that that evidence is insufficient. What that recital of the evidence this morning did not include is what the president did know on June 23, 1972. The president did know that it was Republican money, that it was money from the Committee for the Re-Election of the President, which was found in the possession of one of the burglars arrested on June 17.

What the president did know on June 23 was the prior activities of E. Howard Hunt, which included his participation in the break-in of Daniel Ellsberg's psychiatrist, which included Howard Hunt's participation in the Dita Beard ITT affair, which included Howard Hunt's fabrication of cables

Having set down the law and the gravity of their actions, Jordan moves to the specifics of the case before them, again making the legal case—as she sees it—for the impeachment of Richard Nixon.

Barbara Jordan / "My faith in the Constitution is whole, it is complete, it is total."

108

designed to discredit the Kennedy administration. We were further cautioned today that perhaps these proceedings ought to be delayed because certainly there would be new evidence forthcoming from the president.

Notice how, in this next short sentence, Congresswoman Jordan completely dismisses this last argument for delay and delivers, at the same time, a subtle, but overwhelming challenge to President Nixon. The confidence with which this first-term congresswoman takes on the President of the United States—in just this one sentence alone—is astounding.

The committee subpoena is outstanding, and if the president wants to supply that material, the committee sits here.

Very politely and very judiciously, she makes it clear that she doesn't expect Nixon will take up the challenge. Her use of the words *the American People* and *their president* cleverly implies that Nixon has disappointed far more than just her or the committee.

The fact is that yesterday, the American people waited with great anxiety for eight hours, not knowing whether their president would obey an order of the Supreme Court of the United States.

At this point I would like to juxtapose a few of the impeachment criteria with some of the president's actions.

Watch here as she analyzes the evidence and places the crime squarely in Nixon's office. She leaves little room for rebuttal.

Impeachment criteria: James Madison, from the Virginia ratification convention. "If the president be connected in any suspicious manner with any person and there be grounds to believe that he will shelter him, he may be impeached."

We have heard time and time again that the evidence reflects payment to the defendants of money. The president had knowledge that these funds were being paid and that these were funds collected for the 1972 presidential campaign.

We know that the president met with Mr. Henry Petersen twenty-seven times to discuss matters related to Watergate and immediately thereafter met with the very persons who were implicated in the information Mr. Petersen was receiving and transmitting to the president. The words are "if the president be connected in any suspicious manner with any person and there be grounds to believe that he will shelter that person, he may be impeached."

Justice Story: "Impeachment is intended for occasional and extraordinary cases where a superior power acting for the whole people is put into operation to protect their rights and rescue their liberties from violations."

Departing from her longer, more legalistic sentences, here she uses some short sentences to build cadence and momentum.

We know about the Huston plan. We know about the break-in of the psychiatrist's office. We know that there was absolute complete direction in August 1971 when the president instructed Ehrlichman to "do whatever is necessary." This instruction led to a surreptitious entry into Dr. Fielding's office. "Protect their rights." "Rescue their liberties from violation."

The South Carolina ratification convention impeachment criteria: Those are impeachable "who behave amiss or betray their public trust."

Beginning shortly after the Watergate break-in and continuing to the present time, the president has engaged in a series of public statements and actions designed to thwart the lawful investigation by government prosecutors. Moreover, the president has made public announcements and assertions bearing on the Watergate case which the evidence will show he knew to be false.

These assertions, false assertions, impeachable, those who misbehave. Those who "behave amiss or betray their public trust."

James Madison, again at the Constitutional Convention: "A president is impeachable if he attempts to subvert the Constitution."

The Constitution charges the president with the task of taking care that the laws be faithfully executed, and yet the president has counseled his aides to commit perjury, willfully disregarded the secrecy of grand jury proceedings, concealed surreptitious entry, attempted to compromise a federal judge while publicly displaying his cooperation with the processes of criminal justice. "A president is impeachable if he attempts to subvert the Constitution."

Notice how, without saying whether she personally believes that Richard Nixon has committed impeachable offenses, she continues to inexorably undermine his case.

If the impeachment provision in the Constitution of the United States will not reach the offenses charged here, then perhaps that eighteenth-century Constitution should be abandoned to a twentieth-century paper shredder.

As we come to the climax—an example of truly extraordinary wordsmithing—Jordan still does not say that Nixon should be impeached, but, had she shouted the words, she could not have made her point more powerfully. Her sarcasm speaks louder here than any explicit statement could.

Has the president committed offenses and planned and directed and acquiesced in a course of conduct which the Constitution will not tolerate? That is the question. We know that. We know the question. We should now forthwith proceed to answer the question. It is reason, and not passion, which must guide our deliberations, guide our debate, and guide our decision.

Remarkably, having ripped Richard Nixon's presidency apart more efficiently than "a twentieth-century paper shredder" ever could, she steps back and, as always, defers to the Constitution as she ends, classically, with a stirring triplet.

Fourteen days later, with impeachment imminent, Richard Nixon resigned.

Barbara Jordan

THE SPEECH—WHAT TO LOOK FOR: To make what in essence is one long legal argument flow like poetry and sing like a song is almost impossible. The understatement, the precision, the sarcasm and the eloquence of her words are stunning.

THE DELIVERY—WHAT TO LISTEN FOR: No voice, male or female, has ever generated more authority and gravitas. Jordan knows how to use this gift—the perfect pauses command respect, the building force and energy command attention, and the vocal variation plays the room like a Stradivarius.

THE PERSON—QUALITIES OF GREATNESS: A courageous pioneer. A black woman from the South, she succeeded by being better than white men she confronted at every step of her career. In doing so, she achieved more firsts for blacks and women than just about anyone else in history.

ANWAR SADAT

"Let there be no more wars..."

EGYPTIAN PRESIDENT DEFIES HIS ALLIES AND MAKES PEACE WITH ISRAEL

Born on Christmas day, 1918, into a family of thirteen children just outside of Cairo at a time when Egypt was a British colony, Anwar Sadat played a vital role in the history of modern Egypt. After graduating from the Egyptian Military Academy, Sadat became involved in a group, which included Gamal Abdel Nasser, whose aim was to end British the colonial rule of Egypt. In 1939, they founded, while on duty in the Sudan, the Free Officer's Organization to do just that.

As a result of his efforts in the resistance against the British, he was jailed twice: first in 1942 for plotting with German spies against the British and, then, in 1946, when he was accused of involvement in the assassination of the Prime Minister designate, a pro-British Egyptian. Placed in solitary confinement until 1948, Sadat used the time in jail to better himself, learning both French and English, and writing extensively in his journal on all aspects of life.

Released from jail and back in the army as Captain and then Lieutenant Colonel after a stint in business, Sadat was thrust into the national spotlight as he, Nasser, and the Free Officer's Organization successfully organized a bloodless coup that deposed King Farouk in 1952.

Sadat became Public Affairs and Communications Officer in the new government and also ran its newspaper. In 1953, Egypt became a Republic and in 1956, after the election of his friend, Gamal Abdel Nasser, Sadat became public relations minister, then vice president, and, after Nasser's death in 1970, Egypt's president.

Not as flamboyant as Nasser, and as yet untried, Sadat turned out to be a very strong leader. Almost immediately upon taking office, Sadat released political prisoners being held under Nasser's government, ended internal spying operations against Egyptian citizens, and suspended the practice of arbitrary arrest without trial. In 1972, he threw the USSR's entire military force of 15,000 out of Egypt when they failed to provide support he was requesting after the debacle of the Six-Day War. This action also brought him much political support within Egypt.

On October 6, 1973, Egypt launched a surprise attack on Israel—known as the "Yom Kippur War" because it took place on that Jewish holy day. Despite inflicting heavy damage, the Egyptians—with assistance from Syria, Iraq, Saudi Arabia, Lebanon, Algeria, Tunisia, Jordan, Sudan, Morocco, and other Arab forces—were repelled.

Devastated by the loss and with the economy of Egypt in terrible condition, Sadat began to think of different ways to end the conflict. A student of Mahatma Gandhi's nonviolent approach, Anwar Sadat, in a speech on November 9, 1977, to the Egyptian Parliament, shocked the country and the Arab world when he suggested:

> There is no time to lose. I am ready to go to the ends of the earth if that will save one of my soldiers, one of my officers, from being scratched. I am ready to go to their house, to the Knesset, to discuss peace with the Israeli leaders.

No one believed him. It was unthinkable. Sadat's mentor, President Nasser, only a few years earlier had said publicly that "Our basic aim is the total destruction of Israel." Since 1948, the year the United Nations authorized the creation of the state of Israel, no Arab leader had touched foot inside of Israel. To suggest

Members of the Revolutionary Council pose together (January 4, 1955). Seated are, left to right: Hassan Ibrahim; Zakaria Mohieddin; Gamal Salem; Gamal Abdel Nasser; and Abel Hakim Amer. Standing are, left to right: Hussein Elshafei; Anwar el-Sadat; Kamal Eldin Hussein; Salahm Salem, and Abdel Latif Boghdadi.

"I think he would willingly lay his life down for his country or to carry out the principles in which he believes. He's admirable in every possible way."

Jimmy Carter, quoted in *St. Louis Post Dispatch,* UPI; October 6, 1981

"What made Mr. Sadat into such a catalytic force in Middle Eastern history was a display of courage and flexibility that transformed what had seemed to be an average Arab officer-turned-potentate."

The New York Times, obituary, October 7, 1981

going, not only to the country, but especially to the Knesset, Israel's Parliament, was a revolutionary idea. Israelis were delighted. Finally, there was an Arab leader with whom they might be able to negotiate. The formal invitation from Prime Minister Menachem Begin was issued immediately. President Sadat accepted and, on November 19, 1977, Anwar Sadat landed at Tel Aviv's Ben Gurion Airport to a huge media reception.

In response, a summit of Arab states quickly convened in Tripoli by Libya's Muammar Khaddafi froze relations with Egypt. Undeterred, Sadat, himself, responded by breaking off relations with Syria, Libya, Algeria, Iraq, and South Yemen.

(above) President Anwar Sadat, Muhammad Hosni Mubarak, and Ali, attend the ceremony handing over the El-Arish oil fields from Israel to Egypt as agreed to at Camp David.

(right) President Jimmy Carter, Egyptian President Anwar Sadat, and Israeli Prime Minister Menachem Begin shake hands after the signing of the Middle East peace treaty.

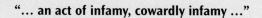

"… an act of infamy, cowardly infamy …"

Excerpts from Statement by President Reagan on the Death of Anwar Sadat, October 6, 1981

…President Sadat was a courageous man whose vision and wisdom brought nations and people together. In a world filled with hatred, he was a man of hope. In a world trapped in the animosities of the past, he was a man of foresight, a man who sought to improve a world tormented by malice and pettiness.…

Anwar Sadat was admired and loved by the people of America. His death today—an act of infamy, cowardly infamy—fills us with horror.

America has lost a close friend; the world has lost a great statesman; and mankind has lost a champion of peace.…

The wheels of peace began moving rapidly. President Jimmy Carter summoned Sadat and Begin to Camp David, the U.S. President's private retreat, for 13 days of secret talks. At the end of those talks, on September 17, 1978, a framework for peace was signed by all parties. Egypt agreed after thirty years to recognize Israel as a state and to cease hostilities. In exchange, Israel agreed to return the entire Sinai Peninsula, which Israel had controlled since the 1967 Six-Day War, to Egypt. In addition, a framework agreement establishing a format for discussions for Palestinian autonomy in the West Bank and Gaza was formulated, but never implemented.

After final details were worked out and the agreements were ratified by the Egyptian and Israeli governments, a formal peace agreement was officially signed by both countries on March 26, 1979.

Camp David was an extraordinary achievement for Carter, Begin, and Sadat and for the cause of Middle East Peace. As a result of these accords, Sadat and Begin received the Nobel Peace Prize in 1978.

As popular as Anwar Sadat became in the United States and around the world, he was not a hero to many Muslims and Palestinians who believed that the UN had no right to create the state of Israel and that land had been illegally expropriated. On October 6, 1981, while reviewing a military parade commemorating the 1973 war against Israel, three soldiers turned their rifles on President Sadat, killing him in Cairo in broad daylight. Sadat's murder was a huge blow to the hopes for peace in the Middle East.

"Let there be no more wars..."

Speech at the Signing of the Egyptian-Israeli Peace Treaty, The White House, March 26, 1979

This is one of the most difficult speeches anyone ever had to deliver. In it, Anwar Sadat had to please three completely different audiences. He had to acknowledge the magnitude of the accomplishment, be gracious to President Carter and his American hosts for their role in the Accords, and acknowledge his former enemy, Israel, for its efforts. At the same time, he had to downplay his role and the magnitude of what Egypt was "giving away" so as not to further inflame his Arab critics.

One of the most courageous things about this speech was what President Sadat decided to leave out. The original draft included strong language about the rights of the Palestinians and the need for a Palestinian state, words seemingly designed to appease the militant factions in Egypt and the rest of the Arab world and reassure them that he had not forsaken them. In the end, Sadat omitted any reference to the Palestinians, which may have endeared him to Israelis, but no doubt created problems for him with Palestinians and Arabs. At the time, Sadat so angered PLO leader Yassir Arafat that, immediately after the speech, he publicly vowed to "cut off the hands" of Sadat.

ANALYSIS	SPEECH
	President Carter, dear friends: This is certainly one of the happiest moments in my life. It is a historic turning point of great significance for all peace-loving nations.
Facing great criticism from those Arabs and Palestinians who wanted to continue a state of war against Israel, Sadat fires a subtle shot at those who weren't *endowed with vision* and flatters those moderates who might be drawn to it. With the words *sacred mission* he imbues it with religious necessity.	Those among us who are endowed with vision cannot fail to comprehend the dimension of our sacred mission.
By pointing to thousands of years of glorious history, he implies that being on the cutting edge of progress is the destiny of all Egyptians, which is both flattering and a very nice way to deflect criticism.	The Egyptian people, with their heritage and unique awareness of history, have realized from the very beginning the meaning and value of this endeavor.
Continuing, he praises the Egyptian people, which, on the one hand, distances him personally from the criticism that he was acting without mandate and against the wishes of the Egyptian people, and on the other, gives them credit for the action he has taken.	In all the steps I took, I was not performing a personal mission. I was merely expressing the will of a nation. I am proud of my people and of belonging to them.
With beautiful, visionary language, Sadat puts the efforts leading up to the agreement in historical context. Notice the use of the words *never before* and the emphasis he places on how long, how complex, how difficult it was to come to this point. At the same time, he is beginning one of the most extensive accolades a head of state has ever paid to another. Notice the plentiful use of hyperbole.	Today a new dawn is emerging out of the darkness of the past. A new chapter is being opened in the history of co-existence among nations, one that is worthy of our spiritual values and civilizations. Never before had men encountered such a complex dispute which is highly charged with emotions. Never before did men need that much courage and imagination to confront a single challenge. Never before had any cause generated that much interest in all four corners of the globe. Men and woman of good will have labored day and night to bring about this happy moment. Egyptians and Israelis alike pursued their sacred goal undeterred by difficulties and complications. Hundreds of dedicated individuals on both sides have given generously of their thought and effort to translate the cherished dream into a living reality.

Egyptian President Anwar Sadat. Sadat (right) with Israeli Prime Minister Menachem Begin after his arrival in Israel, November 19, 1977. The man who had sent his armies against Israel in 1973 stepped down from his plane, saluted the flag and soldiers of Israel, and exclaimed, "No more war!"

But the man who performed the miracle was President Carter. Without any exaggeration, what he did constitutes one of the greatest achievements of our time.

And, in one of the most extensive accolades a head of state has ever paid to another, he attributes it all to Jimmy Carter.

He devoted his skill, hard work and above all his firm belief in the ultimate triumph of good against evil to ensure the success of our mission. To me, he has been the best companion and partner along the road to peace. With his deep sense of justice and genuine commitment to human rights, we were able to surmount the most difficult obstacles. There came certain moments when hope was eroding and retreating in the face of pride. However, President Carter remained unshaken in his confidence and determination. He is a man of faith and compassion. Before anything else, the signing of the peace treaty and the exchange of letters is a tribute to the spirit and ability of Jimmy Carter. Happily, he was armed with the blessing of God and the support of his people. For that, we are grateful to each and every American who contributed in his own way to the success of our endeavor.

He supports his compliments with concrete references to what Carter did. Carter *has been the best companion and partner along the road to peace.*

We are also heartened by the understanding of hundreds of thousands of Israelis who remained unwavering in their commitment to peace. The continuation of this spirit is vital to the coronation of our efforts.

Next he acknowledges the Israeli people, who he knows will be asked to make sacrifices for peace, and reminds them that there's more to be done and that their continued support is vital to the effort.

President Anwar Sadat (left) rides in an open limosine along a road in Cairo on his way to a military parade honoring the October War of 1973. Sadat would be shot dead at the parade. Vice President Hosni Mubarak (right) would succeed him.

Without mentioning either the Palestinians or a Palestinian state by name—a huge and difficult concession to the Israelis and the conciliatory spirit of the ceremony—Sadat pointedly refers to the *comprehensive settlement* and *all parties*. In the language of diplomacy, everyone listening knew to whom he was referring.

We realize that difficult times lay ahead. The signing of these documents marks only the beginning of peace. But it is an indispensable start. Other steps remain to be taken without delay or procrastination. Much will depend on the success of these steps. We are all committed to pursue our efforts until the fruits of the comprehensive settlement we agreed upon are shared by all parties to the conflict.

President Carter once said that the United States is committed without reservation to seeing the peace process through until all parties to the Arab-Israeli conflict are at peace.

The contrast between *morality and ethics* and *power politics and opportunism* is more than just a beautiful juxtaposition of nouns, it is a compliment as well as a strong reminder to President Carter, on whose continued support he knows Egypt will have to rely, of his promise to see the peace process through.

We value such a pledge from a leader who raised the banner of morality and ethics as a substitute for power politics and opportunism.

117

The steps we took in the recent past will serve Arab vital interests. The liberation of Arab land and the reinstitution of Arab authority in the West Bank and Gaza would certainly enhance our common strategic interests.

Notice that he continues to skirt the Palestinian question and that he still does not use the word *Palestinian,* using only the word *Arab.*

While we take the initiative to protect these interests, we remain faithful to our Arab commitment. To us, this is a matter of destiny. Pursuing peace is the only avenue which is compatible with our culture and creed.

In this one short paragraph, he accomplishes two purposes: He asserts his loyalty to the Arab cause and ties the peace agreement (which many felt proved his disloyalty) to their very *destiny.* Contrary to their opinion of many, he states that the initiative is *not* incompatible with the *culture and creed* of the Arab people. Further, he emphasizes, *pursuing peace* is the *only avenue* available. In very skillful words, Sadat is saying that by negotiating and signing this peace agreement with Israel, he and Egypt are furthering Arab interests, while those who oppose them are going against their destiny.

Let there be no more war or bloodshed between Arabs and Israelis. Let there be no more suffering or denial of rights. Let there be no more despair or loss of faith. Let no mother lament the loss of her child. Let no young man waste his life on a conflict from which no one benefits. Let us work together until the day comes when they beat their swords into ploughshares and their spears into pruning hooks. And God does call to the abode of peace. He does guide whom He pleases to his Way. Thank you.

Using parallel construction—six consecutive uses of the word *Let*—Sadat builds momentum. Using concrete human examples, he builds emotion and a human bond with his former enemy and makes the abstract peace agreement all the more real. By quoting the Bible—the same passage ("swords into ploughshares") that, independently, President Carter and Prime Minister Begin used—Sadat lifted himself, his people, and the audience above the hate and bloodshed and made a giant step towards a most difficult peace.

Anwar Sadat

THE SPEECH—WHAT TO LOOK FOR: This was an incredibly difficult speech to write—to graciously celebrate peace with Israel and, at the same time, not further anger other Arabs who already saw him as a traitor.

THE DELIVERY—WHAT TO LISTEN FOR: His perfect English (he learned it in a British prison), rich voice, and poetic cadence communicate a wonderfully reassuring elegance and sophistication that makes it so easy to relate to him and like him.

THE PERSON—QUALITIES OF GREATNESS: A visionary leader with the courage to follow his convictions and go against so many of his former allies, despite the personal and political consequences.

MARIO CUOMO

"There is despair, Mr. President, in the faces you don't see..."

A "TALE OF TWO CITIES": AN IMPASSIONED PLEA FOR A COMPASSIONATE AMERICA

"I could just feel that they were there with me, on every word," he said. And it was true. In his keynote address to the 1984 Democratic Convention, Mario Cuomo lit up the crowd, confirming his place as one of the twentieth century's most stirring political speakers as he set the standard for a more compassionate America and articulated a liberal agenda that continues into the twenty-first century. Often mentioned as one of the most gifted and inspiring political speakers of his generation, many Democrats clamored for the keynoter himself to run for President, a request he never granted.

By the time Governor Cuomo delivered this speech, the adulation of crowds was not an uncommon experience for this first-generation Italian-American, who had been born in a room above the family grocery store in Queens, New York. Top of his class at St. John's University School of Law, clerk for a judge on New York's highest court, practicing attorney and law professor at St. John's, it was obvious to everyone that Mario Cuomo was a rising star. Governor Hugh Carey appointed him New York's Secretary of State in 1975. He was elected lieutenant governor in 1978. He became New York's fifty-second governor in 1982.

Cuomo's intellect, strong handle on economics, visionary approach to many difficult issues, and especially his genuine compassion, made him one of the most popular governors in New York's history. When running for reelection in 1986 and 1990, Cuomo received the highest percentage of votes and the largest margin of victory of any second- and third-term gubernatorial candidate in the state.

This rare combination of qualities sets Mario Cuomo apart as a politician and as a speaker. In an interview with the author, Governor Cuomo explained that he looked for two very different qualities when assessing himself and others—"strength and sweetness." By strength he meant taking decisive action and following through on one's beliefs and convictions. Sweetness is an interesting word; one rarely hears it used in politics. To Cuomo, it stood for compassion, empathy, and actions and policies centered on helping people.

Judging him by his own standard, we can clearly discern both attributes. During his 12-year tenure as governor, his *strength* was amply demonstrated as he balanced the budget twelve times in a row while giving New Yorkers the biggest tax cut in state history, pushed through the largest economic development plan in the history of the state, and improved public safety, among other things, by building more prisons —actions more often associated with tough, bottom line–oriented Republicans.

The *sweet* side of Mario Cuomo is perhaps his defining characteristic. A deeply introspective man, Cuomo keeps a daily journal of his thoughts and feelings, and has seriously studied many religions and philosophies. But this sweetness has a

Ed Koch, Mayor of New York City; Walter Mondale, Democratic Presidential candidate; Geraldine Ferraro, Vice-Presidential candidate; and Governor Mario Cuomo waving during the 1984 Columbus Day Parade on Fifth Avenue, New York City.

(above) Mario Cuomo makes his first State of the State speech in 1983 before a joint session of the New York Legislature.

(left) President Ronald Reagan delivers a speech to exuberant supporters during the 1984 Republican National Convention.

A Shining City on a Hill

It was a favorite phrase of President Reagan's and he returned to this image many times in his career. It came from John Winthrop, a Pilgrim, who in 1630 described his vision of his new American home: "For we must consider that we shall be as a City upon a Hill. The eyes of all people are upon us." Winthrop, in turn, had paraphrased a line from Matthew 5:13–16, "Ye are the light of the world. A city that is set on a hill cannot be hid."

Reagan, in his farewell address to the nation in 1989, said that that phrase, in his mind, communicated "a tall, proud city built on rocks stronger than oceans, windswept, God-blessed, and teeming with people of all kinds living in harmony and peace. . ."

very pragmatic focus. Cuomo created the largest homeless housing assistance program, the most extensive drug treatment network, a nationally recognized plan to help victims of AIDS, the largest program for the mentally ill in the U.S., appointed New York's first two women to serve on the state's high court, and inaugurated "The Decade of the Child" in New York State, introducing programs like "Child Health Plus" and the "Children's Assistance Program." As Governor he appointed the first and second women judges, the first black judge, the first Hispanic judge, and the first woman Chief Judge on the New York Court of Appeals.

In 1984, the Democratic party was facing a difficult election against an extremely popular president, Ronald Reagan, who, for four years had dominated the political landscape. In fact, in a campaign speech, Reagan boldly declared that "Four years ago … we proclaimed a dream of an America that would be a 'shining city on a hill.' . . . Well, now it's all coming together." Employment was indeed up, inflation was down, and prosperity was on the rise, especially for American business.

"I saw, heard and felt a rip-roaring keynote address at the Democratic convention this week. Gov. Mario Cuomo … put those Republicans right in their place…. I emerged convinced that President Reagan could receive no more than 1.5 percent of the vote in November."

Thomas Hazlett, "A Dim View of the Shining City, Circa 1980," *The Wall Street Journal*, July 19, 1984

(above) New York City Mayor Ed Koch and Governor Mario Cuomo show their support for fellow Democrat Walter Mondale, as he campaigns for the Democratic Party's nomination as presidential candidate.

(right) Wendy Moore, from Oakland, CA, pushes her daughter Taylor Woolridge, 11 months, with help from family friend Robbin Davis, from Berkeley, during the women's rights march.

(bottom right) Coal miners with lunch pails.

Mario Cuomo was chosen to deliver the keynote address to rally the Democratic faithful, draw traditional Democrats—who had defected to Reagan in 1980—back into the fold, and to attract independent votes; in essence, he had to highlight Reagan's potential electoral weaknesses. Making a brutal, penetrating attack on Ronald Reagan's presidency and on the conservative agenda, Cuomo pointed out that, yes, America was a "shining city on a hill" (a phrase Reagan had used quite effectively in his 1976 address to the Republican convention) to the rich and the fortunate, but that America was, in fact, "a tale of two cities," taking a phrase from Charles Dickens. He lashed out at Reagan and the Republicans for their indifference to the poor, on the economic policies that he felt hurt the poor, and on what he called their "survival of the fittest" (a phrase from Darwin) philosophy where only the strong could survive to enjoy America's riches.

This speech, written entirely in his own hand, was much more than an attack on Ronald Reagan and his party. This speech was a passionate advertisement for a new kind of America—one where blacks, Hispanics, Native Americans, and all minorities could claim their share of America, where students could afford the education they needed to succeed, where women would truly be treated equally, where seniors and natural resources were truly protected, where the courts would protect freedom of reproductive choice, and where the government was "strong enough to use the words *love* and *compassion.*"

It did not, however, accomplish its immediate goal: Democratic candidate Walter Mondale was crushed by Ronald Reagan in the 1984 election and many of the problems that Cuomo articulated remain. This 1984 keynote, however, serves as a manifesto of sorts for issues that transcend the 1984 political environment.

"It was only after his stem-winder at the 1984 Democratic National Convention ... that Mario Cuomo pierced the larger American consciousness. ... Wherever he speaks, he dazzles audiences with his verbal virtuosity and moves them with the evocation of his oft-repeated theme of family."

Robert Ajemian, "What to Make of Mario: Can Cuomo run for President by not running?" *Time* magazine, June 2, 1986

"A Tale of Two Cities"

Keynote Address, Democratic Convention, July 16, 1984

Mario Cuomo captivated the huge audience at the Democratic Convention at the San Francisco Cow Palace from the first sentence. Everyone sensed it, including the Governor. It was a magical moment for the audience and a career-making one for the speaker.

This long speech transformed the audience by combining Cuomo's own strong and warm personality with masterful speechwriting and delivery. It was a course in the use of visual imagery, parallel sentence construction, emotionally rhythmic speech flow, and the use of a personal and intimate conversational tone. Written entirely in his own hand, Mario Cuomo's keynote address was one of the great American political orations of the twentieth century.

ANALYSIS

We get immediate insight into the workings of his mind and one of the reasons for Mario Cuomo's great popularity in this first sentence. Notice how he describes the people of his state of New York as *the whole family*, setting the tone for a warm, inclusive, family-oriented message.

One sentence into the speech, he cuts to the chase. His no-nonsense directness, like Goldwater's, is a great speech-writing tool, which immediately grabs this audience. By *skipping the stories and the poetry* (for which he is well known as an orator), he adds weight to what he is about to say to them.

He then further grabs the audience's attention by commenting on something very current—still in people's memories—something President Reagan said in a campaign speech just ten days before. In Ronald Reagan's use of the phrase "shining city on a hill," Cuomo saw great contradiction.

Here comes the first stinging jab at what he and Democrats believed was the vulnerable side of a very popular president. Cuomo paints vivid word pictures as he contrasts the stunning vistas from White House porticos and ranch verandas with the other "city" where many live in far different circumstances.

This paragraph is about as good as political speech writing ever gets. Instead of making general statements about how there are poor, elderly, homeless, and adrift youth in this "other city," Cuomo literally brands disturbing visual images deep into our brain with choice phrases like *where the glitter doesn't show.*

SPEECH

On behalf of the great Empire State and the whole family of New York, let me thank you for the great privilege of being able to address this convention.

Please allow me to skip the stories and the poetry and the temptation to deal in nice but vague rhetoric. Let me instead use this valuable opportunity to deal immediately with the questions that should determine this election and that we all know are vital to the American people.

Ten days ago, President Reagan admitted that although some people in this country seemed to be doing well nowadays, others were unhappy, and even worried, about themselves, their families and their futures.

The President said he didn't understand that fear. He said, "Why, this country is a shining city on a hill."

The President is right. In many ways we are "a shining city on a hill."

But the hard truth is that not everyone is sharing in this city's splendor and glory.

A shining city is perhaps all the President sees from the portico of the White House and the veranda of his ranch, where everyone seems to be doing well.

But there's another city, another part of the shining city, the part where some people can't pay their mortgages, and most young people can't afford one, where students can't afford the education they need, and middle class parents watch the dreams they hold for their children evaporate.

In this part of the city, there are more poor than ever, more families in trouble, more and more people who need help but can't find it. Even worse: There are elderly people who tremble in the basements of their houses there, and there are poor who sleep in the city's streets, in the gutter, where the glitter doesn't show. There are ghettos where thousands of young people, without an education or a job, give their lives away to drug dealers every day.

There is despair, Mr. President, in faces you never see, in places you never visit in your shining city. In fact, Mr. President, this is a nation—Mr. President, you ought to know that this nation is more a "Tale of Two Cities," than it is just a "shining city on a hill."

Having described what he believes is the "real" condition of the lives of many Americans, he launches a frontal assault directly on the president. Even his repeated use of the term *Mr. President* is sarcastic, a classic crowd-pleasing technique at political conventions.

Maybe, if you visited more places, Mr. President, you'd understand. Maybe if you went to Appalachia where some people still live in sheds, and to Lackawanna where thousands of unemployed steel workers wonder why we subsidize foreign steel; maybe if you stopped in at a shelter in Chicago and talked with some of the homeless there.

Maybe Mr. President, if you asked a woman who'd been denied the help she needs to feed her children because you say we need the money to give a tax break to a millionaire, or for a missile we couldn't afford to use—maybe then you'd understand.

Note the use of the word *maybe*. He implies that the President has no idea of how Americans live, and then names the places where he might go to see the real America. The places Cuomo names are not chosen randomly; they are places in which there are large numbers of Democrats who have not participated in the boom of the first Reagan term.

Maybe, Mr. President. But I'm afraid not. Because the truth is, ladies and gentlemen, this is how we were warned it would be.

Notice the continued dramatic use of sarcasm. This is tricky to do successfully, but when not overdone and especially when backed up with facts, it is one of the best techniques for building momentum with an already friendly crowd.

President Reagan told us from the very beginning that he believed in a kind of social Darwinism. Survival of the fittest. "Government can't do everything," we were told. So it should settle for taking care of the strong and hope that economic ambition and charity will do the rest. Make the rich richer and what falls from the table will be enough for the middle class and those trying to make it, to work their way into the middle class.

Again, by sticking to verifiable statements, Cuomo exhibits another speech-writing skill as he "spins" those factual statements into something that sounds and feels downright horrible. Reagan never said he believed in "a kind of social Darwinism," but Cuomo's lawyer-like arguments make it as real as if he had.

The Republicans called it "trickle-down" when Hoover tried it. Now they call it "supply-side."

In making the analogy to Hoover, the former Republican president, whom many felt did nothing to alleviate the suffering of the poor during the early stages of the Depression, Cuomo is making a very strong, negative comment about the Republican party and, by inference, Reagan himself.

It's the same shining city for those relative few who are lucky enough to live in its good neighborhoods. But for the people who are excluded—but for the people who are locked out—all they can do is stare from a distance at that city's glimmering towers.

It's an old story. As old as our history.

And now, like a symphony, he returns to the shining city theme and summarizes the differences he's just enunciated with the rest of the country.

The difference between Democrats and Republicans has always been measured in courage and confidence. The Republicans believe the wagon train will not make it to the frontier unless some of our old, some of our young, and some of our weak are left behind by the side of the trail.

With an already worked-up convention audience, Cuomo takes that momentum and expands the scope of the speech to talk about his party. Notice how he uses the Republicans' own favorite theme—family—and makes the case that it is the Democrats who care more for "the whole family." But again, notice how effectively he uses visual imagery.

Paraphrasing the famous Biblical phrase, "The meek shall inherit the earth," Cuomo blasts the Republicans' "Darwinian" philosophy and then accents the Democrats' "family values."	The strong—the strong, they tell us—will inherit the land! We Democrats believe that we can make it all the way with the whole family intact. We have. More than once.
Cuomo extends that image further with a poetic first sentence. Franklin Roosevelt was a hero to most Democrats and many others. But it's not just Roosevelt's image he's invoking, it's Roosevelt saving the country, and, by implication, Roosevelt—the wheelchair-bound man—being left by the wayside. Who could conceive of that? He then leads the audience in a superbly emotional paragraph through his vision of America—and what it could be like.	Ever since Franklin Roosevelt lifted himself from his wheelchair to lift this nation from its knees—wagon train after wagon train—to new frontiers of education, housing, peace. The whole family aboard. Constantly reaching out to extend and enlarge the family. Lifting them up into the wagon on the way. Blacks and Hispanics, people of every ethnic group, and Native Americans—all those struggling to build their families and claim some small share of America.
Now he reminds his listeners of what Democrats have done for them.	For nearly fifty years we carried them to new levels of comfort, security, dignity, even affluence. Some of us are in this room today only because this nation had that confidence. It would be wrong to forget that.
It is always important in a long speech to come back and provide an overview of the purpose of the speech.	So, we are at this convention to remind ourselves where we come from and to claim the future for ourselves and for our children. Today our great Democratic Party, which has saved this nation from depression, from fascism, from racism, from corruption, is called upon to do it again—this time to save the nation from confusion and division, from the threat of eventual fiscal disaster, and most of all, from a fear of a nuclear holocaust.
A critical technique here: Cuomo knows that he and his party are up against a master communicator in Ronald Reagan. To have credibility with his audience, he must acknowledge that and then provide the strategy for overcoming it.	In order to succeed, we must answer our opponent's polished and appealing rhetoric with a more telling reasonableness and rationality. We must win this case on the merits. We must get the American public to look past the glitter, beyond the showmanship—to reality, to the hard substance of things. And we will do that not so much with speeches that sound good as with speeches that are good and sound.
Great word play here, much like that of another extraordinary orator and word artist, Reverend Jesse Jackson.	Not so much with speeches that bring people to their feet as with speeches that bring people to their senses.
And, again, Cuomo returns to his main theme.	We must make the American people hear our "Tale of Two Cities." We must convince them that we don't have to settle for two cities, that we can have one city, indivisible, shining for all its people.
Drawing biblical imagery from the tower of Babel, Cuomo is telling the party, which had had its internal disagreements, that if they want to win, they have to come together.	We will have no chance to do that if what comes out of this convention is a Babel of arguing voices. If that's what's heard throughout the campaign—dissonant voices from all sides—we will have no chance to tell our message.

New York Governor Mario Cuomo delivers the keynote address to the Democratic National Convention.

To succeed we will have to surrender small parts of our individual interests, to build a platform we can all stand on, at once, comfortably, proudly singing out the truth for the nation to hear, in chorus, its logic so clear and commanding that no slick commercial, no amount of geniality, no martial music will be able to muffle the sound of the truth.

We Democrats must unite so that the entire nation can. Surely the Republicans won't bring the country together. Their policies divide the nation into the lucky and the left out, the royalty and the rabble.

The Republicans are willing to treat this division as victory. They would cut this nation in half, into those temporarily better off and those worse off than before, and call that division "recovery."

We should not be embarrassed or dismayed if the process of unifying is difficult, even at times wrenching.

Unlike any other party, we embrace men and women of every color, every creed, every orientation, every economic class. In our family are gathered everyone from the abject poor of Essex County in New York to the enlightened affluent of the gold coasts of both ends of our nation. And in between is the heart of our constituency. The middle class. The people not rich enough to be worry-free but not poor enough to be on welfare. Those who work for a living because they have to. White-collar and blue-collar. Young professionals. Men and women in small business desperate for the capital and contracts they need to prove their worth.

Using alliteration—repetition of initial letters and sounds (*chorus, clear, commanding* and *martial music*)—and powerful one-liners (*Those who work for a living because they have to.*) leave an indelible impression and keep the audience focused during a long speech such as this one.

Governor Mario Cuomo, Jesse Jackson, and Representative Charles Rangel, New York (1990).

Cuomo's compassion for "ordinary" people is strongly evident here as he enumerates six different groups he and the Democratic Party will fight for. Parallel sentence construction using the word *for* gives this section even more power.

We speak for the minorities who have not yet entered the mainstream.

We speak for ethnics who want to add their culture to the mosaic that is America.

We speak for women indignant that we refuse to etch into our governmental commandments the simple rule "thou shalt not sin against equality," a commandment so obvious it can be spelled in three letters: E R A (which stands for Equal Rights Amendment).

We speak for young people demanding an education and a future.

We speak for senior citizens terrorized by the idea that their only security —their Social Security—is being threatened.

We speak for millions of reasoning people fighting to preserve our environment from greed and stupidity and fighting to preserve our very existence from a macho intransigence that refuses to make intelligent attempts to discuss the possibility of nuclear holocaust with our enemy. Refusing because they believe we can pile missiles so high that they will pierce the clouds and the sight of them will frighten our enemies into submission.

We're proud of this diversity. Grateful we don't have to manufacture its appearance the way the Republicans will next month in Dallas, by propping up mannequin delegates on the convention floor.

But while we're proud of this diversity as Democrats, we pay a price for it.

The different people we represent have many points of view. Sometimes they compete and then we have debates, even arguments. That's what our primaries were about. But now the primaries are over and it is time to lock arms and move into this campaign together.

If we need any inspiration to make the effort to put aside our small differences, all we need to do is to reflect on the Republican policy of divide and cajole and how it has injured our land since 1980.

The President has asked us to judge him on whether or not he's fulfilled the promises he made four years ago. I believe as Democrats that we ought to accept that challenge. And just, for a moment, let us consider what he has said and what he has done.

Having acknowledged the varied constituencies that made up the Democratic Party, Cuomo moves to the vital task of uniting these constituencies under one umbrella.

Inflation is down since 1980. But not because of the supply-side miracle promised to us by the president. Inflation was reduced the old-fashioned way, with a recession, the worst since 1932. We could have brought inflation down that way. Now how did he do it? Fifty-five thousand bankruptcies. Two years of massive unemployment. Two hundred thousand farmers and ranchers forced off the land. More homeless than at any time since the Great Depression in 1932, more hungry in this world of enormous affluence, the United States of America. More hungry, more poor—and most of them women. And he created one other thing: a nearly $200 billion deficit threatening our future.

Now we must make the American people understand this deficit, because they don't. The President's deficit is a direct and dramatic repudiation of his promise in 1980 to balance our budget by 1983. How large is it? That deficit is the largest in the history of the universe. President Carter's last budget had a deficit less than one-third of this deficit. It is a deficit that, according to the President's own fiscal advisor, may grow as much as $300 billion a years for "as far as the eye can see." And, ladies and gentlemen, it is a debt so large that almost one-half of our revenue from the income tax goes just to pay the interest on it each year. It is a mortgage on our children's futures that can only be paid in pain and that could bring this nation to its knees. Don't take my word for it—I'm a Democrat.

Ask the Republican investment bankers on Wall Street what they think the chances are this recovery will be permanent. If they're not embarrassed to tell you the truth, they'll say they are appalled and frightened by the President's deficit. Ask them what they think of our economy, now that it has been driven by the distorted value of the dollar back to its colonial condition—exporting agricultural products and importing manufactured ones.

Ask those Republican investment bankers what they expect the interest rate to be a year from now. And ask them what they predict for the inflation rate then.

How important is this question of the deficit?

Think about it: What chance would the Republican candidate have had in 1980 if he had told the American people that he intended to pay for his so-called economic recovery with bankruptcies, unemployment, and the largest government debt known to humankind? Would American voters have signed

In the next part of this speech, Cuomo goes deeply into the details. Notice, as you read this, how expertly he translates policy—something that people have little or no interest in—into examples that have real-life punch. By frequently using rhetorical questions and by translating details into human images (*more hungry, more poor—and most of them women*), he keeps his audience's attention.

the loan certificate for him on Election Day? Of course not! It was an election won with smoke and mirrors and with illusions. It is a recovery made of the same stuff.

And what about foreign policy? They said that they would make us and the whole world safer. They say they have, by creating the largest defense budget in history, one that even they now admit is excessive; by escalating to a frenzy the nuclear arms race; by incendiary rhetoric; by refusing to discuss peace with our enemies; by the loss of 279 young Americans in Lebanon in pursuit of a plan and a policy no one can find or describe. We give monies to Latin American governments that murder nuns and then lie about it. We have been less than zealous in our support of the only real friend we have in the Middle East, the one democracy there, our flesh and blood ally, the state of Israel.

Our foreign policy drifts with no real direction other than a hysterical commitment to an arms race that leads nowhere, if we're lucky. And if we're not, it could lead us to bankruptcy or war.

Of course we must have a strong defense. Of course Democrats believe that there are times when we must stand and fight. And we have. Thousands of us have paid for freedom with our lives. But always when we've been at our best—our purposes were clear.

Now they're not. Now our allies are as confused as our enemies. Now we have no real commitment to our friends or our ideals, not to human rights, not to the *refuseniks* [Russian dissidents], not to Sakharov, not to Bishop Tutu and the others struggling for freedom in South Africa. We have in the last few years spent more than we can afford. We have pounded our chest and made bold speeches. But we lost 279 young Americans in Lebanon and we are forced to live behind sandbags in Washington.

How can anyone say that we are stronger, safer, or better?

That's the Republican record.

Every speaker who speaks on a substantive topic must address the details. Cuomo did this brilliantly. In the end, however, the most critical goal in a speech like this is to inspire the party faithful—to generate an emotional, not an intellectual response.

That its disastrous quality is not more fully understood by the American people is attributable, I think, to the President's amiability and the failure by some to separate the salesman from the product.

It's now up to us to make the case to America. And to remind Americans that if they are not happy with all the President has done so far, they should consider how much worse it will be if he is left to his radical proclivities for another four years unrestrained by the need once again to come before the American people.

With the crowd already worked up, notice how he uses simple language and short sentences to attack, over and over again, the sitting President and the effects of his policies. But especially note how easy it is to follow and pay attention as he does this. This is because he uses eleven successive rhetorical questions—another brilliant oratorical device for hooking an audience.

If July brings back Ann Gorsuch Burford [Reagan's first EPA Administrator]—what can we expect of December? Where would another four years take us? How much larger will the deficit be? How much deeper the cuts in programs for the struggling middle class and the poor to limit that deficit? How high the interest rates? How much more acid rain killing our forests and fouling our lakes?

What kind of Supreme Court will we have? What kind of court and country will be fashioned by the man who believes in having government mandate people's religion and morality? The man who believes that trees pollute the environment, that the laws against discrimination go too far, the man who threatens Social Security and Medicaid and help for the disabled. How high will we pile the missiles? How much deeper will be the gulf between us and our enemies? And, ladies and gentlemen, will four years more make meaner the spirit of our people? This election will measure the record of the past four years. But more than that, it will answer the question of what kind of people we want to be.

We Democrats still have a dream. We still believe in this nation's future, and this is our answer to the question. This is our credo:

We believe in only the government we need, but we insist on all the government we need.

We believe in a government that is characterized by fairness and reasonableness, a reasonableness that goes beyond labels, that doesn't distort or promise to do what it knows it can't do.

We believe in a government strong enough to use the words *love* and *compassion* and smart enough to convert our noblest aspirations into practical realities.

We believe in encouraging the talented, but we believe that while survival of the fittest may be a good working description of the process of evolution, a government of humans should elevate itself to a higher order, one which fills the gaps left by chance or a wisdom we don't understand.

We would rather have laws written by the patron of this great city, the man called the "world's most sincere Democrat," St. Francis of Assisi, than laws written by Darwin.

We believe, as Democrats, that a society as blessed as ours, the most affluent democracy in the world's history, one that can spend trillions on instruments of destruction, ought to be able to help the middle class in its struggle, ought to be able to find work for all who can do it, room at the table, shelter for the homeless, care for the elderly and infirm, and hope for the destitute.

We proclaim as loudly as we can the utter insanity of nuclear proliferation and the need for a nuclear freeze, if only to affirm the simple truth that peace is better than war because life is better than death.

We believe in firm but fair law and order, in the union movement, in privacy for people, openness by government. We believe in civil rights and we believe in human rights.

We believe in a single fundamental idea that describes better than most textbooks and any speech what a proper government should be: The idea of family, mutuality, the sharing of benefits and burdens for the good of all, feeling one another's pain, sharing one another's blessings, reasonably, honestly, fairly, without respect to race or sex or geography or political affiliation.

Launched by a reference to Martin Luther King, Jr.'s speech given over two decades earlier, Cuomo is able to harness the speech's exquisite emotional power, and succinctly and expertly set the course for the future. Once again he uses parallel sentence construction to drive the momentum (twelve uses of the phrase *we believe*).

Labor activists carry a banner featuring New York Governor Mario Cuomo during a 1982 Labor Day parade.

Like Dr. King's use of geographical locations to provide a sense of place and give breadth to his speech, notice how these specific examples make Cuomo's point concrete.

We believe we must be the family of America, recognizing that at the heart of the matter we are bound one to another, that the problems of a retired schoolteacher in Duluth are our problems. That the future of the child in Buffalo is our future. The struggle of a disabled man in Boston to survive, to live decently, is our struggle. The hunger of a woman in Little Rock, our hunger. The failure anywhere to provide what reasonably we might, to avoid pain, is our failure.

Mario Cuomo gained the respect of so many because he infuses so much substance into his emotional orations. Here he condenses fifty years of Democratic history, with specific reference to programs and presidents, stirring pride by mentioning the heroes of the party and backing it up with facts.

For fifty years, we Democrats created a better future for our children using traditional Democratic principles as a fixed beacon, giving us direction and purpose, but constantly innovating, adapting to new realities. Roosevelt's alphabet programs; Truman's NATO and the G.I. Bill of Rights; Kennedy's intelligent tax incentives and the Alliance for Progress; Johnson's civil rights; Carter's human rights and the nearly miraculous Camp David Accord.

Speeches done well are musical symphonies with their own entrancing rhythm. After two long sentences heaped with detail, Cuomo hammers it home with a short sentence with two short, punchy phrases.

And, keeping the music rolling, Cuomo pulls in more parallel construction, this time with five successive *We cans*.

Democrats did it, and Democrats can do it again.

We can build a future that deals with our deficit. Remember this, that fifty years of progress under our principles never cost us what the last four years of stagnation have. And we can deal with that deficit intelligently, by shared sacrifice, with all parts of the nation's family contributing, building partnerships with the private sector, providing a sound defense without depriving ourselves of what we need to feed our children and care for our people. We can have a future that provides for all the young of the present by marrying common sense and compassion.

We know we can, because we did it for nearly fifty years before 1980.

And we can do it again. If we do not forget, forget that this entire nation has profited by these progressive principles. That they helped lift up generations to the middle class and higher. That they gave us a chance to work, to go to college, to raise a family, to own a house, to be secure in our old age, and before that to reach heights that our own parents would not have dared to dream of.

That struggle to live with dignity is the real story of the shining city, and it's a story, ladies and gentlemen, I didn't read in a book or learn in a classroom. I saw it and lived it, like many of you. I watched a small man with thick calluses on both hands work fifteen and sixteen hours a day. I saw him once literally bleed from the bottoms of his feet, a man who came here uneducated, alone, unable to speak the language, who taught me all I needed to know about faith and hard work by the simple eloquence of his example. I learned about our obligation to each other from him and from my mother. And they asked to be protected in those moments when they would not be able to protect themselves. This nation and its government did that for them.

Already a powerful and masterfully written speech, we come now to my favorite part: the extremely loving personal example of Cuomo's own father. See the compelling word pictures that he paints about his father, listen to the rhythm of the sentences, and feel the emotion coming out of this one paragraph!

And that they were able to build a family and live in dignity and see one of their children go from behind their little grocery store in South Jamaica, on the other side of the tracks where he was born, to occupy the highest seat in the greatest state in the greatest nation, in the only world we know, is an ineffably beautiful tribute to the democratic process.

And how beautifully he projects his success onto his parents and then patriotically links it to the values of this country.

And, ladies and gentlemen, on January 20, 1985, it will happen again. Only on a much, much grander scale. We will have a new President of the United States, a Democrat born not to the blood of kings but the blood of immigrants and pioneers. We will have America's first woman Vice President, the child of immigrants, and she will open with one magnificent stroke a whole new frontier for the United States. It will happen, if we make it happen—if you and I make it happen.

Now with the audience exactly where he wants them, Cuomo takes all of this energy and emotion and, exactly as a keynote speaker must, connects it with the candidates, Walter Mondale and Geraldine Ferraro.

I ask you, ladies and gentlemen, brothers and sisters, for the good of all of us—for the love of this great nation, for the family of America—for the love of God, please, make this nation remember how futures are built.

Thank you and God bless you.

In closing he returns to the family theme he began with in the first paragraph, uses the traditional triplet for maximum closing momentum, includes a reference to God, and takes advantage of the relationship he has so carefully constructed with the audience to make a powerful, personal appeal that caps off a magnificent speech and a truly inspiring performance.

Mario Cuomo

THE SPEECH—WHAT TO LOOK FOR: This speech is as soft and sensitive as it is hard hitting, a wonderful and difficult combination. Through a combination of personal stories and inspired use of language, Cuomo brings himself, his life, and his beliefs into the speech. One of the most celebrated political speeches, it achieved its impact with warmth, humanity, and compassion.

THE DELIVERY—WHAT TO LISTEN FOR: Since Cuomo wrote every word of his speech, you can sense his complete "ownership" in the delivery as he pauses, changes voice tone often and rouses the crowd.

THE PERSON—QUALITIES OF GREATNESS: As "The Conscience of the Left," he is admired for his humanity and equally respected for his strong and pragmatic leadership skills, keen intellect, and deep philosophical vision.

RONALD REAGAN

"... they ... 'slipped the surly bonds of earth' to 'touch the face of God.'"

"GREAT COMMUNICATOR" COMFORTS COUNTRY AFTER CHALLENGER DISASTER

In his use of the office as bully pulpit, Ronald Reagan had few peers. A former sportscaster, actor, president of the Screen Actors Guild, and two-term governor of California, Reagan's legacy derives in large part from his amazing ability to communicate. No matter what you thought of his politics, you had to admire his warm, homespun style, his optimistic view of the world, his rich voice, and the certainty with which he spoke.

Ronald Reagan's success came in large part because he knew one of the most important secrets of leadership: the power of compelling communication—both verbal and nonverbal. Reagan always looked and sounded presidential. Like a great actor, he fully "owned" everything that he said. And he did it by focusing on the larger principles or themes that drove his powerful ideological passions. Nowhere were those broad, larger principles more evident than in his "Evil Empire" speech.

The President's passionate conviction that democracy was superior to communism allowed him, four years later, to stand at the Berlin Wall and give one of his most powerful addresses. His speech there is one of the best examples of the Reagan style and the awesome power of simplicity.

The "Evil Empire"

Address to the National Association of Evangelists, March 8, 1983

... Let us pray for the salvation of all those who live in totalitarian darkness, pray—they will discover the joy of knowing God.

But until they do, let us be aware that while they preach the supremacy of the state, declare its omnipotence over individual man, and predict its eventual domination of all peoples on the earth, they are the focus of evil in the modern world....

1979 Iranian militants seize U.S. embassy in Tehran on November 4, taking fifty-two Americans hostage	**1984** Defeats Walter Mondale in landslide, winning forty-nine states.
1980 Landslide victory over Jimmy Carter on November 4; wins 44 states in the general election	**1985** Mikhail Gorbachev becomes Soviet premier; U.S. admits sponsoring armed insurgencies against Soviet-backed governments in the Third World (the "Reagan Doctrine"); U.S. replaces Israeli stocks; Israel ships 604 anti-tank missiles to Iran; Colonel Oliver North is put in charge of the shipment of HAWK anti-aircraft missiles to Iran
1981 Sworn in as 40th President of the United States on January 20; Iran releases the hostages; shot by John Hinckley, Jr. (November)	
1982–1983 U.S. sinks into worst recession since the Great Depression (Fall 1982); approval rating plummets to 35 percent (January); economic recovery begins; biggest peacetime economic expansion in U.S. history (Spring); suicide bomber crashes truck into U.S. Marine barracks in Lebanon, killing 241 members of the U.S. peacekeeping force (October 23); U.S. troops invade Grenada (October 25)	**1986** January 28, U.S. space shuttle *Challenger* explodes 73 seconds after takeoff; December 1, Reagan appoints the Tower Commission to review Iran Contra
	1989 The Berlin Wall opens
	1991 Gorbachev dissolves the Soviet Union

> ### "…tear down this wall!"
>
> *Excerpt of Remarks at the Brandenburg Gate, West Berlin*
> *June 12, 1987*
>
> …There is one sign the Soviets can make that would be unmistakable, that would advance dramatically the cause of freedom and peace.
>
> General Secretary Gorbachev, if you seek peace, if you seek prosperity for the Soviet Union and Eastern Europe, if you seek liberalization: come here to this gate! Mr. Gorbachev, open this gate! Mr. Gorbachev, tear down this wall! …

Although Peggy Noonan, Reagan's speechwriter, is often credited with creating the Reagan "magic," according to Nancy Reagan, the President, himself, did extensive editing of every important speech. Regardless of who wrote the words, the real key to Reagan's success, of course, was his delivery. Without his delivery—the pauses of just the right length, always in the perfect moment, the wonderful changes in intonation, and the solid body language—the words would still have been brilliant, but they would not have dazzled as they did.

At no time during his eight years as president did Ronald Reagan need to use his ability to connect, to capture, and to lead the emotions of the nation more than on January 28, 1986. On that day, with a 39-year-old high school teacher, wife, and mother from New Hampshire on board, the space shuttle *Challenger* exploded.

The tenth flight of the *Challenger* was one of the biggest media events of the decade. Millions of schoolchildren as well as adults—in America and around the world—were glued to their television sets to celebrate the heart-warming milestone of the first "civilian" in space. In the end, it was anything but heart-warming.

Even before it took off that January morning, this launch had something of the nightmare about it. Delayed four times because of scheduling problems with the previous *Challenger* mission; delayed again because of bad weather and its own technical difficulties, there was great pressure to finally get it off the ground. The eyes of the world were on the shuttle, the shuttle program, and NASA. What's

Demonstrators on the west side try to tear down a segment of the wall near the Brandenburg Gate. East German border guard uses hose-pipe to disperse the demonstrators.

(left) The Space Shuttle *Challenger*, its two solid rocket boosters and a new lightweight external fuel tank were captured on film by an automatically-tripped camera.

(right) Crew members of STS 51-L mission walk out of the Operations and Checkout Building on their way to Pad 39B where they will board the Shuttle *Challenger*. From front to back: Commander Francis R. (Dick) Scobee; mission specialists Judith A. Resnik and Ronald E. McNair; pilot Michael J. Smith; payload specialist Christa McAuliffe; mission specialist Ellison Onizuka; and payload specialist Gregory Jarvis.

more, it was Reagan himself who had suggested that a teacher go into space. No one wanted another delay.

But the weather in Florida that morning, although clear with blue skies, was uncharacteristically cold. So cold, in fact, that two-foot icicles had formed at the base of the aircraft. Engineers responsible for the solid rocket boosters expressed grave reservations about the safety of launching in such conditions.

NASA executives feared another postponement would not only damage popular confidence in its programs, but also impact the federal funding it received. Ultimately, top officials (non-scientists) at NASA and Morton-Thiokol (the manufacturer of the O-rings) decided to proceed with the launch despite vehement staff protests.

The President didn't even watch the launch. He was at work with his top advisers preparing for the State of the Union address scheduled for that evening. But millions of schoolchildren all over the country sat transfixed in front of television sets brought in by their teachers, who wanted to celebrate one of their own going into space. The teachers were not alone—in fact, for the first time in years, a space mission had captured the public's imagination, and the nation paused to watch.

The countdown went off as usual. The chest-thumping roar of the lift-off enveloped the spectators watching from the grandstands. Against the perfect blue sky the *Challenger* gloriously rose, as people craned their necks and shaded their

High Flight

by John Gillespie Magee, Jr.

Magee wrote "High Flight" on the back of a letter to his parents. He said: "I am enclosing a verse I wrote the other day. It started at 30,000 feet, and was finished soon after I landed." Three months later his own "high flight," a training mission over England, ended in his death at the age of 19.

Oh! I have slipped the surly bonds of earth,
And danced the skies on laughter-silvered wings;
Sunward I've climbed, and joined the tumbling mirth
Of sun-split clouds—and done a hundred things
You have not dreamed of—Wheeled and soared and swung
High in the sunlit silence. Hov'ring there,
I've chased the shouting wind along, and flung
My eager craft through footless halls of air.
Up, up the long, delirious burning blue
I've topped the windswept heights with easy grace
Where never lark, or even eagle flew.
And, while with silent, lifting mind I've trod
The high untrespassed sanctity of space,
Put out my hand, and touched the face of God.

". . . [Reagan] sought to insure that the initial shock and sadness would evolve, in time, into a renewed sense of determination."
R. W. Apple, Jr., *The New York Times,* January 29, 1986

Words That Shook the World

"The Speech That Was Never Given"

Written for Richard Nixon by William Safire

It was back in '69. We were just about to launch Apollo 11 . . . *I had prepared a speech for President Nixon hailing this event, welcoming the men back. And then one of the astronauts said to me quietly, 'In case of disaster, do you have another speech?' . . . And then it hit me—that these men were, indeed, not just off on a great adventure, but they were taking their lives in their hands. . . . The speech was never given.*

Fate has ordained that the men who went to the moon to explore in peace will stay on the moon to rest in peace.

These brave men, Neil Armstrong and Edwin Aldrin, know that there is no hope for their recovery. But they also know that there is hope for mankind in their sacrifice.

These two men are laying down their lives in mankind's most noble goal: the search for truth and understanding. They will be mourned by their family and friends; they will be mourned by their nation; they will be mourned by the people of the world; they will be mourned by a Mother Earth that dared send two of her sons into the unknown.

In their exploration they stirred the people of the world to feel as one; in their sacrifice, they bond more tightly the brotherhood of man.

In ancient days men looked at stars and saw their heroes in the constellations. In modern times we do much the same, but our heroes are epic men of flesh and blood.

Others will follow and surely find their way home. Man's search will not be denied. But these men were the first and they will remain the foremost in our hearts.

For every human being that looks up at the moon in the nights to come will know that there is some corner of another world that is forever mankind.

(top) Main engine exhaust, solid rocket booster plume and an expanding ball of gas from the external tank is visible seconds after the Space Shuttle *Challenger* accident on January 28, 1986.

(above) Reagan and staff watch *Challenger* explosion on television in the White House.

eyes trying to follow its trajectory. Suddenly, at 73 seconds into its flight, the world stood still as an eerily pretty, but highly unusual double trail of white smoke spiraled down from the shuttle. Something that looked like a rocket booster spun off.

The mission announcer was silent. The *Challenger* had exploded.

Pat Buchanan, Reagan's Communications Director, interrupted preparations for that evening's address to give the President the news. Like the rest of the country and the world, they turned on a television, and everyone in the room—at the hub of world power—watched. The State of the Union address was canceled. Reagan and his advisers felt an upbeat national speech in the face of the tragedy would be inappropriate, yet Reagan knew he had to address the loss that the entire country felt.

With only hours to prepare, the challenge was to find the appropriate tone. Scrambling for the perfect close, Peggy Noonan remembered a poem written by an American pilot who had volunteered to fly for the Canadian Air Force before the U.S. entered World War II. John Gillespie Magee, Jr., wrote "High Flight" three months before he died in a training accident in England in 1941 at the age of 19. Reagan knew and loved the poem, and agreed to use it.

> ## "Suddenly, the celebration stopped."
> *Washington Post,* January 29, 1986

> ## "Soviet people deeply mourn the tragic loss of the seven U.S. astronauts aboard the space shuttle *Challenger*."
> *Moscow News,* February 16, 1986

> ## ". . . they . . . 'slipped the surly bonds of earth' to 'touch the face of God.'"
>
> ### Address to the Nation, January 28, 1986
>
> Ronald Reagan's weakness at details was his greatest strength as a communicator. A man who had little fascination with analysis, his brilliance as an orator and communicator emanated from his ability to simplify the details of life and policy into large, powerful themes.
>
> The Challenger speech was the perfect vehicle for those talents. Clearly not a speech about policy or details, it was the ideal moment for Ronald Reagan to be a leader, to be the warm, fatherly, grandfatherly figure who charmed people all the way from Los Angeles to Sacramento to Washington, D.C.
>
> The speech works brilliantly, despite its painful message, because in it Ronald Reagan is Ronald Reagan: He is warm, personal, eloquent, uplifting, and optimistic even in tragedy, and talks in big, inspiring themes. Simply put, in this short speech he sets the standard for how a leader, a real leader, shows strength and compassion in the face of disaster.

ANALYSIS	SPEECH
Reagan wastes no time opening his remarks with that warm, personal, conversational magic for which he is known.	Ladies and Gentlemen, I'd planned to speak to you tonight to report on the State of the Union, but the events of earlier today have led me to change those plans. Today is a day for mourning and remembering. Nancy and I are pained to the core by the tragedy of the shuttle *Challenger*. We know we share this pain with all of the people of our country. This is truly a national loss.
He acknowledges the tragedy, and, at the same time, he bathes the lost astronauts in positive tones as he introduces his first major theme: *courage*.	Nineteen years ago, almost to the day, we lost three astronauts in a terrible accident on the ground. But, we've never lost an astronaut in flight; we've never had a tragedy like this. And perhaps we've forgotten the courage it took for the crew of the shuttle; but they, the *Challenger* Seven, were aware of the dangers, but overcame them and did their jobs brilliantly. We mourn seven heroes: Michael Smith, Dick Scobee, Judith Resnik, Ronald McNair, Ellison Onizuka, Gregory Jarvis, and Christa McAuliffe. We mourn their loss as a nation together.
He then moves quickly on as he introduces the second and third major themes: *challenge* and *service*.	For the families of the seven, we cannot bear, as you do, the full impact of this tragedy. But we feel the loss, and we're thinking about you so very much. Your loved ones were daring and brave, and they had that special grace, that special spirit that says, "Give me a challenge and I'll meet it with joy." They had a hunger to explore the universe and discover its truths. They wished to serve, and they did. They served all of us.
Next, possibly to deflect criticism of NASA or the government for the failure, but more likely to get us to open our minds to the big picture of space exploration and to further our appreciation of the courage and service of those who died, he takes us back to the beginnings of the space program. Notice how with the use of very short sentences, he starts to make the speech "sing" and lift.	We've grown used to wonders in this century. It's hard to dazzle us. But for twenty-five years the United States space program has been doing just that. We've grown used to the idea of space, and perhaps we forget that we've only just begun. We're still pioneers. They, the members of the *Challenger* crew, were pioneers.
Here, Reagan as grandfather steps in. Notice how in the guise of talking to the children of America, he puts an extraordinarily positive spin on—and sells—one of the most embarrassing disasters in the nation's history.	And I want to say something to the schoolchildren of America who were watching the live coverage of the shuttle's takeoff. I know it is hard to understand, but sometimes painful things like this happen. It's all part of the process of exploration and discovery. It's all part of taking a chance and expanding man's horizons.
He builds on the theme of courage, and adds another theme with this empowering and famous sentence: *bravery*.	The future doesn't belong to the fainthearted; it belongs to the brave.

The *Challenger* crew was pulling us into the future, and we'll continue to follow them.

This line is brilliant! The visual image, that horrible visual image of the *Challenger* exploding, is almost transformed by this one line. No longer can we think of the rocket and its plume of white smoke as a failure. The *Challenger* may have exploded, but the astronauts are still there—leading us.

I've always had great faith in and respect for our space program, and what happened today does nothing to diminish it. We don't hide our space program. We don't keep secrets and cover things up. We do it all up front and in public. That's the way freedom is, and we wouldn't change it for a minute.

Reagan now moves even further from this disaster, as he congratulates the American system and, by implication, the American people. In a not-so-veiled attack, he takes advantage of the opportunity to take another shot at the "Evil Empire," as he introduces his fifth large theme: *freedom*.

We'll continue our quest in space. There will be more shuttle flights and more shuttle crews and, yes, more volunteers, more civilians, more teachers in space. Nothing ends here; our hopes and our journeys continue. I want to add that I wish I could talk to every man and woman who works for NASA or who worked on this mission and tell them: "Your dedication and professionalism have moved and impressed us for decades. And we know of your anguish. We share it."

And now that we've shared our sadness and saluted our fallen heroes, here is how Ronald Reagan moves the space program and the country forward. Notice how he again takes an overtly personal approach as he declares his desire to connect with every one of the NASA workers.

There's a coincidence today. On this day 390 years ago, the great explorer Sir Francis Drake died aboard ship off the coast of Panama. In his lifetime the great frontiers were the oceans, and a historian later said, "He lived by the sea, died on it, and was buried in it." Well, today we can say of the Challenger crew: Their dedication was, like Drake's, complete.

The crew of the space shuttle *Challenger* honored us by the manner in which they lived their lives.

Moving toward a close, he compares the fallen astronauts with another hero—an explorer from another era—and uses it to successfully introduce his sixth theme: *dedication*.

We will never forget them, nor the last time we saw them, this morning, as they prepared for the journey and waved goodbye and "slipped the surly bonds of earth" to "touch the face of God."

Until this last sentence, this is just another very good Ronald Reagan speech and performance. The truly amazing thing to notice here is how one sentence, one poetic, soaring sentence, transforms the speech and bathes the entire tragedy—and the watching world—in a hopeful, spiritual glow, something only a master communicator like Ronald Reagan could deliver.

Ronald Reagan

THE SPEECH—WHAT TO LOOK FOR: See the way in which the President used his personality and simple words to make the country feel better—even proud—in a moment of national disaster, and, of course, how the speech and the event were transformed by one brilliant, closing phrase.

THE DELIVERY—WHAT TO LISTEN FOR: As always with "The Great Communicator," notice the warmth and silky richness of his voice, the perfect pacing and the personal, conversational way in which he speaks that makes every listener feel that they are right there in the Oval Office with him.

THE PERSON—QUALITIES OF GREATNESS: An "Everyman" to whom we could all relate, but one with masterful communication skills, passion, vision, and an infectious, palpable love for his principles and his country.

TENZIN GYATSO,
14TH DALAI LAMA OF TIBET

"...a universal responsibility for one another and the planet we share."

HIGHLIGHTS

1935 Born Lhamo Dhondrub on July 6

1940 February 22, enthronement ceremony in Lhasa, capital of Tibet

1949 Completes the Geshe Lharampa degree (Doctorate of Buddhist Philosophy)

1950 80,000 Chinese People's Liberation Army soldiers invade Tibet; November 17, assumes full political power (head of the state and government)

1954 Visits Beijing to talk peace with Mao Tse-tung and other Chinese leaders

1956 Series of meetings with Indian Prime Minister Nehru about conditions in Tibet

"SIMPLE MONK" SEEKS PEACEFUL SOLUTIONS TO TIBET'S AND WORLD'S PROBLEMS

With its capital city, Lhasa, at 11,975 feet and the rest of Tibet's cities at over 11,000 feet above sea level, the people of Tibet (sometimes called "The Altar of the Earth") live in the rarefied air of the highest country on the planet. It may not be surprising, then, that this Asian culture is firmly rooted in deep religious and spiritual customs and traditions—Tibetan Buddhism.

A fascinating aspect of Tibetan Buddhism is the belief that their leader and chief monk, "Dalai Lama" (literally *oceanic teacher*), is an incarnation of "Bodhisattva Avalokiteshvara," the Buddha of Compassion, who was first born in 1351 and is repeatedly reborn in order to bring Tibetans the consistent spiritual and political wisdom they require. When the Dalai Lama dies, Tibetans believe that his spirit passes into the body of a newborn boy. A nationwide search of all of the villages begins, and only after rigorous tests is the next Dalai Lama proclaimed. The boy is then carefully trained.

The story of the search for, and the life of, the 14th Dalai Lama is extraordinary. In 1935 the 13th Dalai Lama, Thupten Gyatso, died at the age of 57. According to Tibetan lore, that same year the Regent of Tibet had a vision: He saw a monastery, three stories high with a turquoise and gold roof. The monastery had a path running from it to a hill and a small house with an oddly shaped gutter. He also saw the letters Ah, Ka, and Ma.

A search party, with knowledge of the vision, was dispatched. They ultimately found a location that matched the vision: the town of Taktser in the province of

Amdo, where they focused on a three-year-old boy named Lhamo Dhondrub.

Without telling the parents of the reason for their visit, they stayed the night to observe and question the boy. Asked to identify a member of the group, who was disguised as a servant, the little boy responded *Sera aga*, which means "a lama of Sera." Amazingly, he was right.

Other tests followed, including the correct identification of garments and other objects belonging to the 13th Dalai Lama. According to Tibetan history, little Lhamo Dhondrub not only correctly identified the former Dalai Lama's possessions, but he also repeatedly shouted out, "It's mine, it's mine." The meaning of the letters? It is thought that *Ah* stood for Amdo, the name of the province; *Ka* for Kumbum, one of the area's largest monasteries; and the two letters *Ka* and *Ma* also indicated the first name of the Karma Rolpai Dorjer, a monastery located on the mountain above the village.

On February 22, 1940 in Lhasa, the 14th Dalai Lama was enthroned. At the age of five, Lhamo Dhondrub's name was changed to Jetsun Jamphel Ngawang Lobsang Yeshe Tenzin Gyatso, which means "Holy Lord, Gentle Glory, Compassionate, Defender of the Faith, Ocean of Wisdom."

From the age of six until late 1959, when he was 24, the new Dalai Lama was buried in intense training in everything from Tibetan culture to Buddhist philosophy to the English language. His studies continued even after late 1949 when 80,000 soldiers of the Chinese People's Liberation Army (PLA) marched across the

(above) The Dalai Lama shown with crowds during celebration of 10th anniversary of the Tibetan uprising against the Chinese Reds and subsequent exile.

(left) The fourteenth Dalai Lama as a child.

Tenzin Gyatso / "...a universal responsibility for one another and the planet we share."

140

(left) Pursued by Red Chinese troops struggling against the harsh elements of the Himalayas, the Dalai Lama is shown on fourth day of his flight to freedom. The 23-year-old ruler, wearing spectacles, is aboard the white horse. At this point, the escape party is crossing the Zsagola pass in Southern Tibet.

(above) This photograph from the official Communist Chinese Picture Agency shows Chen Yi, vice premier of Communist China (saluting, second from right) on his visit to Lhasa, Tibet, on April 17 to attend ceremonies connected with the inauguration of a preparatory committee to organize Tibet in the Communist Chinese framework. Reviewing local troops with Chen Yi are the Dalai Lama, spiritual leader and chairman of the committee, left, and Panchen Lama, right, named first vice chairman.

Press Release Announcing The Nobel Prize for Peace, 1989

The Norwegian Nobel Committee has decided to award the 1989 Nobel Peace Prize to the 14th Dalai Lama, Tenzin Gyatso, the religious and political leader of the Tibetan people.

The Committee wants to emphasize the fact that the Dalai Lama in his struggle for the liberation of Tibet consistently has opposed the use of violence. He has instead advocated peaceful solutions based upon tolerance and mutual respect in order to preserve the historical and cultural heritage of his people.

The Dalai Lama has developed his philosophy of peace from a great reverence for all things living and upon the concept of universal responsibility embracing all mankind as well as nature. In the opinion of the Committee, the Dalai Lama has come forward with constructive and forward-looking proposals for the solution of international conflicts, human rights issues, and global environmental problems.

border from China, headed to Lhasa. On November 17, 1950 the 15-year-old assumed full political power as head of the state and government. A student of Mahatma Gandhi, the young Dalai Lama attempted to convince Great Britain, the United States, and Nepal to intervene, but unwilling to risk conflict with China, they refused. He sent a delegation to China to try to open a dialogue with them. Instead, news came back that on May 23, 1951 Tibet had formally agreed to a seventeen-point plan for the "peaceful liberation of Tibet," an agreement that some say was signed under threat of invasion and made "official" by a forged seal.

Despite the agreement, negotiations continued and, in 1954, the Dalai Lama himself went to Beijing to speak with Mao Tse-tung and other Chinese leaders to try to negotiate a mutually satisfactory peace, with no success. He continued his efforts until, on March 10, 1959, after demonstrations against Beijing reached their peak, the Tibetan National Uprising was crushed. Disguising himself as a common soldier, His Holiness escaped to India in the dark of night and was given political asylum after a grueling three-week journey. Since 1960 he and the 80,000 refugees who followed him live in Dharamsala, India, the official seat of the Tibetan Government-in-exile.

(left) The 23-year-old "living Buddha," who threaded his way through the towering mountains of his homeland by horse and yakskin barge, reached Tezpur in an Indian Army jeep. In his first public statement since fleeing Tibet, the Dalai Lama accused Red China of treachery and murder in its invasion of the Himalayan kingdom.

(above) Chinese and Tibetan leaders: From left to right: Zhu De, a leader of the Chinese Communists; the Dalai Lama; the Panchen Lama; and Zhou Enlai, premier of the People's Republic of China during a state visit to Peking in September 1954 by the Tibetan Buddhist leaders.

After the Dalai Lama's departure, the vastly superior Chinese forces captured and took over Lhasa and the entire country of Tibet. Despite strong international condemnation, the Chinese occupation continues with more than 250,000 Chinese troops stationed there. According to the Dalai Lama, 1.2 million Tibetans died as a result of the Chinese occupation and more than 6,000 monasteries, temples, forts and other historic landmarks, approximately 90 percent of "the repository of our ancient Tibetan civilization," were destroyed or desecrated.

The Chinese, of course, have a different view of the situation in Tibet. They believe that Tibet historically has been part of China for many centuries. They blame Tibetans for collaborating with Chang Kai-Shek in his struggles with the Communists and for assisting Taiwanese efforts to gain independence from the Chinese mainland.

Despite the constant difficulties inherent in his people's struggle to regain what they believe is their rightful independence, Tenzin Gyatso, the 14th Dalai Lama of Tibet, continues to fight. He takes, as he often states, "from the teachings of love and compassion of the Buddha, and from the practice of non-violence of the great leaders, Mahatma Gandhi and Martin Luther King."

In recognition of his lifelong, nonviolent efforts to liberate Tibet, the Dalai Lama, over the strong objection of China, was awarded the Nobel Peace Prize in 1989.

"His Holiness the Dalai Lama's courageous struggle has distinguished him as a leading proponent of human rights and world peace. His ongoing efforts to end the suffering of the Tibetan people through peaceful negotiations and reconciliation have required enormous courage and sacrifice."

U.S. Congressman Tom Lantos, regarding the Dalai Lama's receipt of the Raoul Wallenberg Congressional Human Rights Award

> ## "... a universal responsibility for one another and the planet we share."
>
> ### Nobel Acceptance Speech, Oslo, Norway, December 10, 1989
>
> The Dalai Lama is neither a fiery speaker like a Martin Luther King, Jr., nor a stirring orator like Winston Churchill. He does not have a rich, soothing voice like Ronald Reagan or a booming, impressive one like Barbara Jordan. Yet, he is as charismatic a personality and speaker as any you can name. The Dalai Lama's secret comes from his absolute simplicity of speech and carriage. With no fancy flourishes, no soaring sentences, no punctuated voice tone and no oratorical techniques designed to stir the audience, he nevertheless has the power to move us by the simple power of who he is—by his authenticity, his moral authority.
>
> Without pretense or technique, he stands before an audience of luminaries and speaks from the heart. Few have the confidence to do this. This speech to the Nobel Academy accepting the 1989 Nobel Peace Prize delivers both a spiritual and political message, and His Holiness does it in a straightforward and honest manner, exuding warmth, optimism, and simplicity.

ANALYSIS

This *simple monk* theme is central to his message of humility and a consistent theme in all his speeches. Were he not perceived as being genuine, phrases like it and his often used *I am no one special* would seem manipulative and be received badly. The way he carries himself, how he smiles as he speaks, the total lack of flourish in his tone of voice, and the consistent focus on other people and their suffering give self-effacing words genuine weight, sets the tone, and add to the simple power of his message.

His Holiness demonstrates here that he has learned much from Gandhi. He effortlessly moves from the idea of his own insignificance to thanking the Academy on behalf of *all who struggle* to his acknowledgment of his mentor to his commitment to non-violence—*truth, courage* and *determination* are their only weapons.

Like Gandhi, the Dalai Lama's philosophy stems from his own deeply held beliefs in the oneness and the universality of all men. Look at the inclusiveness of his language, which has both a spiritual and a more subtle social/political message. If we are one spiritually, then don't we all have the same rights to self-determination? Without saying the words, he simply and passionately makes the case for this position here.

In the preceding paragraph he did not mention Tibet, but by talking about independence movements in Europe and Africa he is clearly trying to convince the world to help support Tibetan independence from China. Now, he focuses not on Tibet, but on Tibet's adversary with a litany of recent Chines efforts to destroy democracy within its borders.

SPEECH

Your Majesty, Members of the Nobel Committee, Brothers and Sisters:

I am very happy to be here with you today to receive the Nobel Prize for peace. I feel honoured, humbled, and deeply moved that you should give this important prize to a simple monk from Tibet.

I am no one special. But I believe the prize is a recognition of the true value of altruism, love, compassion, and nonviolence which I try to practise, in accordance with the teachings of the Buddha and the sages of India and Tibet.

I accept the prize with profound gratitude on behalf of all of the oppressed everywhere and for all those who struggle for freedom and work for world peace. I accept it as a tribute to the man who founded the modern tradition of nonviolent action for change—Mahatma Gandhi—whose life taught and inspired me. And, of course, I accept it on behalf of the six million Tibetan people, my brave countrymen and women inside Tibet, who have suffered and continue to suffer so much. They confront a calculated and systematic strategy aimed at the destruction of their national and cultural identities. The prize reaffirms our conviction that with truth, courage, and determination as our weapons, Tibet will be liberated.

No matter what part of the world we come from, we are all basically the same human beings. We all seek happiness and try to avoid suffering. We have basically the same human needs and concerns. All of us human beings want freedom and the right to determine our own destiny as individuals and as peoples. That is human nature. The great changes that are taking place in the world, from Eastern Europe to Africa, are a clear indication of this.

In China the popular movement for democracy was crushed by brutal force in June this year. But I do not believe the demonstrations were in vain, because the spirit of freedom was rekindled among the Chinese people, and China cannot escape the impact of this spirit of freedom sweeping in many parts of the world. The brave students and their supporters showed the Chinese leadership and the world the human face of that great nation.

Tenzin Gyatso, His Holiness the 14th Dalai Lama of Tibet, at a Kalachakra Initiation ceremony. Two lines of seated lamas join His Holiness in chanting sacred texts, while western devotees assemble in tent beyond

By referring to the killing of 155 and the wounding of 65 students and other demonstrators at Tiananmen Square, and then mentioning recent trials in Tibet, he is reminding the world, which had great sympathy for the Tiananmen demonstrators, that he and his people are fighting the very same enemy.

Like Gandhi's nonviolent struggle against the British in India, the Dalai Lama's and the Tibetan people's struggle has gone on for years. Here he reminds his audience, and indirectly the governments of the world, of the offers he has made to the Chinese to achieve peace, thus far without success. He ends this section of his address with what seems to be an uncharacteristic ultimatum.

Last week a number of Tibetans were once again sentenced to prison terms of up to nineteen years at a mass show trial, possibly intended to frighten the population before today's event. Their only "crime" was the expression of the widespread desire of Tibetans for the restoration of their beloved country's independence.

The suffering of our people during the past forty years of occupation is well documented. Ours has been a long struggle. We know our cause is just. Because violence can only breed more violence and suffering, our struggle must remain nonviolent and free of hatred. We are trying to end the suffering of our people, not to inflict suffering upon others.

It is with this in mind that I proposed negotiations between Tibet and China on numerous occasions. In 1987, I made specific proposals in a Five-Point Peace Plan for the restoration of peace and human rights in Tibet. This included the conversion of the entire Tibetan plateau into a zone of Ahimsa, a sanctuary of peace and nonviolence where human beings and nature can live in peace and harmony.

Last year, I elaborated on that plan in Strasbourg at the European Parliament. I believe the ideas I expressed on those occasions were both realistic and reasonable, although they have been criticised by some of my people as being too conciliatory. Unfortunately, China's leaders have not responded positively to the suggestions we have made, which included important concessions. If this continues, we will be compelled to reconsider our position.

U.S. President George W. Bush (right) welcomes the Dalai Lama (left) at the White House, May 23, 2001, over Beijing's stern objections. Bush "declared his strong support for the Dalai Lama's tireless efforts to initiate a dialogue with the Chinese government," Bush spokesman Ari Fleischer said in a statement after the half-hour meeting.

Having delivered this ultimatum, he presents in effect a legal argument and a legal "document"—dating back over 1,000 years—to support his claim to Tibetan independence from China.

Any relationship between Tibet and China will have to be based on the principle of equality, respect, trust, and mutual benefit. It will also have to be based on the principle which the wise rulers of Tibet and of China laid down in a treaty as early as 823 A.D., carved on the pillar which still stands today in front of the Jokhang, Tibet's holiest shrine, in Lhasa, that "Tibetans will live happily in the great land of Tibet, and the Chinese will live happily in the great land of China."

Here, once again, he speaks as a *Buddhist monk*. Is there an inconsistency between delivering what seems to be a strong ultimatum, presenting a legal "brief," and then speaking as a spiritual leader? Because he established the dominant theme of universal brotherhood so well in the earlier part of the speech and returns to it now, this transition is seen as neither manipulative nor awkward.

He continues his theme of universal brotherhood as the solution to the world's pressing problems and, by implication, the problems of the Tibetan and Chinese people. He starts this transition by going to the core of Buddhist philosophy—the end of suffering by sentient (feeling) beings of all kinds (including animals)—and then expanding to give a very concise overview of the Buddhist, and his, philosophy.

As a Buddhist monk, my concern extends to all members of the human family and, indeed, to all the sentient beings who suffer. I believe all suffering is caused by ignorance. People inflict pain on others in the selfish pursuit of their happiness or satisfaction.

Yet true happiness comes from a sense of peace and contentment, which in turn must be achieved through the cultivation of altruism, of love and compassion, and elimination of ignorance, selfishness, and greed.

The problems we face today, violent conflicts, destruction of nature, poverty, hunger, and so on, are human created problems which can be resolved through human effort, understanding, and a development of a sense of brotherhood and sisterhood. We need to cultivate a universal responsibility for one another and the planet we share. Although I have found my own Buddhist religion helpful in generating love and compassion, even for those we consider our enemies, I am convinced that everyone can develop a good heart and a sense of universal responsibility with or without religion.

The Dalai Lama here extols *universal values—love, compassion, universal responsibility*—which are so important to his Buddhist beliefs, but acknowledges that others—even . . . our enemies—can *develop* these traits *with or without religion*—a clear allusion to the Chinese.

With the ever-growing impact of science in our lives, religion and spirituality have a greater role to play reminding us of our humanity. There is no contradiction between the two. Each gives us valuable insights into each other. Both science and the teaching of the Buddha tell us of the fundamental unity of all things. This understanding is crucial if we are to take positive and decisive action on the pressing global concern with the environment.

I believe all religions pursue the same goals, that of cultivating human goodness and bringing happiness to all human beings. Though the means may appear different, the ends are the same.

In other words, we are all connected and we are all one—a restatement of his essential message to the world to look to the connections and similarities we share rather than our differences. Notice how artfully he says so much in such clean, simple sentences.

As we enter the final decade of this century, I am optimistic that the ancient values that have sustained mankind are today reaffirming themselves to prepare us for a kinder, happier twenty-first century.

Having strongly restated his theme, he begins his conclusion, as he began the speech, on a hopeful note, allying *ancient values* with the nearing twenty-first century.

I pray for all of us, oppressor and friend, that together we succeed in building a better world through human understanding and love, and that in doing so we may reduce the pain and suffering of all sentient beings.

Thank you.

Since His Holiness is a political leader as well as spiritual leader, he combines the two in his concluding prayer. By choosing to use the word *oppressor*, he delivers a pointed attack on China (without mentioning the name) and ends by eloquently suggesting a common purpose toward which all should strive.

The Dalai Lama

THE SPEECH—WHAT TO LOOK FOR: The style is very clean; no words wasted, no more words required. It is a wonderful combination of mind and heart working together in one speech.

THE DELIVERY—WHAT TO LISTEN FOR: This is a lesson in the effectiveness of simplicity. Notice how relaxed and comfortable he is, allowing his naturally warm, joyful personality to come forth with every word.

THE PERSON—QUALITIES OF GREATNESS: A living example of humility, compassion, and simplicity. Exalted almost as a God by his followers, he seems to be completely without ego.

Tenzin Gyatso / "…a universal responsibility for one another and the planet we share."

146

ITZHAK RABIN

"Enough of blood and tears. Enough."

HIGHLIGHTS

1922 Born on March 1 in Jerusalem

1941 Enlists in the Palmach, an underground Labor Zionist commando unit

1947–1948 Appointed Deputy Commander of the Palmach; commands the Harel Brigades that defend Jerusalem during Israel's War of Independence; oversees the expulsion of 50,000 Palestinians from coastal areas; May 14, declaration of Israeli statehood

1964 Becomes chief of staff of Israel Defense Forces

1967 June 5–11, leads Israeli forces in Six-Day War, resulting in Israeli capture of the West Bank, Gaza Strip, Sinai Peninsula, and Golan Heights as well as control of East Jerusalem

PRIME MINISTER PRAYS TO "GIVE PEACE A CHANCE"

The United Nations declared Israeli statehood on May 14, 1948. Within hours of the UN declaration Egypt, Jordan, Syria, Iraq, and Lebanon—promising to wipe Israel off the face of the earth—warned Arabs living within the borders of the new country that they would attack, and suggested it would be safer for them to leave and come back later. True to their word, they did attack, but their prediction did not come to pass. In January 1949 an armistice between Israel and the Arab countries was signed. The victorious new nation had almost doubled in size, Jordan had annexed the Arab-held area adjoining its territory (which became known as the West Bank), and Egypt occupied a coastal strip in the southwest that included Gaza.

In 1956 and again in 1967, Israel was at war with its neighbors. Each time Israel prevailed. As a result of the 1967 war, known as the "Six-Day War" because of the speed of the Israeli victory, Israel unified the Arab and Israeli sections of Jerusalem.

On October 6, 1973, the Jewish holy day of Yom Kippur, Egypt, Syria, Jordan, and Lebanon attacked Israeli positions in Sinai and the Golan Heights. Israel, initially caught off guard, suffered casualties and lost ground, but ultimately pushed them back from their strategic positions. Israel gained land—this time the Sinai Peninsula from Egypt and the Golan Heights from Syria. On October 22 and 23, the UN Security Council called for a cease-fire, which went into effect shortly thereafter.

The constant tension resulting from the continuing warfare and uncertain periods of peace has created many opportunities for greatness in the Middle East. Some, like Anwar Sadat and Yitzhak Rabin, have taken them.

1968	Appointed ambassador to the United States
1973	Elected to the Knesset as a member of the Labor Party; appointed minister of Labor by Golda Meir; October 6, start of Yom Kippur War
1974	Selected by Labor as Prime Minister to succeed Meir, who steps down in aftermath of Yom Kippur War. Signs interim peace agreement with Egypt
1977	Resigns as Prime Minister; succeeded by Shimon Peres
1984–1990	Serves as defense minister in Labor-Likud coalition
1992	July 13, becomes Prime Minister for the second time; campaign promises include intensified peace efforts
1993	September 13, signs the Israeli-Palestinian Declaration of Principles with Arafat and Peres
1994	May 4, Oslo I Accord signed, granting self-rule to Palestinians in Gaza and Jericho; October 26, Israel-Jordan peace treaty signed; awarded the Nobel Peace Prize with Arafat and Peres
1995	September 28, signs Oslo II agreement with Arafat at the White House, expanding Palestinian self-rule in the West Bank; November 4, assassinated after a peace rally in Tel Aviv

Israel's first "Sabra" (native-born) Prime Minister, Yitzhak Rabin, was born in Jerusalem in 1922. His father had emigrated to Israel from the United States. After completing his schooling at Kadoorie Agricultural High School with distinction, Rabin joined the "Palmach," the elite strike force of the "Haganah" (an underground organization fighting for the creation of the state of Israel). He served with them for seven years. In 1948, the state of Israel was formally established, and the Haganah was disbanded and replaced by the IDF, the Israel Defense Forces.

A soldier in the IDF for over two decades, Rabin rose to the rank of Major General. At the age of 32, he was responsible for formulating the IDF's training techniques and creating its leadership style. In 1962, at the age of 40, he was promoted to the rank of Lieutenant General. Later, as Chief of the General Staff, he created the IDF doctrine of "movement and surprise," which was so successful in achieving air and ground supremacy in the 1967 "Six-Day War."

In January 1968, Major General Yitzhak Rabin traded his military uniform, after 27 years of service, for a suit and tie to become Israel's Ambassador to the United States. He served in Washington for five years and was instrumental in solidifying strategic cooperation between the two countries.

Returning to Israel in 1973, just before the "Yom Kippur War," Rabin became an active member of the Labor Party and was elected to the Israeli legislature, the Knesset, later that year. When Golda Meir formed her government in March 1974, she chose Rabin as Minister of Labor, but the coalition supporting her crumbled

(top left) A scene on the Jaffa Road during the capture of Castel by members of the Haganah from the Jewish Army.

(above) Members of the newly created state of Israel gathered to hear David Ben Gurion read the Jewish "Declaration of Independence." Left to right: Baruch Schitrit, Minister of Arab Affairs and Police; David Remez, Minister of Communications; Felix Rosenblueht, Minister of Justice; Fritz Bernstein, Minister of Trade; Rabbi Juda Fishman of Jerusalem; David Ben Gurion, Prime Minister and Defense Minister; Moshe Shapiro, Minister of Immigration; Moshe Shertock, Minister of Foreign Affairs; Eliazar Kaplan, Minister of the Treasury; M. Ben Tov, Minister of Labor; and A. Zisling, Minister of Agriculture (not shown).

(left) Chief of Staff Lieutenant General Moshe Levy, Shimon Peres, Yitzhak Rabin, Haim Bar-Lev, and Yitzhak Navon discuss Israeli Defense Forces manouvers in the Negev.

(above) Officials from Israel and the Palestinian government-in-exile come to Cairo to sign the first direct agreements between them, giving Gaza and Jericho to the Palestinians. From left to right: Shimon Peres, Israeli Foreign Minister, unknown Israeli, Yitzhak Rabin, Prime Minister of Israel, Hosni Mubarak, President of Egypt, Yasir Arafat, Chairman of the PLO, U.S. Secretary of State Warren Christopher, and an unknown Arab official.

"Mr. Rabin, the general-turned-statesman, was nervous and palpably uncomfortable—staring down at his shoes, never applauding anyone, shifting nervously and taking his speech in and out of his pocket. When he delivered that speech, though, Mr. Rabin was both eloquent and frank. He articulated the deep ambivalence that he and so many Israelis felt about this reconciliation with a man they have only known by the name 'terrorist' for 30 years. Mr. Rabin made clear that this was a moment he came to not out of some soaring vision of peace, but out of a grudging acknowledgement of reality: that Israel could no longer go on ignoring the P.L.O., the organization that represents the Palestinian people."

Thomas Friedman, "Rabin and Arafat Seal Their Accord as Clinton Applauds 'Brave Gamble,'" *The New York Times,* September 14, 1993

and, on June 2, 1974, another coalition government, this time with Yitzhak Rabin as Prime Minister (at age 52 Israel's youngest) was formed.

Quickly establishing a reputation for candid, direct, and sometimes blunt leadership, Rabin moved quickly on domestic and international issues. In 1975 he shepherded through an Interim Agreement with Egypt (a precursor to the Camp David Accords) whereby Israel would withdraw from the Suez Canal in exchange for free shipping for Israeli boats through the Canal. As a result, the United States entered into a Memorandum of Understanding, the first between the two countries, which ensured American support of vital Israeli interests.

The controversy surrounding Israel's raid on the Entebbe Airport, internal social and economic problems, a lack of confidence in the military and civilian leadership, internal political conflicts, and scandals led to the elections of 1977, in which Rabin and the Labor party lost to the Likud. As a result, Likud's leader, Menachem Begin, became Prime Minister and Rabin resigned as head of the Labor Party.

From 1977–1992, Rabin continued to serve in the Knesset where between 1984 and 1990, he also served as Minister of Defense. In June 1992, as leader again of the Labor Party, Yitzhak Rabin was once again Prime Minister. This time he was

President Clinton gestures as Israeli Prime Minister Yitzhak Rabin, left, and Palestine Liberation Organization Chairman Yasir Arafat shake hands after signing a peace accord, Monday, Sept. 13, 1993, on the South Lawn of the White House.

"Peace is our goal. It is peace we desire."

Excerpts from Address to the United States Congress on signing Peace Agreement with Jordan, July 26, 1994

...We have come from Jerusalem to Washington because it is we who must say—and we are here to say: Peace is our goal. It is peace we desire.

With me here in this House today, are my partners in this great dream....

I stand here today on behalf of those youngsters who wanted to live, to love, to build a home.... The debate goes on: Who shapes the face of history—leaders or circumstances? My answer to you is: We all shape the face of history. We the people.... And we, the leaders, hear the voices, and sense the deepest emotions and feelings of thousands and millions, and translate them into reality.... We bear the responsibility. We have the power to decide.... We are graced with the privilege of fulfilling this duty for our peoples....

There is much work before us. We face psychological barriers. We face genuine practical problems....

Your Majesty, we have both seen a lot in our lifetime. We have both seen too much suffering. What will you leave to your children? What will I leave to my grandchildren? I have only dreams: to build a better world—a world of understanding and harmony, a world in which it is a joy to live. This is not asking for too much....

Today we are embarking on a battle which has no dead and no wounded, no blood and no anguish. This is the only battle which is a pleasure to wage: the battle for peace....

In the Bible ...in the Book of Jeremiah, we find a lamentation for Rachel the Matriarch. It reads: "Refrain your voice from weeping, and your eyes from tears: for their work shall be rewarded, says the Lord."

I will not refrain from weeping for those who are gone. But... we sense that our work will be rewarded....

---

instrumental in facilitating two historic events: the Oslo Accords, which led to the Declaration of Principles signed with the PLO at the White House in September 1993, and the Treaty of Peace with Jordan in October 1994.

The signing of the Oslo Accords were the result of secret negotiations in Oslo, Norway and an exchange of letters between Arafat and Rabin on September 9, 1993. In his letter, Yasir Arafat, on behalf of the PLO, specifically: (1) recognized "the right of the State of Israel to exist in peace and security" and (2) renounced "the use of terrorism and other acts of violence." In response, Yitzhak Rabin, on behalf of Israel, stated that "in light of the PLO commitments included in your letter, the Government of Israel has decided to recognize the PLO as the representative of the Palestinian people and commence negotiations with the PLO within the Middle East peace process." The Declaration, itself, provided a framework for a solution to the question of Palestinian self-determination, return of land, and other issues.

Assembled in front of the White House, with President Bill Clinton proudly looking on, old foes Arafat and Rabin shook hands, taking the largest step forward

---

"What I shall remember most..."

*Excerpts from Remarks on Receiving the Nobel Prize for Peace
December 10, 1994*

Rabin shared a chilling insight into his lifetime as a soldier.

. . . And of all the memories I have stored up in my seventy-two years, what I shall remember most, to my last day, are the silences: The heavy silence of the moment after, and the terrifying silence of the moment before....

That is the moment you grasp that as a result of the decision just made, people might go to their deaths. People from my nation, people from other nations. And they still don't know it.

At that hour, they are still laughing and weeping; still weaving plans and dreaming about love; still musing about planting a garden or building a house—and they have no idea these are their last hours on Earth. Which of them is fated to die? Whose picture will appear in the black frame in tomorrow's newspaper? Whose mother will soon be in mourning? Whose world will crumble under the weight of the loss?...

Yitzhak Rabin / "Enough of blood and tears. Enough."

150

(left) Arafat Meets Rabin at Erez Checkpoint, 1994.

(above) Palestine Liberation Organization Chairman Yasir Arafat, Israeli Prime Minister Yitzhak Rabin, and Israeli Foreign Minister Shimon Peres accept the 1994 Nobel Prize for Peace from Nobel Committee Chairman Francis Sejersted during a presentation ceremony in Oslo, Norway.

"The achievement of Israel's Yitzhak Rabin lay here: In an age of ever harsher self-serving ethnic politics, he wrenched himself and his country into a quest for feasible accommodation with the people—the Palestinians—with whom Israelis contest for the same national ground."

Stephen S. Rosenfeld, "Rabin Grasped a Vision," *The Washington Post,* November 10, 1995

in the relationship between Israel and the Palestinian people. How difficult it was to get to even this simple gesture, the handshake, was revealed in a speech in 2001 in which Israeli Foreign Minister Shimon Peres recalled Rabin turning to him with the words, "O.K., now you have to do it." This giant step forward earned Yitzhak Rabin, Shimon Peres, and Yasir Arafat the 1994 Nobel Peace Prize "for their efforts to create peace in the Middle East."

In giving the award, the committee further stated that: "By concluding the Oslo Accords, and subsequently following them up, Arafat, Peres and Rabin have made substantial contributions to a historic process through which peace and cooperation can replace war and hate."

To the United States Congress, in 1994, at the signing of the peace accords with Jordan, Rabin powerfully recalled his own transformation:

Allow me to make a personal note. I, military I.D. number 30743, retired general in the Israel Defense Forces in the past, consider myself to be a soldier in the army of peace today. I, who served my country for 27 years as a soldier, I say to you, Your Majesty, the King of Jordan, and I say to you, American friends: Today we are embarking on a battle which has no dead

(left) U.S. President Bill Clinton (center) walking through the Great Hall at the White House with (left to right) King Hussein of Jordan, Israeli Premier Yitzhak Rabin, PLO chairman Yasir Arafat, and Egyptian President Hosni Mubarak after ceremonies in the East Room where Israel and the PLO signed a West Bank autonomy accord.

(above) Bill Clinton speaks at Prime Minister Yitzhak Rabin's funeral.

and no wounded, no blood and no anguish. This is the only battle which is a pleasure to wage: the battle for peace.

Unfortunately for the peace process, two years after the handshake and eleven months after accepting the Nobel Prize, Yitzhak Rabin was dead. At a huge peace rally in Tel Aviv on November 4, 1995, the Prime Minister ended his very last speech with these words:

This rally must send a message to the Israeli public, to the Jewish community throughout the world, to many, many in the Arab world and in the entire world, that the people of Israel want peace, support peace, and for that, I thank you very much.

Afraid that he would give away too much to the Palestinians, seconds later, an Israeli radical walked up to Prime Minister Rabin and shot him.

> ### "It was he who brought us together … for peace."
>
> *Excerpts from President Bill Clinton's Eulogy for Rabin, Mt. Herzl, Jerusalem November 6, 1995*
>
> … He was a man completely without pretenses; all of his friends knew. I read that in 1949 after the War of Independence, David Ben-Gurion sent him to represent Israel at the armistice talks at Rhodes and he had never before worn a necktie and did not know how to tie the knot. So, the problem was solved by a friend who tied it for him before he left and showed him how to preserve the knot, simply by loosening the tie and pulling it over his head. Well, the last time we were together, not two weeks ago, he showed up for a black tie event, on time but without the black tie. And so he borrowed a tie and I was privileged to straighten it for him. It is a moment I will cherish as long as I live.…
>
> Today, my fellow citizens of the world, I ask all of you to take a good, hard look at this picture. Look at the leaders from all over the Middle East and around the world who have journeyed here today for Yitzhak Rabin, and for peace. Though we no longer hear his deep and booming voice, it is he who has brought us together again here, in word and deed, for peace.…
>
> *Shalom, haveer.*" (Goodbye, friend.)

Remarks on the Signing of the Israeli–Palestinian Declaration of Principles, Washington, D.C., September 13, 1993

After 27 years in the military fighting against Yasir Arafat and those he represented, it was exceedingly difficult for Yitzhak Rabin to shake his hand. News footage shows that it actually took a nudge from President Bill Clinton. But after the historic handshake, his remarks were, in the words of the *New York Times,* both "eloquent and frank" as he cut through the decades of hostilities with a moving prayer for peace. His down-to-earth qualities; his simple language; his deep, gravelly voice; and his reserved demeanor drew trust and love from Israelis and many around the world. Those qualities and his power as a leader are evident in this short speech, one of his most touching orations.

ANALYSIS

As with Sadat's speech after the Camp David Accords, Prime Minister Rabin's first task is to acknowledge and calm the anxieties of his own people. He shows in these first few words that he is mindful of the sacrifices made and that they weigh heavily on him. In a speech like this one, it is very important to immediately connect with the thoughts and feelings of your audience. Knowing that you think and feel as they do, they can suspend their resistance and more readily accept what you have to say.

Again, as he pays respect to the dead, Rabin poignantly reminds his audience of the lives that have been lost along the road to this day.

The status of Jerusalem is the most important consideration for Orthodox and other religious Israelis. It is also a major holy site for all Moslems. He mentions Jerusalem by name, adding *the ancient and eternal capital of the Jewish people* so that Israelis know he is fully aware of Jewish concerns. At the same time, he is sending a more indirect but very clear message to Moslem Arabs.

With the world watching, he uses this opportunity to humanize (*mothers weeping for their sons*) something that, for most around the world, are only casualty statistics in their morning newspapers. Perhaps more important, he is also, like Sadat before him, trying to sell this peace agreement to one of his most difficult audiences, those in Israel who are wary of the Palestinians and unwilling to give anything away to them.

Rabin was famous and respected for his "no-nonsense" communication style. Notice how he makes a special point of turning from addressing Israelis and the world to speak directly *to* the Palestinians. This personal approach is a highly unusual technique in a speech such as this since formal speeches tend to be more abstract and less conversational in tone. The shifting of gears and the direct, personal focus give the words that follow much more impact and

SPEECH

Mr. President, Ladies and Gentlemen,

This signing of the Israeli-Palestinian Declaration of Principles, here today, is not so easy neither for myself, as a soldier in Israel's wars, nor for the people of Israel, nor to the Jewish people in the Diaspora (the dispersion of Jews all over the world) who are watching us now with great hope, mixed with apprehension. It is certainly not easy for the families of the victims of violence, terror, and war, whose pain will never heal. For the many thousands who have defended our lives with their own, and even sacrificed their lives for our own, for them, this ceremony has come too late.

Today, on the eve of an opportunity for peace and perhaps an end of violence and wars we remember each and every one of them with everlasting love.

We have come from Jerusalem, the ancient and eternal capital of the Jewish people. We have come from an anguished and grieving land.

We have come from a people, a home, a family, that has not known a single year, not a single month, in which mothers have not wept for their sons. We have come to try and put an end to the hostilities, so that our children, our children's children, will no longer experience the painful cost of war, violence and terror. We have come to secure their lives and to ease the sorrow and the painful memories of the past to hope and pray for peace.

Let me say to you, the Palestinians: We are destined to live together on the same soil, in the same land.

importance because audiences, taken by surprise at the unexpected, tend to be more attentive. Also, less formal and more conversational styles are easier to follow.

What he chooses to say—*We are destined to live together on the same soil, in the same land*—are probably the most significant fourteen words of the speech. For 45 years prior to this agreement, most Palestinians did not recognize Israel's right to exist or accept the idea of Israelis and Palestinians sharing the land.

We, the soldiers who have returned from battle stained with blood, we who have seen our relatives and friends killed before our eyes, we who have attended their funerals and cannot look into the eyes of their parents, we who have come from a land where parents bury their children, we who have fought against you, the Palestinians—

Rabin's next job is to show the Palestinian audience that they, the Israelis, have endured suffering just as the Palestinians have. He does this not with cold concepts or dry statistics, but with powerful imagery of the human destruction and despair the fighting has caused. Notice the anger that is evident from the use of the word *we* five times in just the first part of this sentence. He is trying to get the Palestinians to understand that it is not only they who have suffered.

---

we say to you today in a loud and a clear voice: Enough of blood and tears. Enough. We have no desire for revenge. We harbor no hatred towards you.

And then, using the word *we* three more times, he quickly moves to the heart of the speech, which he states for greatest impact with short, exceedingly simple sentences. No one can misinterpret or fail to understand his message.

We, like you, are people who want to build a home, to plant a tree, to love, to live side by side with you in dignity, in empathy, as human beings, as free men. We are today giving peace a chance, and saying again to you: Enough. Let us pray that a day will come when we all will say: Farewell to arms.

In a logical progression, he moves from *we harbor no hatred towards you* to an emotional recitation of how they are, in so many ways, the same. The use here of specific examples makes this work, and the use of *build a home* as the first such example, a clever, perhaps subliminal, message also reinforces the idea that Israel ia a *home* or homeland for the Jewish people.

He again addresses their common humanity and common desires: Who would not want these things? He uses some interesting phrases, *give peace a chance*, no doubt aware of the anthem of the U.S. anti-war movement; and *farewell to arms*, alluding to the title of Hemingway's world-famous anti-war novel.

We wish to open a new chapter in the sad book of our lives together, a chapter of mutual recognition, of good neighborliness, of mutual respect, of understanding. We hope to embark on a new era in the history of the Middle East. Today, here in Washington, at the White House, we will begin a new reckoning in relations between peoples, between parents tired of war, between children who will not know war.

Going from the image of one book to that of a new book yet to be written, Rabin again brings the end of the conflict down to the human level of parents and children rather than abstract ideas like country or people. By humanizing his message, he gives it greater power.

Yitzhak Rabin / "Enough of blood and tears. Enough."

154

People take to the streets of Jericho to celebrate an agreement between the Israeli prime minister, Yitzhak Rabin, and Yasir Arafat, the leader of the Palestine Liberation Organization, for the signing of a historic peace accord.

At the White House, fifteen years earlier, both Menachem Begin and Anwar Sadat ended their speeches at the signing of the Camp David Accords with a quotation from the Bible. Rabin continues that tradition. To this point in his speech, he has done an excellent job of lifting the discussion from abstract issues to human issues. Here, he gives the discussion and the speech a spiritual dimension, with Biblical words on which most people can agree. He chose a passage whose message was perfectly suited to the occasion, one with simple words, simple sentences, and a simple yet supremely powerful message. Note too how he calls attention to what he is about to say, by addressing his audience, in effect, by name.

President of the United States, Ladies and Gentlemen,

Our inner strength, our high moral values, have been derived for thousands of years from the Book of Books, in one of which, Koheleth, we read:

"To every thing there is a season, and a time to every purpose under heaven: a time to be born, and a time to die; a time to kill, and a time to heal; a time to weep and a time to laugh; a time to love, and a time to hate; a time of war, and a time of peace."

Words That Shook the World

Ladies and Gentlemen, the time for peace has come.

Here he underscores the power of this Biblical verse in one simple sentence, by again addressing the audience *Ladies and Gentlemen*. He wants to be certain that everyone is really listening, and, with this device he, in essence, says "pay attention."

In two days, the Jewish people will celebrate the beginning of a new year. I believe, I hope, I pray, that the New Year will bring a message of redemption for all peoples: a good year for you, for all of you. A good year for Israelis and Palestinians. A good year for all the peoples of the Middle East. A good year for our American friends, who so want peace and are helping to achieve it, for Presidents and members of previous administrations, especially for you, President Clinton, and your staff, for all citizens of the world: may peace come to all your homes.

As he concludes, his tone and his words become even more personal. Instead of talking as the Israeli Prime Minister, he addresses his audience as one human being to another. Using the metaphor of the impending Jewish New Year, he acknowledges everyone and extends prayers and best wishes as one would to friends. This human touch is the right close to a speech that consistently focused on humanity over abstract policy.

In the Jewish tradition, it is customary to conclude our prayers with the word "Amen." With your permission, men of peace, I shall conclude with words taken from the prayer recited by Jews daily, and whoever of you volunteer, I would ask the entire audience to join me in saying "Amen":

"*Oseh shalom bimromav, hu ya'aseh shalom aleinu v'al kol yisrael. V'imru. Amen.*"

("He maketh peace in His high places. He shall make peace for us and for all of Israel. And they shall say: Amen." [*translation from Hebrew*])

More than just a custom, the symbolism of having the entire audience say *Amen* together is akin to a stamp of approval on the messages and prayers he has offered throughout the speech. To have everyone participate on the last word is a perfect finale to a speech in which his desire is to emphasize shared values and common goals.

Yitzhak Rabin

THE SPEECH—WHAT TO LOOK FOR: Beautiful in its simplicity and chilling in its soulful cry for a real peace for his people, Rabin transcends issues and policy, speaks directly to the Palestinian people, and brilliantly translates the issues into deeply felt human experience.

THE DELIVERY—WHAT TO LISTEN FOR: The thick accent and deep voice add great depth and feeling to the human message and warm, everyman quality of this passionate but simple man.

THE PERSON—QUALITIES OF GREATNESS: A celebrated army general who became a true warrior for peace and touched his nation and the world with his warmth, authenticity, and humanity.

Yitzhak Rabin / "Enough of blood and tears. Enough."

156

PRINCESS DIANA

as remembered by Earl Charles Spencer

"... the unique, the complex, the extraordinary and irreplaceable Diana ..."

"A FAMILY IN GRIEF, IN A COUNTRY IN MOURNING, BEFORE A WORLD IN SHOCK"

The emotion kept building. We knew we weren't supposed to applaud or cheer—this was, after all, Westminster Abbey. The tombs of eighteen monarchs of England; Sir Isaac Newton; Mary Queen of Scots; the poets Chaucer, Browning, and Tennyson; and many other British notables lay under our feet. But we couldn't help it.

As the hundreds of thousands outside huddled together to share a grief that surprised everyone, a handful of us inside listened to brotherly words of passion that reverberated off every sculpted angle of the venerable walls.

Princess Diana hated speaking in public, but her brother, Earl Charles Spencer, clearly didn't. A student at Oxford, a journalist, and former contributing correspondent for NBC's *Today* show, his words captured every nuance of the complex personality that had held the world spellbound. The vulnerability and the power, the sophistication and the childishness, the nursery school teacher and world icon, a woman who had the ultimate power brokers waiting in line to shake her hand and the lonely princess spending Christmas Eve alone—Diana's brother caught it all.

But it wasn't only the brilliance of the observations that caused us to sit frozen on our wooden benches. It was that the tears, the anger, and the anguish of the millions filling the streets outside had somehow entered the cathedral and lifted Earl Spencer's words to spiritual heights.

Why had this former nursery school teacher touched so many, not only in London, but also around the world? Why was her death, and the funeral that followed six days later, an event that touched millions?

1991 First visit to AIDS patients at English hospital

1992 December 9, Buckingham Palace announces Diana and Charles's separation

1996 August 28, Charles and Diana are divorced

1997 Visits Angola and launches campaign against land mines; Christie's New York auctions 79 of Diana's gowns, raising more than $4 million for AIDS and cancer research; travels to Bosnia to further campaign against land mines; August 31, Diana and companion Dodi Al Fayed and their driver, Henri Paul, die in car crash in Paris; September 6, funeral at Westminster Abbey

Based on the time I spent with her, I can attest to her extraordinary charisma. You simply had to be in her presence for seconds and you could feel it. It emanated from her in the way she held her body—tall and regal, but completely approachable; it shined from her smile; and, as her brother remarks in the eulogy, it came from "the sparkle in those unforgettable eyes."

Diana's impact came not just from her personal charisma, but from the almost fairy-tale story of her life. Born into an aristocratic family, Diana Spencer lived her adult life under the world's microscope. From the moment Prince Charles named her his princess-to-be on February 24, 1981, when she was only 19, to the glamour and pomp of her wedding at St. Paul's Cathedral on July 29, 1981, until her untimely death in a Paris tunnel in the early morning hours of August 31, 1997, the world thrilled to her story and came to admire the shy, awkward, young girl who had become a full-fledged princess, a woman, and a mother before our eyes.

The world continued watching as her marriage fell apart; as she divorced; as the intimate details of eating disorders, mutual infidelities, and scandal rocked the Royals. Despite personal turmoil, Diana worked to fill a role beyond that of the glamorous or troubled princess. After her divorce from Prince Charles, she took up a number of humanitarian causes—most notably the anti-land mine cause, traveling to Angola and Bosnia, bringing international attention to the issue as she consoled victims and visited ruins and grave sites. Diana also used her celebrity to call

(above) Earl Spencer escorts his daughter, Diana Spencer (soon to be Princess Diana) down the aisle during her wedding ceremony.

(left) Young Diana.

"…an international angel of mercy."
Daily Express, January 17, 1997, on Diana's work on land mines

"She was the people's princess and that's how she will stay, how she will remain, in our hearts and in our memories forever."
British Prime Minister Tony Blair, August 31, 1997

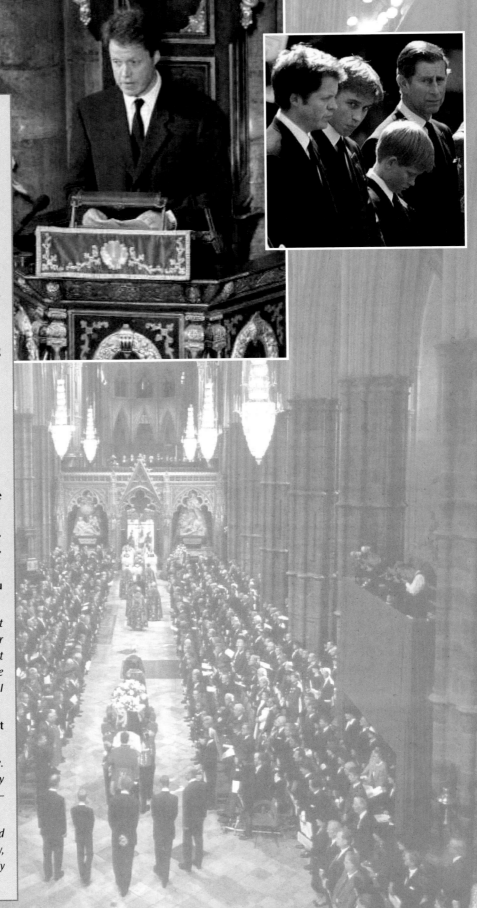

Earl Spencer Talks About His Eulogy to Diana, Princess of Wales

Did you know that this was an extraordinary address when you had finished it?

No, that was never a concern. Doing justice to Diana was all I aimed to do. I was confident that every word I'd written was true and fair, in my view.

What is your favorite line in the speech?

The one about the name Diana, and the irony of it being that of the ancient goddess of hunting. It was a thought I had never had before writing the speech early that Wednesday morning, and yet it is such a strikingly obvious point in retrospect.

Did the Queen or any member of the Royal Family say anything to you about the speech?

No.

What was the reaction of William and Harry to it?

They were extremely positive about it.

Did they feel you had described their mother well?

I hope so.

Did they know the contents of it before you delivered it at the funeral?

No, none of my family did. I had read it to my then girlfriend, who said it sounded "fine," and to my two senior employees, who were clearly moved by it.

Was there a point in the delivery of the speech where you thought you would lose control and break down and cry?

Yes, this was a real concern throughout. From reading it through out loud beforehand, I knew there were danger points, where the emotion was particularly charged. The last few sentences, addressed to the boys, were almost impossible to complete. My throat had almost closed up. I didn't think I was going to make it.

Were you nervous, knowing that this was probably the largest audience for any speech ever given?

The size of the audience was so vast as to be unimaginable. The small section of the congregation in the part of the abbey where my family was seated—a couple of hundred people— was the audience I concentrated on.

I was so wrung out that I never heard the applause at the end of the tribute. Another point: I did not want to speak that day, but knew that I had to—a conclusion that my family fully endorsed.

159

Princess Diana Speaking Out About...

Single-Parent Families
Excerpts from Speech at Dr. Barnardo's Conference, London, The Daily Telegraph, October 19, 1988

"I know that family life is extremely important and, as a mother of two small boys, I think we may have to find a securer way of helping our children, to nurture and prepare them to face life as stable and confident adults. . . . One in eight children lives in single-parent families. These children's experience of family life may be different but I do not believe it need necessarily be any less satisfying or effective."

The Handicapped
Excerpts from Speech at Christ's and Notre Dame College, Liverpool, The Daily Post, September 21, 1989

"We need to bring home to everyone the message that young people with mental handicap should have somewhere to live; should have something to do; and should have the opportunity to enjoy life to the full."

Family
Excerpts from Speech at International Congress for the Family, East Sussex, November 2, 1990

"I doubt whether there is any standard formula for a successful family. The family is, after all, the most human (and hence the most imperfect) of institutions. Instead, I could only point to those mothers, fathers and children—in lonely isolation or in comfortable conformity—who simply do their best with what they have. Their success is measured by the care they have for each other and, I suspect, there is no better form of judgment. To all of them, and to all who help them experience the warmth and strength of family life, I offer my support."

Compassion
Excerpts from Speech at Humanitarian Awards Dinner, New York United Cerebral Palsy, December 11, 1995

"I'm often struck by the reaction of people when a major tragedy occurs, when a natural disaster happens. Certainly, people seem to rise up and rush to support those in need. It's almost as if they were waiting for something to happen before they felt able to act . . . I would wish to say that today is the day of compassion. Let's not wait to be prompted, but let us go out tonight, tomorrow and the days that follow, and let us demonstrate our humanity. Let us not wait to be asked, but let us act today."

(top) Handshake with leprosy sufferer, Leprosy Hospital, Indonesia.

(center) Meeting the "Untouchables," India, 1992.

(left) Opening The Markfield Project, a family resource centre for families with disabled children and for young people, London, 1986.

attention to the AIDS crisis. In 1991 she began visiting AIDS patients. Later, following her divorce, she took an active role in bringing attention to and raising research funds for AIDS. In 1996, she donated 79 of her dresses and gowns to the AIDS Crisis Trust, to be auctioned to raise funds for the organization, and she named the National AIDS Trust as one of her patronages. She made highly publicized visits to AIDS clinics, bringing renewed international attention to the crisis.

Throughout it all, the press never turned their eyes from her and an eager public soon discovered the fantasy and reality, the dream life and the all-too-painful real life. A princess to admire and the vulnerable human being just like the rest of us. That was the unique and compelling combination that mesmerized the world while she lived and touched the world far more deeply than we could ever imagine when she died.

"... the eulogy of her younger brother, Earl Spencer, burst forth yesterday as an undiluted cry of pain and anger..."

The New York Times, September 7, 1997

(opposite page) The funeral of Diana, Princess of Wales, Westminster Abbey, September 6, 1997

(left inset) Princess Diana's brother, Earl Charles Spencer, addresses the congregation during the funeral service for his sister.

(right inset) Earl Charles Spencer, Prince William, Prince Harry, and Prince Charles stand by the hearse as it pulls away from Westminster Abbey carrying the body of Princess Diana.

EARL CHARLES SPENCER'S EULOGY FOR PRINCESS DIANA

Westminster Abbey, London, September 6, 1997

More than any other kind of speech, a eulogy has potential for enormous impact because of the pools of emotion that are just waiting to be stirred and emptied in a satisfying tear-filled catharsis.

Rarely has there been the kind of ambient emotion surrounding a eulogy as there was when Earl Charles Spencer, Princess Diana's younger brother, took his place above the crowd at Westminster Abbey and before the world's television cameras.

Remarkably, Spencer was able to hit all of the right notes, and created, as famed speechwriter Peggy Noonan called it, "A breathtaking address."

I agree.

ANALYSIS	SPEECH
Notice how the rhythm captures us when phrases are grouped in threes.	I stand before you today the representative of a family in grief, in a country in mourning before a world in shock.
By acknowledging the audience and their feelings, Spencer makes everyone feel personally connected to the speech.	We are all united not only in our desire to pay our respects to Diana but rather in our need to do so. For such was her extraordinary appeal that the tens of millions of people taking part in this service all over the world via television and radio who never actually met her, feel that they too lost someone close to them in the early hours of Sunday morning. It is a more remarkable tribute to Diana than I can ever hope to offer her today.
I love this last phrase. It immediately tells us who Diana is and cleverly introduces the theme of Diana's personality—her contradictions—and reinforces her role as the world's "Queen of Hearts."	Diana was the very essence of compassion, of duty, of style, of beauty. All over the world she was a symbol of selfless humanity, a standard bearer for the rights of the truly downtrodden, a truly British girl who transcended nationality,
This is a wonderful contradiction that says so much.	… someone with a natural nobility who was classless,
See how elegantly he takes aim at the "mourner" sitting in the first row—Queen Elizabeth II, who many believe insisted on the removal of Diana's title, "Her Royal Highness," as part of the divorce settlement with Prince Charles.	… who proved in the last year that she needed no royal title to continue to generate her particular brand of magic.
A healing perspective for the millions who were so visibly pained by her passing. Notice how effortlessly he shifts from talking *about* Diana to talking directly *to* her, generating intimacy in the process.	Today is our chance to say thank you for the way you brightened our lives, even though God granted you but half a life. We will all feel cheated always that you were taken from us so young and yet we must learn to be grateful that you came along at all. Only now that you are gone do we truly appreciate what we are now without and we want you to know that life without you is very, very difficult.
Note the effective use of repetition: with the word *strength*.	We have all despaired at our loss over the past week and only the strength of the message you gave us through your years of giving has afforded us the strength to move forward.

There is a temptation to rush to canonise your memory. There is no need to do so. You stand tall enough as a human being of unique qualities not to need to be seen as a saint. Indeed, to sanctify your memory would be to miss out on the very core of your being, your wonderfully mischievous sense of humour with the laugh that bent you double, your joy for life transmitted wherever you took your smile, and the sparkle in those unforgettable eyes, your boundless energy which you could barely contain.

But your greatest gift was your intuition and it was a gift you used wisely. This is what underpinned all your wonderful attributes. And if we look to analyse what it was about you that had such a wide appeal we find it in your instinctive feel for what was really important in all our lives.

Notice how he makes his sister come to life, as he names the very specific human qualities that made her special. Specific references to real-life qualities or behaviors, in any speech, are almost always greatly appreciated by an audience.

Without your God-given sensitivity we would be immersed in greater ignorance at the anguish of AIDS and HIV sufferers, the plight of the homeless, the isolation of lepers, the random destruction of landmines. Diana explained to me once that it was her innermost feelings of suffering that made it possible for her to connect with her constituency of the rejected.

Great phrase—*constituency of the rejected*—and a wonderful public relations turn as well. Spencer is addressing those critics who accused Diana of being too self-absorbed or insincere or manipulative in her work with her charities.

And here we come to another truth about her. For all the status, the glamour, the applause, Diana remained throughout a very insecure person at heart, almost childlike in her desire to do good for others so she could release herself from deep feelings of unworthiness of which her eating disorders were merely a symptom.

Shifting back into the third person he continues the public relations effort, describing how Diana transcended her struggle with eating and other disorders and turned them to the benefit of the world.

The world sensed this part of her character and cherished her for her vulnerability, whilst admiring her for her honesty.

Now, he confirms that this princess was really just like "regular" people, something everyone felt in their deep connection to her.

The last time I saw Diana was on July the first, her birthday, in London, when typically she was not taking time to celebrate her special day with friends but was guest of honour at a special charity fund-raising evening. She sparkled of course, but I would rather cherish the days I spent with her in March when she came to visit me and my children in our home in South Africa. I am proud of the fact that apart from when she was on public display meeting President Mandela, we managed to contrive to stop the ever-present paparazzi from getting a single picture of her.

That meant a lot to her.

These were days I will always treasure. It was as if we'd been transported back to our childhood when we spent such an enormous amount of time together, the two youngest in the family.

Fundamentally she had not changed at all from the big sister who mothered me as a baby, fought with me at school and endured those long train journeys between our parents' homes with me at weekends.

Personal touches like this are always wonderful. By letting us see their relationship, Spencer allows us to feel closer to him and to Diana. By making this oblique reference to the fact that they came from a broken family, he reinforces another connection many felt they shared with Diana.

It is a tribute to her level-headedness and strength that despite the most bizarre-like life imaginable after her childhood, she remained intact, true to herself.

With the slang term *bizarre-like*, he shifts gears and resumes his beautifully worded attack—this time on the media.

From left, the Duke of Edinburgh, Prince William, Earl Spencer, Prince Harry, and Prince Charles wait near St. James's Palace to follow the coffin of Diana, Princess of Wales, to London's Westminster Abbey. In the background are representatives of charities that had been supported by Princess Diana. They also followed the coffin.

The casual phrase, *It is baffling* makes this part of the speech even more personal. Next comes one of my favorite phrases, which is simultaneously powerful yet subtle. In just a few words he cements the theme of Diana's goodness and simultaneously delivers a direct shot at, presumably, anyone who was in any way her critic—*the opposite end of the moral spectrum.* Wow!

There is no doubt that she was looking for a new direction in her life at this time. She talked endlessly of getting away from England, mainly because of the treatment she received at the hands of the newspapers. I don't think she ever understood why her genuinely good intentions were sneered at by the media, why there appeared to be a permanent quest on their behalf to bring her down.

It is baffling. My own, and only, explanation is that genuine goodness is threatening to those at the opposite end of the moral spectrum.

This is Earl Spencer's own favorite line (see interview). He has taken her very name and eternally bound up her image with ancient mythology, with something larger than life, with a goddess, no less! In addition, to say that she was *hunted* creates in the audience a visceral image as well as real empathy with the feelings Diana must have experienced on a daily basis.

It is a point to remember that of all the ironies about Diana, perhaps the greatest is this: that a girl given the name of the ancient goddess of hunting was, in the end, the most hunted person of the modern age.

Another salvo at the Royal Family. Notice both the anger and the protectiveness that comes with the words *we, your blood family*, and how an already powerful speech becomes even more powerful as Earl Spencer shifts from third to first person, again speaks directly to his sister and allows his own emotions, his own vulnerability, to come through as he speaks.

She would want us today to pledge ourselves to protecting her beloved boys William and Harry from a similar fate. And I do this here, Diana, on your behalf. We will not allow them to suffer the anguish that used regularly to drive you to tearful despair.

Beyond that, on behalf of your mother and sisters, I pledge that we, your blood family, . . .

will do all we can to continue the imaginative way in which you were steering these two exceptional young men so that their souls are not simply immersed by duty and tradition but can sing openly as you planned.

We fully respect the heritage into which they have both been born, and will always respect and encourage them in their royal role. But we, like you, recognise the need for them to experience as many different aspects of life as possible to arm them spiritually and emotionally for the years ahead. I know you would have expected nothing less from us.

William and Harry, we all care desperately for you today. We are all chewed up with sadness at the loss of a woman who wasn't even our mother. How great your suffering is we cannot even imagine.

I would like to end by thanking God for the small mercies he has shown us at this dreadful time; for taking Diana at her most beautiful and radiant and when she had so much joy in her private life.

Above all, we give thanks for the life of a woman I am so proud to be able to call my sister: the unique, the complex, the extraordinary and irreplaceable Diana, whose beauty, both internal and external, will never be extinguished from our minds.

He hits his target. Ever so diplomatically, he essentially tells the Queen, "We won't let you squash their spirits like you tried to do to their mother's!"

These words—*spiritually and emotionally*—were carefully chosen. (It was just days before that Queen Elizabeth had seemingly been forced to take to the airwaves to show that she was emotionally affected by Diana's death.) Spencer also uses an excellent communication technique designed to reduce resistance to what will follow: He begins by asserting the traditionalists' (the Royal Family's) beliefs and then talks about less traditional (Diana's) beliefs on how her children should be reared.

[Here Earl Spencer became so overcome with emotion that he almost could not continue (see interview).]

Saying what so many were thinking here, notice how graphic the phrase *chewed up* is. You can almost feel what he is feeling.

This is a beautiful way to end. Can you feel the rhythm that he builds with the words *the unique, the complex, the extraordinary*? With this uplifting close, Spencer allowed those inside Westminster Abbey and those listening outside and around the world to let go and celebrate this amazing life. The entire Abbey echoed with thunderous applause.

The Eulogy and Princess Diana

THE SPEECH—WHAT TO LOOK FOR: With his great use of imagery, Earl Charles Spencer vividly captured both his sister's magical qualities and the tragedy of her life. At the same time, he subtly and gracefully criticized those he felt had made her unhappy: the press and, especially, the Queen and the Royal Family.

THE DELIVERY—WHAT TO LISTEN FOR: The largest audience ever to hear a speech heard a calm, composed, flawless oration, well-paced as it rose to a crescendo, which created such emotion that it caused a highly inappropriate but irresistible reaction—thunderous applause.

THE PERSON—QUALITIES OF GREATNESS: Diana was a mass of contradictions that were played about on the world stage almost daily: The pinnacle of royalty with the needs and problems of many women; a confident, charismatic enchantress and a lonely insecure woman. She was, as her brother said, "The unique, the complex, the extraordinary and irreplaceable Diana."

FRANKLIN DELANO ROOSEVELT

AND

GEORGE W. BUSH

Days of Infamy

Standing on the deck of the USS *Enterprise* on December 7, 2001, exactly sixty years after that first "date that would live in infamy," George W. Bush connected the events of 1941 and 2001—not only for the devastation they wrought, but for the strength that America and its people exhibited in their aftermath. As Bush eloquently put it:

> What happened at Pearl Harbor was the start of a long and terrible war for America. Yet out of that surprise attack grew a steadfast resolve that made America freedom's defender.

> And that mission, our great calling, continues to this hour, as the brave men and women of our military fight the forces of terror in Afghanistan and around the world.

On December 7, 1941 as on September 11, 2001, the United States was attacked on its own soil. Almost immediately, Presidents Franklin D. Roosevelt and George W. Bush—two very different men confronting two very different attacks—rose to the challenge of rallying a frightened nation while at the same time explaining that defending the country could cost lives and would require sacrifice.

On December 7, 1941 at 7:53 A.M., the Japanese air attack on the U.S. Pacific Fleet stationed at Pearl Harbor began; a second strike hit at 8:55. The attack was over at 9:55. In the first wave 183 Japanese warplanes—in the second, 167—swooped in and killed a total of 2,335 American soldiers and 68 civilians. Another 1,178 were wounded in the surprise attack on Honolulu, Hawaii. In addition, five

(above) President Franklin Roosevelt signs the official Declaration of War with Japan.

(above right) President George W. Bush speaks to his staff inside his private dining room prior to his address to the nation, September 11, 2001.

(right) Minutes after the dust settles from the outer wall of the Pentagon, September 11, 2001, rescue personnel return to the scene to continue efforts after the terror attack.

battleships were damaged, another three were sunk; nine other ships were destroyed along with 188 aircraft. The Japanese lost 27 planes and five midget submarines.

On September 11, 2001 at 8:45 A.M., a huge passenger plane crashed into the North Tower of New York City's World Trade Center; at 9:03 A.M., a second airliner hit the South Tower. At approximately 9:40, a third struck the Pentagon. At around 9:48, the South Tower collapsed; the North Tower came down at around 10:28. At 10:10 A.M., a fourth plane crashed near Shanksville, in rural western Pennsylvania (about 80 miles southwest of Pittsburgh). In all, it is believed that about 3,000 people died in the attacks that were carried out by nineteen Muslims led by Osama bin Laden, leader of a fundamentalist Muslim group called al Qaeda, who lived in Taliban-controlled Afghanistan.

The United States and the rest of the world were stunned.

Franklin D. Roosevelt
and
George W. Bush
"Days of Infamy"

At the same podium in the same historic room in the Capitol building—separated by sixty years of history and technology, but united by tragic events—Franklin Delano Roosevelt and George W. Bush addressed the Congress, the nation, and the world in times of ultimate crises.

But while there are great similarities, there were also great differences in what the two men needed to accomplish as well as in their styles. Roosevelt, the experienced president, was a polished orator; Bush, in office less than a year, has no natural gift for oratory. Nevertheless, called to this high purpose, the tone and impact of these two addresses are remarkably similar. As we read Roosevelt's speech, it becomes immediately apparent that, in 1941 before the advent of television and twenty-four-hour news coverage, Roosevelt—to a large extent—had to provide the news to many who would not yet have heard it, or if they had heard, fully understood its meaning. The situation was completely different by the time Bush delivered his speech. Not only was it delivered nine days after the attacks on the World Trade Center and the Pentagon, but also many listening to his speech had seen the events as they occurred, almost from the very beginning. Few could avoid seeing them replayed and analyzed from every perspective in the days preceding Bush's address to Congress. He, therefore, did not have to present the facts as much as he had to give them meaning and provide direction.

Franklin Delano Roosevelt
". . . a date which will live in infamy. . ."

Request for Declaration of War after Bombing of Pearl Harbor, Joint Session of the Congress, December 8, 1941

When giving speeches, as with any form of communication, many times less is more. Abraham Lincoln's 1863 Gettysburg Address, for example, was only 266 words. Like Lincoln, Roosevelt wrote this speech himself. It, too, is short on words but long on punch. As was his style, Roosevelt begins by getting right to the point, and, like the Gettysburg Address, he places it in time by starting with a date.

ANALYSIS

Roosevelt gets right to the point with a concise statement of events. But what makes this one sentence—one of the most famous of Roosevelt's long career—so memorable are seven little words. With those seven words—*a date which will live in infamy*—Roosevelt conveys the importance of that historic moment as well as his own strong feelings about it. Yet as powerful as the words themselves are, it is the rich, booming, enormously expressive tone of his voice—on this one phrase—that truly elevates this sentence to epic heights.

Notice how crisp his sentences are as he presents the details, like a lawyer presenting a case to a jury. No "filler," just to-the-point, direct information.

SPEECH

To the Congress of the United States:

Yesterday, December 7, 1941—a date which will live in infamy—the United States of America was suddenly and deliberately attacked by naval and air forces of the Empire of Japan.

The United States was at peace with that nation and, at the solicitation of Japan, was still in conversation with its government and its emperor looking toward the maintenance of peace in the Pacific. Indeed, one hour after Japanese air squadrons had commenced bombing in Oahu, the Japanese ambassador to the United States and his colleagues delivered to the Secretary of State a formal reply to a recent American message. While this reply stated that it seemed useless to continue the existing diplomatic negotiations, it contained no threat or hint of war or armed attack.

It will be recorded that the distance of Hawaii from Japan makes it obvious that the attack was deliberately planned many days or even weeks ago. During the intervening time the Japanese government has deliberately sought to deceive the United States by false statements and expressions of hope for continued peace.

The attack yesterday on the Hawaiian Islands has caused severe damage to American naval and military forces. Very many American lives have been lost. In addition, American ships have been reported torpedoed on the high seas between San Francisco and Honolulu.

Yesterday, the Japanese government also launched an attack against Malaya. Last night, Japanese forces attacked Hong Kong. Last night, Japanese forces attacked Guam. Last night, Japanese forces attacked the Philippine Islands. Last night, the Japanese attacked Wake Island. This morning, the Japanese attacked Midway Island.

> Still setting out the facts, he uses tight, short sentences, one after the other to build momentum.

Japan has, therefore, undertaken a surprise offensive extending throughout the Pacific area. The facts of yesterday speak for themselves. The people of the United States have already formed their opinions and well understand the implications to the very life and safety of our nation.

As Commander in Chief of the Army and Navy, I have directed that all measures be taken for our defense.

> It's interesting in this age of POWs, to note the unequivocal assumption Roosevelt makes about public opinion.

Always will we remember the character of the onslaught against us. No matter how long it may take us to overcome this premeditated invasion, the American people in their righteous might will win through to absolute victory.

I believe I interpret the will of the Congress and of the people when I assert that we will not only defend ourselves to the uttermost, but will make very certain that this form of treachery shall never endanger us again.

Hostilities exist. There is no blinking at the fact that our people, our territory and our interests are in grave danger.

> Having made this very clear statement of control and authority, Roosevelt is now free to focus on the emotional needs of the American people and to address their feeling of righteous indignation and to assure them of ultimate victory.

With confidence in our armed forces—with the unbounding determination of our people—we will gain the inevitable triumph—so help us God.

> As the President draws to a close, he raises the "goosebump factor" a notch with two surefire oratorical devices in one sentence: the use of triplets—three short, punchy phrases back to back—and the use of a spiritual reference.

I ask that the Congress declare that since the unprovoked and dastardly attack by Japan on Sunday, December seventh, a state of war has existed between the United States and the Japanese empire.

> Because this is both an address to the American people, as well as a formal request for a Declaration of War with Japan, Roosevelt wanted to make certain the "man-on-the-street" connected emotionally to the coming war effort. The word *dastardly*—a somewhat old-fashioned word (even for 1941!)—resonates and is memorable precisely because it was not commonly used, and when it was, it was almost always associated with villains and despicable acts.

Franklin D. Roosevelt

THE SPEECH—WHAT TO LOOK FOR: As in his Inaugural Address eight years earlier, Roosevelt's words are strong, unequivocal, direct, and inspire enormous confidence in a moment of national crisis.

THE DELIVERY—WHAT TO LISTEN FOR: As in his Inaugural Address, the solid, deep voice—highly punctuated with pauses and exaggerated expression—amplify the inherent confidence of the words and make it almost impossible not to feel secure under this man's leadership.

The Person—Qualities of Greatness: A true leader. Knowing what is required in the moment, FDR replaces his patented wit with steely determination, his lofty eloquence with a concise, matter-of-fact message and, nevertheless, stirs the nation with his strength and supreme confidence.

George W. Bush

". . . we are a country awakened to danger and called to defend freedom."

On the Bombings of the World Trade Center and the Pentagon, Address to a Joint Session of Congress, September 20, 2001

The moment was there for a great speech and the writing was masterful, but the real reason this speech worked was because George Bush owned every word. These were not abstract concepts to him, there were no words with which he was uncomfortable. Although he did not write the words, it is clear that he felt every feeling and controlled every syllable. His speechwriters had done what only the best can do: They captured the words and emotions—the very personality—of their boss.

ANALYSIS	SPEECH
Setting the tone, with no word wasted, George Bush gets right to the point and compliments his audience, accenting the patriotic fervor that had been spreading across the nation.	Mr. Speaker, Mr. President Pro Tempore, members of Congress, and fellow Americans: In the normal course of events, Presidents come to this chamber to report on the state of the Union. Tonight, no such report is needed. It has already been delivered by the American people.
By naming a hero and pointing to his wife, Bush puts a human face on the issue and gives the audience (all of America) a concrete reason to support his plan. In this media-savvy age, this has become a very common technique.	We have seen it in the courage of passengers, who rushed terrorists to save others on the ground—passengers like an exceptional man named Todd Beamer. And would you please help me to welcome his wife, Lisa Beamer, here tonight.
Those words are not only poetic. By making reference to the three languages, Bush is beginning to make the very important point that this event, and the U.S. response to it, is not about one religious or ethnic group against another, and that America, with its diverse population, is united.	We have seen the state of our Union in the endurance of rescuers, working past exhaustion. We have seen the unfurling of flags, the lighting of candles, the giving of blood, the saying of prayers—in English, Hebrew, and Arabic. We have seen the decency of a loving and giving people who have made the grief of strangers their own.
Excellent way to nail the theme.	My fellow citizens, for the last nine days, the entire world has seen for itself the state of our Union—and it is strong. Tonight we are a country awakened to danger and called to defend freedom. Our grief has turned to anger, and anger to resolution.
What a great sentence! The symmetry of the images, the three short phrases, and the use of the word *justice* in all three.	Whether we bring our enemies to justice, or bring justice to our enemies, justice will be done.
Notice how much more Bush's thank-yous mean and how much more we feel his gratitude because he has spelled out the specifics.	I thank the Congress for its leadership at such an important time. All of America was touched on the evening of the tragedy to see Republicans and Democrats joined together on the steps of this Capitol, singing "God Bless America." And you did more than sing; you acted, by delivering $40 billion to rebuild our communities and meet the needs of our military. Speaker Hastert, Minority Leader Gephardt, Majority Leader Daschle and Senator Lott, I thank you for your friendship, for your leadership and for your service to our country. And on behalf of the American people, I thank the world for its outpouring of support. America will never forget the sounds of our National Anthem playing at Buckingham Palace, on the streets of Paris, and at Berlin's Brandenburg Gate. We will not forget South Korean children gathering to pray outside our embassy in Seoul, or the prayers of sympathy offered at a mosque in Cairo. We will not forget moments of silence and days of mourning in Australia and Africa and Latin America.

Nor will we forget the citizens of 80 other nations who died with our own: dozens of Pakistanis; more than 130 Israelis; more than 250 citizens of India; men and women from El Salvador, Iran, Mexico and Japan; and hundreds of British citizens. America has no truer friend than Great Britain. Once again, we are joined together in a great cause—so honored the British Prime Minister has crossed an ocean to show his unity of purpose with America. Thank you for coming, friend.

Usually numbers are boring, but these are chilling and they are included for just that reason.

In contrast, Bush's acknowledgment of the presence of Tony Blair is made warmer—particularly with his use of the word *friend*.

On September the 11th, enemies of freedom committed an act of war against our country. Americans have known wars—but for the past 136 years, they have been wars on foreign soil, except for one Sunday in 1941. Americans have known the casualties of war—but not at the center of a great city on a peaceful morning. Americans have known surprise attacks—but never before on thousands of civilians. All of this was brought upon us in a single day—and night fell on a different world, a world where freedom itself is under attack.

Analogies like this are a very effective tool. In one sentence Bush connects an unknown, al Qaeda, to images of mafia mayhem and violence that exist in the minds of every American and many around the world.

Americans have many questions tonight. Americans are asking: Who attacked our country? The evidence we have gathered all points to a collection of loosely affiliated terrorist organizations known as al Qaeda. They are the same murderers indicted for bombing American embassies in Tanzania and Kenya, and responsible for bombing the USS *Cole*.

Al Qaeda is to terror what the mafia is to crime. But its goal is not making money; its goal is remaking the world—and imposing its radical beliefs on people everywhere.

The question-and-answer technique was used extensively by Winston Churchill; Bush will use it four times in this speech.

The terrorists practice a fringe form of Islamic extremism that has been rejected by Muslim scholars and the vast majority of Muslim clerics—a fringe movement that perverts the peaceful teachings of Islam.

Because of the fear of a violent Muslim reaction to any action by the United States, Bush had to make a clear distinction between the terrorists and the Islamic religion. In the next sentence he uses seven subtle and not-so-subtle words and phrases to make this distinction: *fringe, extremism, rejected by Muslim scholars,* (rejected by) *the vast majority of Muslim clerics, fringe* (again), *perverts the peaceful teachings of Islam.*

The terrorists' directive commands them to kill Christians and Jews, to kill all Americans, and make no distinction among military and civilians, including women and children.

This group and its leader—a person named Osama bin Laden—are linked to many other organizations in different countries, including the Egyptian Islamic Jihad and the Islamic Movement of Uzbekistan. There are thousands of these terrorists in more than 60 countries. They are recruited from their own nations and neighborhoods and brought to camps in places like Afghanistan, where they are trained in the tactics of terror. They are sent back to their homes or sent to hide in countries around the world to plot evil and destruction.

The leadership of al Qaeda has great influence in Afghanistan and supports the Taliban regime in controlling most of that country. In Afghanistan, we see al Qaeda's vision for the world. Afghanistan's people have been brutalized—many are starving and many have fled. Women are not allowed to

To make the country receptive to his leadership in this crisis, it is essential that he strike some fear in his audience's hearts. He pulls no punches in doing so here.

By introducing al Qaeda's *vision for the world* before enumerating some of the terrible things the Taliban had inflicted on the people of Afghanistan, Bush both draws the audience in and "demonizes" the enemy. (Specifics are always more powerful than abstract concepts.)

Firefighters comb the remains of the World Trade Center after the collapse, September 11, 2001. In the worst attack on American soil since Pearl Harbor, three hijacked planes slammed into the Pentagon and New York's landmark World Trade Center, demolishing the two 110-story towers that symbolize U.S. financial might.

attend school. You can be jailed for owning a television. Religion can be practiced only as their leaders dictate. A man can be jailed in Afghanistan if his beard is not long enough.

Two nice logical progressions here: The Taliban is different than the people of Afghanistan and that the Taliban, *by aiding and abetting* al Qaeda, are murderers.

The United States respects the people of Afghanistan—after all, we are currently its largest source of humanitarian aid—but we condemn the Taliban regime. It is not only repressing its own people, it is threatening people everywhere by sponsoring and sheltering and supplying terrorists. By aiding and abetting murder, the Taliban regime is committing murder.

Notice how he gives these seven demands more weight by listing them one after another.

And tonight, the United States of America makes the following demands on the Taliban: Deliver to United States authorities all the leaders of al Qaeda who hide in your land. Release all foreign nationals, including American citizens, you have unjustly imprisoned. Protect foreign journalists, diplomats and aid workers in your country. Close immediately and permanently every terrorist training camp in Afghanistan, and hand over every terrorist, and every person in their support structure, to appropriate authorities. Give the United States full access to terrorist training camps, so we can make sure they are no longer operating.

171

These demands are not open to negotiation or discussion. The Taliban must act, and act immediately. They will hand over the terrorists, or they will share in their fate.

Bush lays down the gauntlet. This last line, especially, is terrific. Notice how much is said in that last phrase.

I also want to speak tonight directly to Muslims throughout the world. We respect your faith. It's practiced freely by many millions of Americans, and by millions more in countries that America counts as friends. Its teachings are good and peaceful, and those who commit evil in the name of Allah blaspheme the name of Allah. The terrorists are traitors to their own faith, trying, in effect, to hijack Islam itself.

The enemy of America is not our many Muslim friends; it is not our many Arab friends. Our enemy is a radical network of terrorists, and every government that supports them.

Our war on terror begins with al Qaeda, but it does not end there. It will not end until every terrorist group of global reach has been found, stopped and defeated.

The major challenge of this speech is to heal the wounds, rally the country for the fight ahead, and, at the same time, not offend the United States' and the world's Muslim population. Talking directly to them, Bush emphasizes that the war is not against them. The reference to the hijacking of Islam does more than subtly recall the four hijacked planes, it says to Muslims that the United States knows that it is not Islam or Muslims who are responsible. He continues this theme more directly in the next sentence.

Americans are asking, why do they hate us? They hate what we see right here in this chamber—a democratically elected government. Their leaders are self-appointed. They hate our freedoms—our freedom of religion, our freedom of speech, our freedom to vote and assemble and disagree with each other.

They want to overthrow existing governments in many Muslim countries, such as Egypt, Saudi Arabia, and Jordan. They want to drive Israel out of the Middle East. They want to drive Christians and Jews out of vast regions of Asia and Africa.

The use of a question is not only a surefire way to make even a long speech interesting (because it alters the rhythm of the speech), it also is an excellent way to focus the audience on the answers you want them to hear. This is the second use of Churchill's technique.

These terrorists kill not merely to end lives, but to disrupt and end a way of life. With every atrocity, they hope that America grows fearful, retreating from the world and forsaking our friends. They stand against us, because we stand in their way.

Again, using the same word (*stand*) in different ways makes a poetic and powerful sentence.

We are not deceived by their pretenses to piety. We have seen their kind before. They are the heirs of all the murderous ideologies of the 20th century. By sacrificing human life to serve their radical visions—by abandoning every value except the will to power—they follow in the path of fascism, and Nazism, and totalitarianism. And they will follow that path all the way, to where it ends: in history's unmarked grave of discarded lies.

You can almost feel the anger and determination drip from Bush's voice as he catalogs the *evil empires* of the past century and ends with a startling and visually overwhelming last sentence in which he dramatically consigns the terrorists to the fates of their predecessors. It is a beautiful sentence, and one that rightly received enormous applause. By making the sentence subtle, visually rich, and poetic, Bush makes a much more effective point than by simply saying, "We will defeat them."

Americans are asking: How will we fight and win this war? We will direct every resource at our command—every means of diplomacy, every tool of intelligence, every instrument of law enforcement, every financial influence, and every necessary weapon of war—to the disruption and to the defeat of the global terror network.

And, using Churchill's "blood, toil, tears, and sweat" speech as a model, he continues asking and answering questions. Compare the language in this paragraph with Churchill's: "you ask, what is our policy," "you ask, what is our aim."

At the edge of the "Ground Zero" site of the World Trade Center disaster, United States flags adorn a memorial board with the names of all those lost in the September 11, 2001 attacks.

An effective leader uses a speech to set realistic expectations…

This war will not be like the war against Iraq a decade ago, with a decisive liberation of territory and a swift conclusion. It will not look like the air war above Kosovo two years ago, where no ground troops were used and not a single American was lost in combat.

Our response involves far more than instant retaliation and isolated strikes. Americans should not expect one battle, but a lengthy campaign, unlike any other we have ever seen. It may include dramatic strikes, visible on TV, and covert operations, secret even in success. We will starve terrorists of funding, turn them one against another, drive them from place to place, until there is no refuge or no rest. And we will pursue nations that provide aid or safe haven to terrorism.

and make the options very clear.

Every nation, in every region, now has a decision to make. Either you are with us, or you are with the terrorists. From this day forward, any nation that continues to harbor or support terrorism will be regarded by the United States as a hostile regime.

Our nation has been put on notice: We are not immune from attack. We will take defensive measures against terrorism to protect Americans. Today, dozens of federal departments and agencies, as well as state and local governments, have responsibilities affecting homeland security. These efforts must be coordinated at the highest level. So tonight I announce the creation of a Cabinet-level position reporting directly to me—the Office of Homeland Security.

And tonight I also announce a distinguished American to lead this effort, to strengthen American security: a military veteran, an effective governor, a true patriot, a trusted friend—Pennsylvania's Tom Ridge. He will lead, oversee and coordinate a comprehensive national strategy to safeguard our country against terrorism, and respond to any attacks that may come.

These measures are essential. But the only way to defeat terrorism as a threat to our way of life is to stop it, eliminate it, and destroy it where it grows.

Many will be involved in this effort, from FBI agents to intelligence operatives to the reservists we have called to active duty. All deserve our thanks, and all have our prayers. And tonight, a few miles from the damaged Pentagon, I have a message for our military: Be ready.

Because he is not by nature erudite or long-winded, Bush is much more comfortable with and excels at delivering short, punchy sentences or phrases. Notice the power and authority invested in and the emotion he is able to generate with those two short words. *Be ready!*

I've called the Armed Forces to alert, and there is a reason. The hour is coming when America will act, and you will make us proud.

This is not, however, just America's fight. And what is at stake is not just America's freedom. This is the world's fight. This is civilization's fight. This is the fight of all who believe in progress and pluralism, tolerance and freedom.

We ask every nation to join us. We will ask, and we will need, the help of police forces, intelligence services, and banking systems around the world. The United States is grateful that many nations and many international organizations have already responded—with sympathy and with support. Nations from Latin America, to Asia, to Africa, to Europe, to the Islamic world. Perhaps the NATO Charter reflects best the attitude of the world: An attack on one is an attack on all.

The last sentence is critical, and perhaps his most important argument in his effort to enlist countries from NATO and around the world in his fragile coalition against al Qaeda and global terrorism.

The civilized world is rallying to America's side. They understand that if this terror goes unpunished, their own cities, their own citizens may be next. Terror, unanswered, can not only bring down buildings, it can threaten the stability of legitimate governments. And you know what—we're not going to allow it.

That last sentence is surprisingly casual, but it is consistent with Bush's personality, which is what makes it work.

Americans are asking: What is expected of us? I ask you to live your lives, and hug your children. I know many citizens have fears tonight, and I ask you to be calm and resolute, even in the face of a continuing threat.

I ask you to uphold the values of America, and remember why so many have come here. We are in a fight for our principles, and our first responsibility is to live by them. No one should be singled out for unfair treatment or unkind words because of their ethnic background or religious faith.

I ask you to continue to support the victims of this tragedy with your contributions. Those who want to give can go to a central source of information, libertyunites.org, to find the names of groups providing direct help in New York, Pennsylvania, and Virginia.

The thousands of FBI agents who are now at work in this investigation may need your cooperation, and I ask you to give it.

I ask for your patience, with the delays and inconveniences that may accompany tighter security; and for your patience in what will be a long struggle.

I ask your continued participation and confidence in the American economy. Terrorists attacked a symbol of American prosperity. They did not touch its source.

For the fourth time, he again becomes Churchillian and resumes the question–answer mode. His short sentences, in reply, are perfectly suited to Bush's style.

Moving now to bring the country together, Bush repeats the words *we* and *our* seven times apiece.

By inviting Pataki and especially Giuliani to be in the audience, Bush brings the visceral emotions that people had about New York into the Capitol and into the speech.

As he begins to close, Bush wisely moves from specifics to larger, loftier themes—from details to talk of ages and generations and global values.

He ends this philosophical portion of the speech with another powerful threesome of short phrases, again adopting the cadence and message of Churchill's war speeches.

But nothing, not even lofty poetry, is more emotionally compelling than real-life, human experience that the audience can relate to in their gut and in their heart. Here Bush brings it down to the common level that everyone can see and feel.

America is successful because of the hard work, and creativity, and enterprise of our people. These were the true strengths of our economy before September 11th, and they are our strengths today.

And, finally, please continue praying for the victims of terror and their families, for those in uniform, and for our great country. Prayer has comforted us in sorrow, and will help strengthen us for the journey ahead.

Tonight I thank my fellow Americans for what you have already done and for what you will do. And ladies and gentlemen of the Congress, I thank you, their representatives, for what you have already done and for what we will do together.

Tonight, we face new and sudden national challenges. We will come together to improve air safety, to dramatically expand the number of air marshals on domestic flights, and take new measures to prevent hijacking. We will come together to promote stability and keep our airlines flying, with direct assistance during this emergency.

We will come together to give law enforcement the additional tools it needs to track down terror here at home. We will come together to strengthen our intelligence capabilities to know the plans of terrorists before they act, and find them before they strike.

We will come together to take active steps that strengthen America's economy, and put our people back to work.

Tonight we welcome two leaders who embody the extraordinary spirit of all New Yorkers: Governor George Pataki and Mayor Rudolph Giuliani. As a symbol of America's resolve, my administration will work with Congress, and these two leaders, to show the world that we will rebuild New York City.

After all that has just passed—all the lives taken, and all the possibilities and hopes that died with them—it is natural to wonder if America's future is one of fear. Some speak of an age of terror. I know there are struggles ahead, and dangers to face. But this country will define our times, not be defined by them. As long as the United States of America is determined and strong, this will not be an age of terror; this will be an age of liberty, here and across the world.

Great harm has been done to us. We have suffered great loss. And in our grief and anger we have found our mission and our moment. Freedom and fear are at war. The advance of human freedom—the great achievement of our time, and the great hope of every time—now depends on us. Our nation—this generation—will lift a dark threat of violence from our people and our future. We will rally the world to this cause by our efforts, by our courage. We will not tire, we will not falter, and we will not fail.

It is my hope that in the months and years ahead, life will return almost to normal. We'll go back to our lives and routines, and that is good. Even grief recedes with time and grace. But our resolve must not pass. Each of us will remember what happened that day, and to whom it happened. We'll remember the moment the news came—where we were and what we were doing. Some will remember an image of a fire, or a story of rescue. Some will carry memories of a face and a voice gone forever.

And I will carry this: It is the police shield of a man named George Howard, who died at the World Trade Center trying to save others. It was given to me by his mom, Arlene, as a proud memorial to her son. This is my reminder of lives that ended, and a task that does not end.

I will not forget this wound to our country or those who inflicted it. I will not yield; I will not rest; I will not relent in waging this struggle for freedom and security for the American people.	He wisely takes the emotion he has just stirred and brings it back to himself with short, punchy phrases.
The course of this conflict is not known, yet its outcome is certain.	This is a great line! And so much more effective and even more confident than "We will prevail."
Freedom and fear, justice and cruelty, have always been at war, and we know that God is not neutral between them.	This is another example of adding power by being indirect rather than straightforward—a technique used consistently throughout this speech.
Fellow citizens, we'll meet violence with patient justice—assured of the rightness of our cause, and confident of the victories to come. In all that lies before us, may God grant us wisdom, and may He watch over the United States of America. Thank you.	And, as Roosevelt did, Bush defers to God in a spiritual and patriotic close.

George W. Bush

THE SPEECH—WHAT TO LOOK FOR: Smooth and flowing with great energy, this speech is filled with memorable, beautifully written sound bites. It is a hard-hitting, practical speech that also has just the right amount of high principle and lofty values to energize the speaker, the Congress, and the country.

THE DELIVERY—WHAT TO LISTEN FOR: When a speaker fully "owns" every word of a speech, as is the case here, it transforms the speech into a conversation and the speaker into an orator, no matter how natural or awkward he or she is.

THE PERSON—QUALITIES OF GREATNESS: The emotion and call to arms of the events of September 11 allow the former Yale yell leader to be fully himself and, impressively, own his words.

ACKNOWLEDGMENTS

We would like to thank and congratulate Ellen Schneid Coleman, our publisher and editor, whose patience and perseverance steadily guided this project home. Her love and passion for history and words—which were ever present—kept her going when lack of sleep, frustration, and blown deadlines dictated otherwise.

Our thanks and gratitude go to:

Our research assistant, Wendy Calhoun, for her exceptional work and superlative organization.

Our "everything assistants" Elise Ballard and Lauren Levy for their help and for charming everyone they met.

Andrew Carroll, the co-editor of the wonderful *In Our Own Words,* who gave generously of his time, wisdom, and resources, and whose suggestions showed an unparalleled lack of ego and a true dedication to the cause of knowledge. Thank you for your friendship.

Jeff Greenfield and Helen Thomas for adding their incomparable experience and prestige and meaningful words.

Edmund Morris for his wonderful reading of Theodore Roosevelt's never-recorded speech at the Grand Canyon.

James Gandolfini and his agent, David Brownstein, for helping to reproduce a missing moment in history with James's poignant rendition of Lou Gehrig's Farewell Address.

Governor Mario Cuomo for his reflections.

Larry King for his insights.

Melody Miller for her passionate dedication to the memories of John and Robert Kennedy.

Earl Spencer for his interview, and Lady Sarah McQuorcodale, Paul Burrell, Linda Tempel, and David Fawkes for their help with the chapter on his eulogy to Princess Diana.

Historian Deborah Mark for her research; Tsetin Panchenchurias and Tenzin Geyche Tethong for their assistance with the Dalai Lama; John Gable, for so many great stories about Theodore Roosevelt; Ted Lapkin and Anthea Morton for Winston Churchill; Israel's Counsel General Yuval Rotem, Minister Yulli Tamir and Avi Gott for their help with Yitzhak Rabin; Col. Davis for Gen. MacArthur; Alida Black for Eleanor Roosevelt; Congressman Rick Lazio for his playful advocacy on behalf of every Republican who ever gave a speech; Nick Morgan, for his great knowledge of speeches; George Stephanopoulis, Dee Dee Myers, Noelia Rodriguez, Pat Caddell, and Richard Riordan for their input; and to White House speechwriters Chris Matthews, Michael Waldman, Tony Snow, Andrei Cherney and Mike Gerson for their vauable insights.

Several people provided access to individuals and/or materials that were critical: Jon Biel; Linda Woolridge; Carolyn Ross and Joanne Goldwater; George Solomon at *The Washington Post;* Dawn Conchie; Anne Dorte Krause at Deutsches Historisches Museum; Michael Dolan, for researching materials at NARA Sound Archives; Richard Fairman at The British Library National Sound Archives for Churchill audio recordings; and the excellent research staffs at the Beverly Hills Public Library and UCLA's Young Research Library.

Tony Seidl and Gene Brissie for bringing this project to us, and Yvette Romero, Sally Hertz, and so many others at Prentice Hall Press for believing in it so strongly.

Richard Greene would also like to thank:

My tremendously supportive father, Martin Greene, for always holding the bar so high and my remarkable mother, Eileen Greene, a real life "Wonder Woman" who, in addition to being there for everyone else, was there for me—as she always has been—when I needed anything and the rest of my extraordinary family, Ed, Larry, Debbie, Susan, Lindsay and Jennifer Greene, Celia and Harry Greene, Sam and Edith Rosenberg. I love you all.

My friend Tony Robbins for inspiring me to leave the practice of law to enter a profession where I wake up every day with a passion to share what I know.

Jennifer Durst, Lord Anthony St. John, Randy Firestone, Meg Mortimer, Katy Selverstone, Gretchen Babarovic, Frank Speno, Tom Healey, Linda Mallis, Paul Gregorowitsch, Wayne Williams, Ron and Osnat Belkin and Dee Riggs for their encouragement and feedback.

My dear friend, Carole Black, for always believing in me and for always telling me to "write a book!"

Brenda Exline, for her love and friendship.

Florie Brizel would also like to thank:

Hashem.

Gesine Thomson, dear friend, mentor and source of inspiration.

Felice and Marc Baritz; Toni Benson; Jonathan Novak; Shelley Elizabeth Reid; and Brad Schreiber.

Rita and Robert Weissmann, who give more than any container can hold; David and Beth Brizel; Farnoush Amid, Mahin "Mommyjoon" Amid and the entire Amid, Nassim and Kamran clans; Aunt Selma; and my extraordinary parents, Nancy and Herb Brizel, who are the finest examples of love, devotion, honor, integrity and charity. Thank you for always believing in me. I love you.

SOURCES

All credits are listed by page numbers. We have made every effort to correctly identify and credit all materials used in *Words That Shook the World*. If any errors have been made, they will be corrected in future editions.

Speeches and Other Print Material

If all material on a page or chapter comes from one source, the source is listed only once.

Lou Gehrig 21 Excerpt from "This Morning with Shirley Povich (7/5/39)," © 1939, The Washington Post Company; *Leonard Shapiro*; 22 Excerpt from a memorial tribute to Shirley Povich (6/5/98, p A01), written by Leonard Shapiro, *Washington Post* staff writer, © 1998, The Washington Post Company; 22 ™/© 2002 Estate of Eleanor Gehrig, by CMG Worldwide Inc., www.LouGehrig.com.

Winston Churchill 27 Excerpt from Speech to House of Commons, June 4, 1940; 28 Speech to House of Commons, June 18, 1940; 29 Speech to Students at The Harrow School, October 29, 1941; 29 Speech given at Westminster College, Fulton, Missouri, March 5, 1946; 31 Address to the House of Commons, May 13, 1940 reproduced with permission of Curtis Brown Ltd., London on behalf of Winston S. Churchill; Copyright Winston S. Churchill.

Douglas MacArthur 36 Statement to Press, March 21, 1942; 37 Farewell Address to a Joint Session of Congress, April 20, 1951; 39–40 Speech On Receiving West Point's Sylvanus Thayer Award, May 1962; 41 Surrender Ceremony on the U.S.S. *Missouri*, September 2, 1945 courtesy The General Douglas MacArthur Foundation, Norfolk, VA.

Albert Einstein Albert Einstein™ HUJ, Represented by The Roger Richman Agency, Inc., www.the richman agency.com.

Eleanor Roosevelt 56 Originally published by the Department of State in "Human Rights and Genocide: Selected Statements; United Nations Resolution Declaration and Conventions," 1949.

John F. Kennedy 63–4 Inaugural Address, January 20, 1961; Remarks at Berlin Wall, June 26, 1963, courtesy The John F. Kennedy Library.

Martin Luther King, Jr. 72 Letter from Birmingham Jail, April 26, 1963, all material copyrighted by Dr. Martin Luther King, Jr. All material copyright renewed by Coretta Scott King and the heirs to the Estate of Dr. Martin Luther King, Jr. and reprinted by arrangement c/o of Writer's House, LLC, as agents for Estate of Dr. Martin Luther, King, Jr.; 73 Speech Accepting Nobel Peace Prize, Nobel Foundation, December

10, 1964, copyright © Nobel Foundation; 74 Speech to Meeting of Clergy and Laity Concerned, April 4, 1967. All material copyrighted by Dr. Martin Luther King, Jr.; 75 Speech in Support of the Striking Sanitation Workers, April 3, 1968; 76 Speech at the March on Washington for Jobs and Freedom, August 28, 1963; 77 *Autobiography of Martin Luther King, Jr.* All material copyright renewed by Coretta Scott King and the heirs to the Estate of Dr. Martin Luther King, Jr., and reprinted by arrangement c/o of Writer's House, LLC as agents for Estate of Dr. Martin Luther King, Jr.

Barry Goldwater 85–92 Republican Presidential Nomination; 1964 Republican National Convention July 16, 1964, courtesy Personal and Political papers of Senator Barry M. Goldwater, Arizona Historical Foundation and the Barry M. Goldwater Family.

Robert F. Kennedy as remembered by Edward M. Kennedy 96 RFK's Remarks on the Death of Dr. Martin Luther King, Jr., April 4, 1968; EMK's Eulogy for Senator Robert F. Kennedy, June 8, 1968, courtesy The John F. Kennedy Library.

Barbara Jordan 106 Democratic National Convention Keynote Address, July 12, 1976; 107–10 Watergate Testimony courtesy the Estate of Barbara Jordan.

Anwar Sadat 113 Address to the Israeli Knesset, November 20, 1977; 113 Statements on Signing Camp David Accords, September 17, 1978: Anwar Sadat, reprinted with permission from Jehan Sadat, Ph.D, widow of President Anwar Sadat, Senior Fellow of the Anwar Sadat Chair for Development and Peace, University of Maryland, College Park; and active public speaker; Menachem Begin, courtesy State of Israel; Jimmy Carter, courtesy Jimmy Carter Library; 114 President Ronald Reagan's Statement on Death of Anwar Sadat, October 6, 1981 courtesy Ronald Reagan Library; 115–18 Speech on the Signing of the Egyptian–Israeli Peace Treaty, March 26, 1979, reprinted with permission from Jehan Sadat, Ph.D., widow of President Anwar Sadat, Senior Fellow of the Anwar Sadat Chair for Development and Peace, University of Maryland, College Park; and active public speaker.

Mario Cuomo 123–32 courtesy Mario Cuomo.

Ronald Reagan 133 Address to the National Association of Evangelicals, Public Papers of the Presidents, courtesy The Ronald Reagan Library; 134 Remarks at the Brandenburg Gate courtesy The Ronald Reagan Library; 135 "High Flight" from "John Magee: the Pilot Poet," which is available from *This England Magazine,* P.O. Box 52, Cheltenham G150 1YQ, UK; 136 Memo; William L. Safire to H.R. Haldeman; 18 July 1969; [H.R. Haldman Personnel Material]; Box 294;

White House Special Files; Staff member and office Files: H.R. Halde-man; Richard M. Nixon Presidential Materials Staff, National Archives at College Park, MD. 137–38 Address to the Nation on the Explosion of the Space Shuttle *Challenger* courtesy The Ronald Reagan Library.

Tenzin Gyatso, 14th Dalai Lama of Tibet 141 Press Release Announcing the Nobel Peace Prize for 1989 Copyright © Nobel Foundation; 143–46 Nobel Acceptance Speech, December 10, 1989, Copyright © Nobel Foundation.

Yitzhak Rabin 150 Address to the United States Congress on Signing Peace Agreement with Jordan, courtesy Dalia Rabin-Pellosof and Yitzhak Rabin Center for Israel Studies; 150 Remarks on Receiving Nobel Prize for Peace, Copyright © Nobel Foundation; 152 Bill Clinton's Eulogy for Rabin, Public Papers of the Presidents, courtesy of National Archives and Records Service; 153–56 Remarks on Signing of the Israeli–Palestinian Declaration of Principles, courtesy Dalia Rabin-Pellosof and Yitzhak Rabin Center for Israel Studies.

Princess Diana as remembered by Earl Spencer 159 Earl Spencer Talks About His Eulogy to Diana, Princess of Wales, reproduced with permission of Earl Spencer and the Althorp Charitable Trust, www.althorp.com; 160 Princess Diana Speaking Out About... courtesy The Diana, Princess Of Wales Memorial Fund, www.theworkcontinues.org; 161–64 Earl Charles Spencer's Eulogy for Princess Diana, reproduced with permission of Earl Spencer and the Althorp Charitable Trust, www.althorp.com.

Photography Credits

If more than one photo appears on a page, credits are listed from left to right (top to bottom). If all photos on a page come from one source, the source is listed only once.

Theodore Roosevelt 1 Bettmann/*CORBIS*; 2 CORBIS; 3 CORBIS; Theodore Roosevelt Collection/Harvard College Library; 4 CORBIS; 5 Library of Congress; PhotoDisc, Inc.; 6 Theodore Roosevelt Collection/Harvard College Library.

Franklin Delano Roosevelt 9 AP/ Wide World Photos; 10 and 11 *(all)*, Courtesy the Franklin D. Roosevelt Library Digital Archives; 12 Courtesy the Franklin D. Roosevelt Library Digital Archives; Bettmann/ *CORBIS*.

Lou Gehrig 19 George Brace/AP/Wide World Photos; 20 and 21 *(all)* Bettmann/*CORBIS*; 22 PictureQuest; Bettmann/*CORBIS*; Bettmann/ *CORBIS*; ™/© 2002 Estate of Eleanor Gehrig, by CMG Worldwide Inc., www.LouGehrig.com.

Winston Churchill 25 Getty Images Inc.; 26 CORBIS; 27 CORBIS; Library of Congress; 28 Bettmann/*CORBIS*; 30 Getty Images Inc.; 32 AP/Wide World Photos; 33 Getty Images Inc.

Douglas MacArthur 35 and 36 The Douglas MacArthur Foundation, Norfolk, VA; 37 The Douglas MacArthur Foundation, Norfolk, VA; AP/Wide World Photos; The Douglas MacArthur Foundation, Norfolk, VA; 38 The Douglas MacArthur Foundation, Norfolk, VA; 39 Getty Images, Inc.; 40, 43 The Douglas MacArthur Foundation, Norfolk, VA.

Albert Einstein 45 Albert Einstein™ HUJ, Represented by The Roger Richman Agency, Inc., www.therichmanagency.com; 42 American Institute of Physics/Emilio Segre Visual Archives; 46 AP/Wide World Photos; Bettmann/*CORBIS*; 47 Austrian *Archives/CORBIS*; Bettmann/*CORBIS*; Bettmann/*CORBIS*; Getty Images Inc.; 50 Underwood & Underwood/*CORBIS*; 51 Getty Images Inc.

Eleanor Roosevelt Courtesy the Franklin D. Roosevelt Library Digital Archives.

John F. Kennedy 61, 62, 63 courtesy The John F. Kennedy Library; 64 Getty Images Inc.; 65 National Archives and Records Administration: Bettmann/*CORBIS*; 66, 67, 69 Deutsches Historisches Museum GmbH.

Martin Luther King, Jr. 71 Flip Schulke/*CORBIS*; 72 The Granger Collection; Bettmann/*CORBIS*; 73 Bettmann/*CORBIS*; Bettmann/*CORBIS*; 74 AP/Wide World Photos; 75 Flip Schulke/*CORBIS*.

Barry Goldwater 81 Prentice-Hall, Inc.; 82 The Barry M. Goldwater Family; 83 Hulton-Deutsch Collection/*CORBIS*; 84 Bettmann/*CORBIS*; 90 Getty Images Inc.

Robert F. Kennedy 93, 94 courtesy The John F. Kennedy Library; 95 courtesy The John F. Kennedy Library; AP/Wide World Photos; 96 courtesy The John F. Kennedy Library; Burt Glinn/Magnum Photos; 97 AP/Wide World Photos; AP/Wide World Photos; 98 courtesy The John F. Kennedy Library; AP/Wide World Photos; 101 AP/Wide World Photos.

Barbara Jordan 103 AP/Wide World Photos; 104 Bettmann/*CORBIS*; 105 *CORBIS*; Bettmann/*CORBIS*; 106 Bettmann/*CORBIS*.

Anwar Sadat 111 Getty Images Inc.; 112 Bettmann/*CORBIS*; 114 David Rubbinger/*CORBIS*; AP/Wide World Photos; 116 David Rubbinger/ *CORBIS*; 117 Kevin Fleming/*CORBIS*.

Mario Cuomo 119 Governor's Office, New York State; 120 Bettmann/ *CORBIS*; 121 White House Photo Office; UPI/*CORBIS*; 122 Wally MacNamee/*CORBIS*; AP/Wide World Photos; David Tumley/*CORBIS*; 126 Bettmann/*CORBIS*; 127 David Tumley/*CORBIS*; 131 Prentice-Hall, Inc.

Ronald Reagan 133 The Reagan Library; 134 AP/World Wide Photos; 135 NASA 136 NASA; The Reagan Library.

Tenzin Gyatso, 14th Dalai Lama of Tibet 139 Galen Rowell/*CORBIS*; 140 Hulton-Deutsch Collection/*CORBIS*; Bettmann/*CORBIS*; 141 AP/Wide World Photos; Bettmann/*CORBIS*; 142 Bettmann/*CORBIS*; Hulton-Deutsch Collection/*CORBIS*; 144 Sheldan/*CORBIS*; 145 AFP/*CORBIS*.

Yitzhak Rabin 147 AFP/*CORBIS*; 148 Hulton Getty/Liaison Agency, Inc.; Bettmann/*CORBIS*; 149 David Rubbinger/*CORBIS*; 150 AP/Wide World Photos; 151 David Rubbinger/*CORBIS*; AP/Wide World Photos; 152 AFP/*CORBIS*; David Tumley/*CORBIS*; 155 Miki Kratsman/*CORBIS*.

Princess Diana 157 CORBIS; 158 © Bettmann/*CORBIS*; Althorp Charitable Trust 159 AP/Wide World Photos; AP/Wide World Photos; Camera Press; 160 Tim Graham/*CORBIS*; 163 AP/Wide World Photos. Reproduced with permission of Earl Spencer and the Althorp Charitable Trust, www.althorp.com, and The Diana, Princess Of Wales Memorial Fund, www.theworkcontinues.org.

Franklin D. Roosevelt and George W. Bush 165 Hulton Getty/Liaison Agency, Inc.; FDR Library; Reuters NewMedia Inc./*CORBIS*; 166 Reuters NewMedia Inc./*CORBIS*; AP/Wide World Photos; Reuters NewMedia Inc./*CORBIS*; Reuters NewMedia Inc./*CORBIS*; 171 Reuters NewMedia Inc./*CORBIS*; 173 Reuters NewMedia Inc./*CORBIS*.

Audio Credits
Narration by Richard Greene.

Recording of Richard Greene narration and Edmund Morris reading of Theodore Roosevelt Grand Canyon Speech by Aaron Baron, Creative Audio Post, New York, New York.

Additional recording of Richard Greene by Sunburst Studios and The Village, Los Angeles, CA.

Archival audio footage for
   Lou Gehrig and James Gandolfini reading of Gehrig's Farewell speech Major League Baseball audio courtesy Major League Baseball Properties, Inc.
   Winston Churchill provided by Universal Music Group.
   Douglas MacArthur provided by The General Douglas MacArthur Foundation, Norfolk, VA.

John F. Kennedy, Robert F. Kennedy and Edward M. Kennedy provided by John F. Kennedy Library.
   Mario Cuomo, Barbara Jordan, Yitzhak Rabin, and Anwar Sadat provided by and copyright of NBC News Archives.
   Dalai Lama is taken from NRK Norwegian Broadcasting.
   Earl Spencer eulogy for Princess Diana copyright © BBC Production and engineering by Jacques Boulanger, Creative Audio Post, New York, New York.
   Lyndon Baines Johnson Courtesy LBJ Library Audio Collection.

Lou Gehrig ™/© 2002 Estate of Eleanor Gehrig, by CMG Worldwide Inc., www.LouGehrig.com.

Winston Churchill Reproduced with permission of Curtis Brown Ltd., London on behalf of Winston S. Churchill; Copyright Winston S. Churchill.

Albert Einstein Copyright © Nobel Foundation; Albert Einstein™ HUJ, represented by The Roger Richman Agency, Inc. www.therichman agency.com.

Martin Luther King, Jr. All material copyrighted by Dr. Martin Luther King, Jr. All material copyright renewed by Coretta Scott King and the heirs to Estate of Dr. Martin Luther King, Jr., and reprinted by arrangement c/o of Writer's House, LLC, as agents for Estate of Dr. Martin Luther King, Jr.

Barry M. Goldwater Courtesy The Barry M. Goldwater Family.

Barbara Jordan Courtesy the Estate of Barbara Jordan.

Anwar Sadat Reproduced with permission from Jehan Sadat, Ph.D., widow of President Anwar Sadat, Senior Fellow of the Anwar Sadat Chair for Development and Peace, University of Maryland, College Park; and active public speaker.

Mario Cuomo Courtesy Mario Cuomo.

Tenzin Gyatso, 14th Dalai Lama of Tibet Copyright © Nobel Foundation; courtesy Tenzin Gyatso.

Yitzhak Rabin Copyright © Nobel Foundation; reproduced courtesy Dalia Rabin-Pellosof and Yitzhak Rabin Center for Israel Studies.

Earl Spencer Reproduced with permission of Earl Spencer and the Althorp Charitable Trust, www.althorp.com.

INDEX